DYING TO LIVE
A TAPESTRY OF REINVENTION

Michael Bianco-Splann

"The writing is superb! It has humor as well as extremely painful moments. Michael's ability to tell his story carried me effortlessly through the pages.

Dying to Live is a thoughtful, original, and extremely well written account of the transformational passage that Joseph Campbell has described as "the Hero's Journey."

This book provides a bonus, _Insights and Tools_, at the end of each chapter that describe the lessons Michael learned from each of his life experiences. These sections make the book even more valuable because they will enable the reader to make Michael's lessons applicable to their own lives."

Raye C. Mathis, MSW, LSW

To my son, Matthew, my guiding North Star, whose perpetual love and encouragement has brought such joy, blessing and direction into my own life. Truly, the arc of my legacy resides within his heart and entwines with mine. For it is only through loving that we find ourselves.

FOREWORD

This story is a fascinating account of a young man's journey through, not only his own darkness but also the darkness of his family of origin and the culture within which he finds himself.

This is a true story of Michael, an intelligent young man caught up in the dark world of alcohol and drugs and the resulting destructiveness of that path. His story demonstrates that in the end we do have free will and the ability to make constructive choices that can lead us out of the shadows in which we find ourselves, however painful the path.

Michael's "reinvention" of himself is a celebration of the potential of the human spirit and is an inspiration for all of us when he describes his growth and maturation as his unique life mission came into focus.

Raye C. Mathis, MSW, LSW

Palmetto Publishing Group
Charleston, SC

Dying to Live

Visit the author's website:
www.illuminateambitions.com

ISBN-13: 978-0-9962296-2-3 (paperback)
ISBN-13: 978-0-9962296-3-0 (ebook)

CONTENTS

INTRODUCTION

Life is fleeting and filled with uncertainty, adventure, infinite opportunities and untold challenges. What we do with these challenges
ultimately defines who we are and the reality of our purpose. Over the
decades my journey has required seeing with eyes wide open and ears to
hear beyond the spoken word, for what appears on the surface of living is
so much more. Change, evolution, redefinition and growth are constants
in my life. They have brought me moments of joyful beauty along with
deep treks into the dark night of the soul. And despite what superficially
looks like conflicting pathways, all intertwine as luminescent threads adding texture to the fabric of transformation and self-exploration.

Leadership, a noble enterprise, demands more than rote learning of
corporate policy, established principles and toeing-the-line managerial
duties. Leadership incorporates the whole person, calling us to be more
than we are, more than our title, more than our own limitations. True
leadership is an amalgamation of life experiences; the leader reaches other
human beings from a base of authenticity, genuineness and prudent risk-
taking. The lessons you draw from your past experiences, both good and
bad, determine your output. If we measure success in accordance with
what companies, organizations and established systems ordain as competencies to master, we conform to a limited and constricted framework that
ultimately leaves us half-filled, dissatisfied and living well below our human capacity. So what is necessary? My story is one of moving through
duress, charting a course into the unknown and setting aside fear and

insecurity to gain understanding, compassion and love. It is a story of resilience and redemption.

I woke up in my life. But not without understanding that the quality of my life had nothing to do with how well people treated me or what my title was or any of the external trappings our consumer-oriented, self-serving way of life calls us to garner. It did, however, demand introspection, ownership of my subconscious firestorms and an expanded sense of self that acknowledges and embraces the triune self of body, mind and spirit.

We know how important it is to treat our bodies as sacred temples, to value diet and exercise as integral necessities for good physical health. And mental health, a complex, misunderstood, and woefully underfunded realm in our collective human experience, remains a central focus across many areas of our greater global community. But spiritual health, largely infused with religious dogmas and constraints, is often viewed as detached and separate from complete health and wellness. Our religious precepts and beliefs tend to operate in a different domain from health and wellness, falsely pretending to support holistic spiritual health. The nature of divinity, as defined by organized religion, is that God is theirs, exclusively constructed to neatly fit into their doctrine. This view leaves us confused, separated from others and in many cases, separated from ourselves. Mine is a journey of integration, creation and awakening. Truly, the fabric of my soulful quilt is an interwoven chronology of experiences, positive and challenging, yet deeply insightful.

The principles elucidated in my book *Conscious Leadership: 7 Principles That WILL Change Your Business and Change Your Life* are real-life practical foundations upon which I live, lead and honor. Arriving at a place of knowing is the culmination of my experiences, both personal and professional. These principles are the keys to transforming rote leadership into something quite different, a purposeful leadership structure that consciously acknowledges and supports the very best in you and in those you lead and serve. Lifting others up to their full potential is a precious gift, one our current world order desperately needs.

This is the resilient story of my journey to transformation, a view into my psyche, my history and my life on the run, filled with reckless risk taking, adventures into the dark netherworld and transitions of magnanimous impact. My hope is that you will be inspired to undertake your own journey to transformation.

This is *Dying to Live: A Tapestry of Reinvention*.

AUTHOR'S NOTE

There are no surprises in life, only unfolding opportunities. I have come to understand by my own unique experiences, that there is an orchestration, a storyboard that is determined by where I place my thoughts, intentions and the choices I make. Combine this with divine influence and you will have a mustard seed of understanding.

My life as told in the words that follow does not align to a strict cadence of chronology, nor is it intended as an autobiographical account of my life. Rather, I provide the reader with chapters of my journey, illustrating the genesis of each of the conscious leadership principles from my first book. These principles are guideposts for living a whole life, one of resilience, expansion, understanding and love. Within the text of this book there are numeric markers which denote further explanation and context found at the end of each chapter as 'reflections.'

It is not my aim to tell you how to interpret or feel about the events, people and circumstances of my adventures; I leave that to you. My goal is to share with you my story, my heart's path so that you may tap into your own resilience to better understand your innate power and live with an awareness that elevates the experiences of your lifetime. It is not my intention to in any way tarnish, impugn or cast disparaging shadows on any of the individuals that I share in the chapters that follow. To this end, names, dates, locations and other detailed information have been changed to protect both the identity and character of those I bring forward in this book.

As is the rhythm of our lives, we are the composite of our experiences, from this life and those of the past. Putting the pieces together across different parts of my journey brings to light understandings that are the colors of the palette enjoining to illuminate and give context to those principles that I share with you. May you find peace, enjoyment and encouragement to be all that you are and will become.

1

BE THE REAL YOU

From Darkness into the Light

Looking back on my life, with its twists and turns, ups and downs, many successes and abysmal failures, I am drawn to a place of reflection and awareness, a level of consciousness not possible in my earlier days. I am the sum of my collective experiences, a harmony of understanding and a messenger of good news. We have the ability to move through challenges to find a new path, one of integrity, genuineness and wellness. Our output as leaders, as human beings living among other human beings, is largely the product of our inner psychic world.

I could see in her eyes the love that I had always dreamed possible. Standing beside Janeen, as we shared in our marriage vows with the small assembly of friends and co-workers witnessing our union on that late December, 2007, evening, I was struck by how far my life had come to have arrived at a place of genuine love and caring. We had both overcome harsh beginnings and great disappointments, divorce, loss of family ties, death, sickness, job loss, addiction and challenges that rocked us to our cores. Yet here we stood, joining our lives together and entering into a shared adventure that would catapult us into new chapters and textures of life otherwise unknown. In her eyes lay the grace of honesty, desire and the hope of a union blessed and received with enormous gratitude and comfort.[1]

I turned to my bride. Our eyes met, and we shared a kiss as husband and wife. We turned to the gathering and walked together, the applause exploding and a harmony of well wishes showering us in a Kodak moment. How many times had I longed for love, pleaded for sanity, searching aimlessly for a glimmer of light? A spark of pain flashed across my consciousness as I looked lovingly at my beautiful bride.

The Beginning

My life started out as both a gift and a challenge. Barbara Cavanaugh, my birth mother, the second youngest of four girls, became pregnant in 1954, when she was fifteen. She attended Ballston Spa High School in upstate New York, where she was fortunate to have Ruth Massey as her business education teacher. Mrs. Massey was a close family friend to my great aunt and godmother, Bernadine O'Hearn, also a school teacher in the Saratoga Springs school district, a bordering district to the north. The two of them were instrumental in supporting young Barbara with her pregnancy. As challenging as it is in modern day America for an unwed pregnant teen, being pregnant at fifteen in 1954 was a disaster of monumental proportion. Exactly what happened with Barbara remains a mystery. But one thing is certain; being adopted by the Splann family was a gift. This would be confirmed as I pursued trying to find my birth mother in 2001.

During my early years my mother, Kathleen Splann, usually late at night with friends and family after imbibing with several gin and tonics and thinking me asleep, would have conversations mentioning adoption. My brother, Danny, and I were both adopted. I also remember digging through old boxes in the attic of my mother's house in Schenectady, New York, finding dated newspaper clippings. One stood out. It talked about Kathleen and Larry adopting a baby.

So I had developed my suspicions early on. I confronted my mother in a moment of anger when I was eighteen. "Am I adopted?"

"Yes."

"Why didn't you ever tell me?"

She paused, visible tears welling up in her eyes. "I always thought of you as mine."

Her sorrow was palpable to me. I recall my own silence that followed. And that was the extent of our conversation around this admission. In truth, I believed her and I loved my mother. The gift of adoption was that someone actually wanted me and, in 1955, had to work hard to make the adoption happen.

Barbara, knowing that she would be giving me up for adoption, may have infused in me a prenatal sense of abandonment that persisted as I grew. This knowing was a turbulent undercurrent that would find its way into my developing a strong defense system, hiding my true nature, playing the good soldier and not wanting to rock the boat, lest I be given up again. Subconsciously, the hidden fears would undermine my intimate relationships and place internal limits on full self-expression and success. My fear of abandonment—that I would be left naked and exposed to a terrifying world that would find me less-than, unlovable and unprotected—led to the adoption of a false self. It would take years before I was able to bring forward these subconscious and destructive limitations and to show up as the real Michael.

While the story of my beginnings was still vaporous with unknowns, I intentionally put finding my birth parents on hold. I decided years ago that I would pursue finding them, but not until my adoptive mother and father passed away. I had bits and pieces of the truth that I carried with me for years, until I finally decided to find my birth parents.

Growing up in the Splann household had its own challenges.

Family Dysfunction Rears Its Head

Early on, especially living abroad, while my father was still active Air Force, nothing catastrophic occurred, at least that I was aware of. It wasn't until we returned to the USA, with my father being stationed in rural Pennsylvania outside Harrisburg, that trouble started to manifest with my father's drinking. Soon after arriving back in the States and moving to New Cumberland, Pennsylvania, my father was diagnosed with a spot on his lung that required surgery. My brother, Danny, and I were kept from knowing what was happening.

It wasn't unusual for my father to leave on missions that would take him away for long stretches. While we were living in the Philippines, the Cuban Missile Crisis put Clark Air Force Base on red alert and all active military were dispatched, my father included. He left quickly and was gone for what felt like weeks. So keeping Danny and me in the dark was expected.

When Danny and I returned to the United States in early 1963, we were eight and nine. Our father was sent to Walter Reed Army Hospital for the lung surgery. I later found out it was suspected that the spot on his lung was cancer. Only upon opening him up was it determined to be a spot of encapsulated tuberculosis, which was removed successfully. The operation left him with a scar that looked as though he had been cut in two.

Some months after his surgery, he was gone again. This time it was the winter of 1964. I was nine and, unbeknownst to me, my father had been in a serious car accident on the Pennsylvania Turnpike, on the mile-long bridge that crossed the Susquehanna River. He was so intoxicated late one evening that he fell asleep at the wheel of his Olds 98 crashing into the center median.

No other car was involved and my father was the only person injured. And injured he was. Many years later I found out that had he not been in his full Air Force uniform winter coat he would have surely been killed.

4

The accident put him in the hospital for three weeks. Teeth had to be surgical removed from his sinus cavity due to the impact of his head going through the windshield. My mother complained until the day she died of how the accident ruined my father's perfect nose. Because my father was an Air Force officer and Second World War veteran, the Pennsylvania State Police never filed charges against him. I have often thought that unfortunate. Perhaps their doing so would have mitigated my father's continued struggles with complications of prolonged alcohol abuse and his ultimate demise. Despite surviving the accident, my father continued his love affair with alcohol. Looking back on this period, it is no wonder that my brother and I were living in a reality that all seemed dangerous and fleeting. We boys did not connect alcohol to the tempest of events ensnarling our young lives. Instead, it was just a normal part of life in the Splann family.

I Hated Holidays

Holidays were painful. I vividly remember Thanksgiving 1966, when I was eleven. My father was drunk. He sarcastically and loudly shot barbed arrows at my mother for insignificant acts, criticizing her harshly and obnoxiously. All my brother and I could do was hide. Aunt Bernadine was visiting, as she often did on holidays. My father was more intoxicated than his usual sloppy, miserable self that November day. The screaming and verbal abuse were overwhelming. My brother and I retreated to our bedroom in tears, without consolation. I wanted so badly to tell my father to stop, to end his drunken behavior. But there was no way for me to voice my anger.

I went to my great aunt looking for her to hug me or to at least acknowledge my despair, only to be met with scorn. She told me to "stop crying." This would be a memory of my godmother that I would carry with me my entire life. It was years later, when she was on her death bed, at age ninety-five, that I realized how cold and cruel she was in her heart.

Little was I aware at the time, but I came into this iteration of life with the spirit and archetype of soldier, assassin and warrior. I manifested feelings of anger and frustration coupled with a fierce desire to forcibly stop the insanity of destruction caused by my father. During holidays especially I wanted to not only verbally assault him but physically take him out, eradicate his sarcastic barbs and break him apart limb by limb. Of course, for an eleven-year old this was a fantasy of impossible proportions. Yet, it was vivid and palpable in my psyche. I dreamt of killing him.

I had a recurring dream during this period. My father, mother, aunt and brother were together in a cemetery in the dark of night. The wind blew the leaves that had fallen from the craggy trees. Clouds passed by as a silver moon shone on the scene. My family was gathered around the dinner table. In a drunken stupor my father spit harsh rebukes out at my mother in his typical slurred manner. I watched from outside the scene, standing beside a large gravestone, grimacing as the tears flowed from my brother Danny's eyes. Danny was not able to process any of my father's behavior. He was simply the victim, and it broke my heart to see him in such distress. My mother took my father's anger and venom, not retaliating but trying to remain calm. My Aunt Bernadine, in her parochial-school sternness, was attempting to defuse the situation. What I was witnessing in the dream was painfully familiar to me, but this time I would take action. My heart racing to the cadence of the scene, I looked down, and in my right hand was a hunting knife with an eight-inch razor-sharp blade.

I turned my gaze back to the family scene, feeling the pulse of purposeful anger rise, screaming, "No more! Not this time." From behind my father I raced into the dining room, coming up to where my father was seated and proceeded to cut off his head. The decapitated body slumped over onto the table as his head fell to the ground. A hush of horror consumed my family as I met their eyes, and in an instant their emotion changed to relief. Just as this occurred, an overwhelming feeling of terror swept over me, and I heard my father's voice laughing aloud, "You think you've gotten revenge?" I turned to the fallen head to see my father's eyes looking at me. The head began to move toward me. I quickly turned from my family and saw a lane through the cemetery leading to a large wrought iron gate in the distance. I had to escape. I started running. But my father's head was right behind me, chasing me and laughing insidiously, his voice echoing, "Come back here!" As I ran down the cemetery lane, overhanging branches swayed back and forth, with the wind now stronger and blowing right into my body. I ran as fast as my legs would carry me, yet the distance to the gate and my escape grew farther and farther away. Turning to look behind me I saw my father's head gaining on me. His head was evil and illuminated with light from hell. I awoke from the nightmare shaken to my core. This dream haunted me for years.[2]

The Last Year of Active Duty

Our father left for one year to serve out his last year in the military at Kelly Air Force base south of San Antonio, Texas. He returned in the summer of 1968 to our suburban home in Pennsylvania, retiring a lieutenant colonel after twenty-eight years of service. The story goes that had it not been for my father's drinking he would surely have been a general. A drunk he was, but an intelligent one.

Having my father home for an extended period created mixed emotions for us. As with most young boys of my generation, I had a troubled emotional attachment to the war hero. On one hand, Larry Splann was bigger than life, standing tall in his military regalia, strong and handsome. On the other hand, he was a person who, when drinking, managed to infuse such harsh negativity into our home that it made our lives unbearable. It is hard to glamorize the effects of alcoholism on the family. Even today as holidays approach, I experience a rush of horror attached to the memories of so many childhood holidays ruined by my father's drinking.

Family Tradition

"What would you like to drink?" was as common a question as you'd ever hear in my home. I visited my great aunt Bernadine's home in Schenectady when I was eighteen. It was the summer of 1973, after I returned from two months living in San Diego, just before starting college. I arrived around lunchtime and my aunt had made meatloaf sandwiches with mustard and relish on rye bread. I loved the combination. As a matter of course she opened a bottle of red wine and we polished off the bottle for lunch, not thinking anything of doing so.

In my family, drinking alcohol was part of the fabric of daily life. It was just one of the things that everyone did. Being brought up in the military as I was, I don't remember a time when alcohol wasn't the central part of all kinds of events and get-togethers and the afternoon pre-dinner routine. I can remember when I was six, living in the Philippines as an officer's son, that my parents would have formal military dinners, casual cocktail parties and officers' club weekly parties that invariably centered on alcohol consumption. Drinking was just expected as part of that culture, and my home was certainly part of it.

Awakening to Confusion

The familiar dull pounding came as I opened my eyes. Adjusting to focus once, twice, a third time brought into view another pair of eyes looking down at me staring intensely into mine. The three EMTs standing in my fourth-floor prewar walkup on 147th Street in Flushing, New York, had been dispatched earlier that Wednesday morning as the result of an emergency call from a concerned neighbor leaving for work who walked out of the adjacent apartment to find what was described by one of the EMTs as a bloodbath. The last flight of concrete steps was splattered with blood, as were the walls and railings. Blood pooled at the entrance to my studio apartment and the keys still dangled from the lock. The doorknob was caked in misery as well.

I was thirty-three. How had my life become a tragedy of self-destruction and endless pain?

When I graduated from Syracuse University in 1977 with my BA in International Relations, I thought that by my early thirties I would be a successful, dynamic international attorney working for Amnesty International in London or Paris, representing high-profile political prisoners and charting a course to change the world. By this time, I would have found love, married and had children. Certainly a man with so much to offer wouldn't now be living each day courting a mistress of drugs and alcohol, trying desperately to hold on to some small residue of sanity. And yet the concerned eyes of the EMT looking down at me lying on my couch were another vivid reminder of the hell that encapsulated me. "What happened? Why are you here?" I asked.

The year was 1988. By then, I had not gone one day without a drink in ten years. What began with drinking beer as a college student, an everyday event in my family, had become a goal, an object of desire and compulsion.

As I lay on my couch that morning, an unspoken truth lay hidden under veils of self-justification, layers of pain, loss, abandonment and unrealized love. I was an alcoholic in denial about my self-destruction. I was incapable of rational thought process, or healthy self-reflection, or even a mustard seed of honesty. The insanity was perpetual and I would remain in this toxic spiral for the next two years.

I had lived in Flushing, Queens, for eight years, most of that time with my girlfriend and her four cats in a three-and-a-half-room apartment on a secluded block off Kissena Boulevard. When that long-term relationship ended badly, my deterioration accelerated. I was fired from my position as an Eastern Airlines in-flight supervisor in March 1988 and demoted back to flying as a flight attendant. I looked forward to days off from flying and the freedom to drink alcohol and snort cocaine.

Late Tuesday afternoon, I arrived at LaGuardia Airport after a two-day trip bouncing between cities in a Boeing 727. I caught the employee bus from the lower level of the terminal, found my 1979 Chrysler Le Baron and made my way back to the small apartment on 147th Street, a six-mile trip up the Van Wyck and into the bowels of Flushing. I had stowed three sixteen-ounce cans of Budweiser under my driver seat and downed two of them before I got home. Ah, the edge was gone, and now three free days were mine. My mistress awaited, and I was a ready and willing lover.

Finding a parking place on the streets of Flushing was tricky business especially for drunks and drug addicts, since alternate side rules applied and the wrong spot could mean towing and fines, not to mention feeling like a rat in a maze after forgetting where I parked.[3]

The three beers on my ride home led to another three while I showered and got ready to walk the four blocks to the Triangle Lounge. Tonight I was hoping to run into Jerry, Johnny or Pauly, all of whom were heavy cocaine users and dealers. You never knew who would show up at the lounge on any given night, yet I felt confident that at least one of my sources would show up and deliver the goods. I had built enough connections over the years with people who took good care of me with drugs, especially cocaine. The 1980s in New York City was a decade of cocaine use. The Colombian connection out of Jackson Heights brought huge amounts of the white powder to the City, along with violent crime. Both Johnny and Pauly were frequently armed to the hilt.

I got to the lounge at 7:00. Some of the regulars were tippling their beers, copping their regular buzzes, as Marty, the bartender, greeted me with a glass of beer. "Been to any fun cities?" he asked. As usual I would smile and say, "Sure Marty, they're all fun." For some time now, I had been blackout drinking on occasion, the result of huge amounts of cocaine and nonstop alcohol. This night was no different. Pauly and Johnny came into the bar together around 9:30, both wired and in rare form. I could see that they were high as a kite. Johnny came up from behind and slapped me on the back. He shook my hand and said, "Hey Mikey, let's fire it up in the bathroom." I got up from my barstool and followed him to the back of the smoky bar to the men's room.

The Triangle Lounge was a drug haven. Men and women rotated in and out of the bathroom frequently. It was quite common to hear sniffing sounds from the regulars following a trip to the bathroom and see the occasional white powder left on the tips of their noses. Many off-duty NYC police officers frequented the bar and partook of these adventures. The lounge was a safe haven of illicit activities.

Johnny pulled out his little brown cocaine vial with its accompanying spoon and proceeded to shovel several helpings of cocaine up my nose. Casually he mentioned that he had just scored two kilos of rock worth a huge amount in street value. Johnny and Pauly were dealing over a hundred grand in drugs a week.

My drunken state was instantly replaced with a clarity of thought and feeling that had been lost in the alcohol high. The seductive and compelling attribute of cocaine was the instant rush of euphoria and confidence. The feeling of *more* was addictive. Snorting cocaine counteracted the depressive effect of alcohol. The problem was the illusion of being in control. At some point I would black out. That Tuesday evening, I lost conscious awareness. I have no memory of my actions, my thoughts or my place in reality.

While the EMT attended to the two-inch gash on my forehead that resulted from my slipping and falling as I climbed the stairs to my apartment, I had a flicker of recall, remembering the thud of hitting my head hard on one of the stair steps. My memory flirted with flashes of fighting to stand up and scramble for my keys while wiping my eyes enough to find the keyhole to open the door. After that, there was complete loss of what happened next. The young EMT, sending the other two back to their mobile unit, attempted to ask me the details. I said, "I'm not very clear as to exactly what happened." He told me that the stairs and landing looked as if someone had been knifed or shot, there was so much blood. I told him that I would clean it up.

After a last check to make sure my vital signs were stable, he packed his medical kit, and with a final "be careful," he left my apartment. What I witnessed upon opening the door was even worse than my pickled imagination had conceived. A bucket of hot water, Ajax and old T-shirts, accompanied the pounding in my head as I scrubbed the entire area clean. I eventually posted a note on the neighbor's door with a simple and lame apology. It was Wednesday afternoon and the events of the previous night leading to my meeting three nice young EMTs were history. What was on my mind was my next drink. There were two more days before my next flight, more than enough time to drink and drug.[4]

When I went into the bathroom to clean myself up from the nightmare of Tuesday night there was a moment of reflection. As I looked at myself in the mirror, examining the gash on my forehead at the hairline, I saw my bloodshot eyes, the same red eyes of little Michael crying in the bathroom on Thanksgiving at age eight while my father ruined another holiday with his drunken abusive yelling and sarcastic barbs. How I hated him for drinking and ruining our holidays. But that was the family tradition I was adopted into, one of dysfunction, pain and sickness.

CHAPTER 1 REFLECTIONS

[1]*Transitions in life mark turning points, and my life is no different from others in that regard. Until I met Janeen, I lived a life hidden from the view of others, one of false pretenses, of being who I thought others wanted me to be. I set aside my own unique essence; I had an ill-conceived notion that if I showed you the real Michael, you would not like me. I compartmentalized my life into segments, always being cautious not to expose my insecurities and fears, lest you find me an impostor or a less-than human being. These inner firestorms burned feverishly throughout my first five decades, leading to failed marriages, superficial friendships and near-death choices. And it was through these challenges that great opportunities emerged. I knew intuitively that finding safe haven with an intimate partner was a missing element in my life. My failures led me to self-examination and slowly I cast aside the armor enough to open up to love, not love in a narrowly confined construct, but rather love shared with openness, vulnerability and respect. I found a partner who did not care about the trappings of success, the possessions accumulated or the level of my educational achievement. I found honest and intimate friendship and a willingness to join spirits together in a bond of unity.*

[2] *I desperately wanted my father to stop drinking, yelling and treating my mother and brother so badly. My mother worked very hard at keeping me quiet. I was much too young to understand how the combination of my father's behavior and my mother's directive to keep quiet was affecting my spirit.*

This dynamic would play out in pervasive ways throughout my adulthood. The anger associated with her repeated requests was buried so deep that it took grueling therapy to eventually arrive at my inner rage at being told over and over again to "be quiet," not to speak my truth. Being the good soldier played out in my childhood, leaving me in a place where speaking, acting and being truthful about my feelings and my desires became risky business. Shielding the true Michael embodied a defense system that would have grave consequences as I made my way into adulthood. The drinking continued.

[3] When I reflect on this period, I often wonder what was impelling me to live a life that was essentially killing me. It was a life on the run, and while I didn't see it at the time, I had been running my entire life. This Tuesday evening was no different from so many nights before or so many that would follow. The primary thought that began my day and occupied me on a cellular level was my next drink. The internal dialogue was incessant, with fierce justification and determination. I had to be totally self-absorbed and self-centered to maintain a life of active alcoholism and drug addiction. Living in the darkness that consumed me required manipulation, lying and extraordinary energy. Only with years of sobriety did I recognize the intensity and overwhelming consumption of body, mind and spirit this pattern of living and dying required.

[4] I see my alcoholism and drug addiction as having been a necessary catalyst for transformation, propelling me forward, chiseling a rebirth of spirit and intellect. The mistress of addiction was a stealthy enemy concealed as a willing and able partner. But the killer stood beside me carefully plotting my demise.

We have the ability to move through challenges to find a new path. The question is whether you and I have done the work necessary to speak the truth and to own our thoughts, intentions and choices so that we can create a life centered on giving back, moving forward and adhering to a higher order—a life of love, compassion and understanding. The work goes on. The courtship with alcohol and drugs nearly killed me, a daily reminder of the seduction in the dark side of life. And the memory of my own self-destructive behavior lingers after all these years.

INSIGHTS AND TOOLS

Be the Real You - listen to your inner voice. Take the time each day to be quiet, a few moments of calm, easy breathing and intentional focus. Understand and embrace loving and accepting your true self, not the one portrayed by your professional title, your worldly possessions or by superficial manifestations. Your soul is divine. Your true essence is a reflection of the divine, despite the circumstances, events and external happenings that frame your present state. Let your true essence shine.

2

BE A RISK-TAKER

From Reckless to Prudent

Reckless risk-taking characterized my youth. It is clear to me now that I was in search of myself, attempting to balance my fears against a desire for meaning and substance in my life. But where does a kid turn in seeking to find himself? The internal turmoil of abandonment, the feelings of inadequacy and the natural awkwardness of adolescence prevented peace-building and developing a true sense of self. It was a scary time, one of risky exploration, of walking a thin line between acceptable and dangerous. I was attempting to thread a needle in a tornado.

The year was 2002. We marched into the executive conference room at our headquarters in Latham, New York, for our weekly sales meeting like lieutenants walking into a flight briefing, gathering around the table to await our battle orders. I recall the tension and anxiety on the faces of the regional sales managers readying themselves for the slaughter. In walked Gladys Christenson, senior vice president of retail banking. From her point of view, we were rats in the corporate maze of management by intimidation. Our meeting was to address weekly strategies for driving high performance sales, but most importantly beating the other divisions to afford Gladys bragging rights and the opportunity for self-aggrandizement. Her monologue was barbed and attacking, directly calling out less than satisfactory results by chiding us and accusing all of us of stupidity and weakness.[5]

I protected myself from Gladys. I had established an elaborate defense system that surely would protect me against any and all intruders, or so I thought. I had always found a way to protect Michael, even as a child, afraid and insecure as I was. Self-protection, justified under the right conditions, requires prudent risk-taking to open oneself to learning, growth and greater self-expansion.

I learned how to open that door just enough to survive as young Michael.

The Defense System

As a child I was driven by an intense need to defend against being given away. Finding my way through the family dysfunction required discovery and resilience. I had a voice and needed to find a way to gain some semblance of control in a world that felt literally out of control.

My defense took the form of a passion and talent for the arts. *You're a Good Man, Charlie Brown* was the musical that catapulted me into the arts. Yes, it was the same smash hit 1960s Broadway show, but this was a fourth grade production in my elementary school. I was living in a suburban community between Middletown and Highspire, Pennsylvania. After my father's military career, my parents agreed that moving us from place to place needed to stop. The decision was made to put down roots at our home on Richard Avenue.

Our school district had acquired arts funding to bring music to the students. I had been identified as having some talent and I began to learn music. My interest and aptitude were instant, and I found the structure of music easy to assimilate. Somehow the music teacher decided that I would make a great French horn player. So my new best friend became a French horn, which was bigger than I was. This presented huge issues for toting it from school to home and back. I eventually switched to a clarinet, largely because of the ease of carrying a clarinet. While I was learning to read music, the school started an elementary choral group. Surprise! The new group included me. I was off on a new adventure that gave me a way to have my voice heard—in more ways than one. This was life-changing for me. Until this time, I lived in my psychic world where I had to remain quiet and not express my true feelings lest I be given up again, but now I could express myself. And more importantly, music allowed me to avoid expressing the words that I wanted to speak and the fear that I would be given away again if I did so. At the age of nine, I had found a sure-fire defense mechanism upon which I could build a young life with some level of individual expression. Music allowed me to keep in place my complex defense system, yet find enough voice to empower and sustain young Michael.

Not only did I possess the musical ability to play and sing, but later the same year I was cast as Snoopy in *You're a Good Man, Charlie Brown*, which was going to be performed in the spring at Kunkel Elementary School. Yes, a bunch of kids performing for their parents, grandparents, teachers and administration. But it just so happened that on the evening of my debut performance there were community theatre producers in the audience. I stole the show, bringing down the house with my rendition of "Suppertime."

Acting, singing and performing became a passion that would carry through public education as well as into Equity theatre over time. I pursued this passion by moving to New York City in late 1978.

It makes sense that I would be skilled in playing someone else, taking on a character that kept my true identity locked inside, safe from anyone getting too close, too intimate with the real me—a person you would dislike, not love, throw away. This became my shield, my defense that I would carry into my adolescence, college career and adulthood. But the seething rage associated with my adoptive parents creating a family environment of dysfunction and repression would manifest over the next twenty years with the unconscious, yet lethal self-destructive behavior that would wreak untold terror on my physical, emotional and spiritual self.

I made a name for myself throughout my school years on stage, both acting and singing, with occasional dance routines as well. Our drama leader, Asher Halbleib, a mathematician who settled for a career in teaching, had identified my talent early on in elementary school. He had his Equity card and managed to pull me along into summer stock theatre in Ephrata, Pennsylvania, at the Ephrata Star Playhouse. My first summer stock show was *Man of La Mancha*, in the summer of 1970; it became my all-time favorite musical. Years later, in Auburn, New York, I auditioned for a touring company production of *Jesus Christ Superstar* using the opening song from *Man of La Mancha* as my audition piece, singing it a cappella and landing a lead role.

Mr. Halbleib thought it would be a wonderful learning experience for his star teen prodigy to accompany him on a weekend trip to New York to see several Broadway shows. My parents assented to his generous offer and blessed the trip. We attended *No, No, Nanette*, *1776* and *Hair*. We shared a hotel room in the New Yorker Hotel. In the morning upon waking we had what I thought was an innocent pillow fight. We were wrestling with each other playfully when Mr. Halbleib reached for my genitals. I pulled away and told him not to do that again. I was sixteen and our relationship changed profoundly after that incident.

Drama, music and song were the tools by which I was able to turn childhood repression into expression of a true part of me. But the depth of my true self remained defended.

Discovering Drugs

In 1965, the Lunt family moved to our small suburban community from the east coast of Florida. Like Danny and me, the Lunt boys were military brats and lived a few suburban blocks from me in a typical split-level four-bedroom ranch. Their father was of English heritage and their mother was direct from southern Italy, along with her sister, the boys' aunt, her son, the boys' cousin, and the four-foot-six grandmother who spoke only Italian and who spent endless hours in the kitchen cooking the most delicious Italian food on the planet. Jordan, the third son, was my age and we bonded quickly. His tales of surfing, girls and brotherly adventures excited my curiosity. Jordan was a great addition to my small circle of guy friends. After all, we were ten going on eleven. But almost as fast as the Lunts arrived, they went back to Florida. Having recently retired from the Air Force, Mr. Lunt's expertise was highly valued back in Cape Canaveral.

My brother and I were accustomed to making new friends only to then move away, never to see them again. But in this case, the Lunts returned four years later, in early 1970. Rick, the oldest Lunt brother was in eleventh grade; Nick, second oldest, was in tenth grade, Jordan and I were in ninth grade and Vinnie was in junior high school.

It was a typical school day in February 1970 when as I walked from my homeroom into the hallway en route to my first class, I saw Jordan Lunt. At first, I didn't recognize him. He was well ahead of me in the puberty department, showing stubble on his face. His hair, usually a coarse brown, showed blonde highlights, as did his bushy eyebrows. Being of southern Italian descent, his skin tone was always darker than mine, but in the school hallway he had a sun-weathered appearance, not your typical rural Pennsylvania February look, and he was wearing an unusual, brightly colored shirt. His older brothers had changed as well, having much more radical, progressive appearances that drew immediate notice from the principal and his administrative staff.

The Lunt brothers brought with them an infusion of counterculture attitudes, styles and behaviors that for the first time in our conservative, right-wing small town high school challenged the very foundation upon which the local culture was built and sustained over generations. For the school, this was a serious threat. It became apparent to me almost immediately; the Lunts were trouble.

Yet I hungered for change and self-expression. The 1970s for most of us was a frightening decade. It was as though the rules of the game were changing and we, the adolescents, were aircraft pilots without a map, flying on a wing and a prayer.

During the rest of my freshman year and well into tenth grade, I remained curious about the counterculture, but refrained from taking the leap into it—especially using drugs—although the Lunts made it a priority to find marijuana, not a small task given the area and the times. Despite my renewed friendship with the Lunts, I continued to excel in academics, the arts and in sports, particularly baseball which was my primary sport. As I became closer to Jordan and his older brothers, they would share their stories of smoking grass, and hash and taking LSD. Living in a beach community in Florida provided the environment for their cultural enlightenment, or rather their adventures into the wild, including sexual exploration.

The feminist movement was well underway in the country, but our little community was slow in accepting most progressive ideas and practices. Nonetheless, the small satellite Penn State campus where my mother worked allowed for many students, particularly from the Philadelphia area, to infiltrate the neighborhood. They brought with them rock 'n' roll music, long hair, unshaven, braless women, sex, bell-bottom jeans and drugs. The impact was visceral and profound. I was compelled to move toward the light, albeit a strobe light in an opium den with naked vixens dancing to the music of the Beatles' *White Album*. Or so I imagined. On one hand there was complacency and on the other, a brand new world. I started playing guitar seriously as well as smoking grass the summer of 1971, between my sophomore and junior years of high school. I had been smoking cigarettes since I was twelve, so the transition to smoking dope seemed a logical choice. The high was either scary or exhilarating, depending on the place and circumstances.

Nick Lunt, our primary drug dealer, now going into senior year, had been in perpetual trouble in school, being sent home many times for wearing clothes inappropriate under the school dress code, not to mention his failing classes and at one point challenging the principal, Mr. Bannen, by calling him a dictator. That was as bold a move as I had witnessed. Mr. Bannen, a Charles Bronson lookalike, was a violent, abusive man who terrorized the student body. During every class change he could be seen standing at the apex of a busy student crossing, arms folded, with his clipboard clutched in his hand. Many times I witnessed him slamming the clipboard over the head of some errant teenage boy, or picking up a boy by his shirt collar and smashing him into a locker for some small infraction. Chewing gum would do it. He would not hesitate to take a large wooden paddle and beat students on their rear ends for the most mundane violations. In my public school up until my senior year, jeans were not permitted to be worn. The dress code required men's hair to be worn at a moderate length.

At sixteen I was not quite still a boy and not yet a man, but somewhere in between. In early summer 1971 a group of friends gathered to plan an outing to Lake Meade, a manmade lake community an hour and a half south of our town. My parents had purchased a lot in the hope of eventually building a small vacation home. There were picnic areas and small boat and paddleboat rentals available in what was a serene and picturesque setting. The lake was fairly large, with ten miles of shoreline offering great fishing, swimming and summer activities. Seven of us decided to take a summer Saturday trip to Lake Meade, *trip* being the operative word. Ed Glasser, a quirky older teen and brother of Meg, an on-and-off girlfriend of mine, had purchased strips of "Space-Ship" LSD. There was enough for all of us to share and what better place than a beautiful lake, or so the original plan went. What occurred was nothing remotely close to a serene beautiful lake experience. The only person who had taken LSD previously was Ed. He reassured us that it would be fun. The seven of us gathered early on Saturday morning, fitting into Ed's 1965 Chevy Impala, four in the back and three up front; and off we went on our adventure.

When we arrived, around 9:30am, Ed proceeded to distribute the LSD, which was in the form of small discolored drops on small strips of blotter paper. There were four drops of acid split in half, giving us eight half-tablets. Our friend Gary Swanson decided last minute to not take the drug. He was not ready to jump into the abyss and none of us pushed him. In reality, he was the only kid being truthful, for all of us except Ed were scared. Ed chose to take a full dose of two halves and prodded me to do the same. I acquiesced, a decision I later regretted. Mary, Joan, Karen and Joe all took a half, and we were off to the races.

After about an hour I started to feel unusual. At first my senses became more acute. I sensed physical pulsing. I could feel the beat of my heart and my thoughts were elongating with a fluidity that was noticeably different. Time started to evaporate. The distinction between past and future was gone; there was only the present moment. Colors became more and more vivid. The reds were deeper. The trees were lush green, thick and textured, deep and rich. The drug continued to take me deeper and deeper into a reality completely unfamiliar and increasingly hallucinogenic. Just when I thought I was at the peak of the effects, I would be taken further. This continued for hours. There was one major issue that I had not fully thought through. My parents had decided to join us at the lake around noontime.

Nowhere in the planning stage had I anticipated having six teens in the middle of an extreme altered state of reality having to communicate and interact with my parents. This was a problem. And to make matters more challenging, I still had not reached a pinnacle in the effects of the drug, nor had my five friends. Panic now mixed with an LSD trip.

By this time, sight and sound were so intense that I could see right through the skin in my friends' faces. I could see bone structure, blood being pumped through veins and arteries, clothes hiding nothing and the ebb and flow of energy being emitted by the person I was speaking with. What I was witnessing was incredible, but if it was not checked it could have easily taken me into insanity.

I spoke with Gary and tried to tell him how high I was, what I was experiencing. The look on his face was one of fear as well as amazement. The voice inside of me spoke as though I was two separate people, one living and breathing the experience of the altered reality and the other coming from a viewpoint of logic and protection. I have often wondered who that second voice was and where it came from. Was this the voice of the Divine or my ego playing its positive role?

Gary had a watch.

"What time is it Gary?"

"It's 11:30," he said.

"Gary, I need you to tell me what you see. Help me to know what looks unusual and weird so we can do something before my parents arrive." The words coming out of my mouth echoed loudly, every consonant like the reverb in a canyon. I could see the sound waves from my mouth and Gary's, first as bursts of light then, with split-second delays, reaching my ears as actual sound waves. I saw every movement as fragmented, leaving elongated trails of light and energy. The stubble on Gary's face moved ever so slightly on his porcelain, see-through skin.

Gary looked around the picnic area and saw friends huddled near some flowers close to the lake edge. They were laughing and playing with the flowers; he said it was unusual and would be seen as very strange.

"Do you see anywhere where we could go to be less conspicuous?"

Gary pointed to a boat rental dock adjacent to the picnic area. The lake had pontoon swimming platforms quite a distance off shore where swimmers could go to lie in the sun and play. I knew all of us were good swimmers, so the voice from within saw this as a possible getaway place to provide safe haven from others, especially my parents.

I proceeded, along with Gary, to round up my friends and tell them that we were going to play on the lake. I told Gary to take them to the rental booth to rent enough paddleboats to get us on the lake and out to the floating raft. Just as they were moving toward the rental area, I turned to see my parents driving up to the parking lot. I asked Gary, "How do I look to you?"

He gave me a critical glance and said, "You look okay. Try to keep your gaze indirect, because your pupils are larger than normal."

I could feel my heart racing as I walked over to my father and mother. They were getting out of their Olds 98, opening the trunk to get out their lounge chairs and small cooler. It was one of the most difficult experiences of my life talking to my parents at that moment. I was close to peaking in the effects of the drug. Sight and sound were so distorted from any normal reality that every word and movement was straight out of a Salvador Dali painting, psychedelically imbued with the deepest colors imaginable. The words "Hi Dad. How was the trip down?" sounded as though every syllable in every word had twenty separate parts to it.

My father's face moved and swirled, his eyes not stationary, nostrils opening and closing like a bull's and the trailing sound of each word as though thrown off a deep ravine endlessly echoing into an unknown darkness. He answered, "Just fine. How are you guys doing?"

I managed to collect myself, saying, "Great, we are renting paddle-boats and going out on the lake. We ate a big breakfast on the way down and are going to have some fun on the lake."

I heard my mom in the background saying, "Do you want some lunch?"

Unbeknownst to my parents, eating was impossible. I said, "No, we are good, Mom."

Trying to limit my interaction with my parents, I needed an excuse to escape. I said, "I need to use the lav."

I turned and walked to a Porta-Potty set up at the picnic grounds. Entering the enclosed unit to relieve myself was surreal. The boomerang-shaped patterns on the fiberglass walls were flying around and jumping at me.

I returned to where my father had set up the chairs beside a small grill. I said, "I'm going to join my friends. See you later."

Their response gave me no indication they knew how desperately high I was. As I walked toward the paddleboat area, I could see the wind blowing the tree limbs back and forth like arms of loving parents reaching out to capture the air into their leaves, all aglow and alive with breath and energy. The wildflowers on the ground each had faces, smiling and dancing together as the breeze touched them. My steps were as though connected to something greater than my body, united to the air, sunlight and energy surrounded me. I saw every single element as different from normal reality. I heard all sounds intensified with reverb amplification. I perceived physical movement as energy in motion, long and streamlined. Time became elastic. Each second became longer, not static but rather experienced in the context of other moments past and future. I could see deeper, past the three-dimensional limitations of earthly material, through layers of skin and bone, through deception and untruth; all seemed to peel away under the effects of the drug. It was overwhelming on one hand and absolutely stunning on the other.

We paddled our boats—two paddleboats and one rowboat manned by Gary and me—out into the lake. Joan and Karen were paddling in one boat, laughing hysterically and pointing up toward a stand of large oak and maple trees on shore. We were quite a distance out in the lake, when I turned to see what they were looking at: I saw the trees smiling at us as their limbs swayed in the breeze. The trees opened up their faces, looking down on us smiling with love and kindness as though telling us how much they loved us connecting with them.

Joan brought their paddleboat close to our rowboat and as I looked at her from across the bow of the boat, I saw a luminescent angel shine through her naked body. I remember the smile on her face as she turned to me in slow motion, the light of the Divine surrounding her. Our eyes met and I smiled back, telling her that she was the most beautiful person I had ever seen. She replied in a voice other than Joan's, "Thank you, Michael. I am only a reflection of you." Then she stood up and dove into the warm lake waters. In what felt like minutes but was only seconds, she emerged from the water. To my surprise I saw her large tail fin come out from behind her to propel her through the water, a mermaid swimming with such ease and grace. Gary then decided to take a swim. Standing up in our rowboat, he took off his tank top, tossed it in the boat and dove into the water. As he came to the surface it wasn't Gary, but rather a dolphin joyfully swimming through the water, jumping repeatedly above the lake surface, playful and at home.

We gathered together on the floating raft and spent the rest of the afternoon on the lake. It was a safe haven for the tripping clan. My parents stayed at the picnic area for several hours. Then they waved to us from the shoreline, yelled that they were leaving and departed.

The seven of us waved back to them and continued our adventures. We had not been caught. It was after three in the afternoon and the trip continued. It was half past seven when we were able to drive home. The effects of the drug lingered for many hours after, but the experience never left me. I would take LSD twice more, both times in a more controlled environment.

Emerging into Myself

The music of the late 1960s and early 1970s captured my creative energies. Jordan Lunt and I both played guitar. We covered many groups and songs of the time, learning their guitar chords and leads and memorizing lyrics. Early on in my guitar playing I was heavily influenced by the Beatles; the Rolling Stones; Led Zeppelin; the Doobie Brothers; James Taylor; Crosby, Stills & Nash; the Eagles and the Allman Brothers Band. The first song I learned was "Eleanor Rigby," from the Beatles' *Revolver* album. I added "House of the Rising Sun," "You've Got a Friend" and "Stairway to Heaven" to my repertoire in the early years of learning guitar and eventually performing. Jordan and I would smoke pot and play guitar for hours, experimenting and jamming to what are now the classics. From 1971 through my college career, I played guitar and sang. I traveled everywhere carrying a guitar and surrounded myself with other musicians.

It was a natural transition for me to embrace the guitar; it provided a rich connection to a hip culture through a magically creative instrument that combined self-expression with passion. It let me continue to hide the real Michael behind the music, with occasional snippets of true identity emerging in moments of singing and performing.

I became a master at controlling just how much I would give you, always careful to conceal the pain and sorrow, the insecurity attached to abandonment and loss. Poet–musicians of this era composed ballads that especially moved me. Early Jackson Browne songs, "Fountain of Sorrow" and "Rock Me on the Water" as well as Dan Fogelberg's, *Home Free* album and Loggins and Messina's "Danny's Song," "Angry Eyes" and "Pathway to Glory" all moved me in an acoustic direction that would define my musical bent.

I managed to remain buoyant through my junior year. I was selected to be the president of the student council and I was nominated for National Honor Society.

By the start of my senior year, my physical appearance mirrored the internal growth and attitude I developed that summer. Within a week I was called into the principal's office to discuss the length of my hair. I was to abide by the dress code or suffer the consequences of suspension. Two other students, both from respectable families, were also pulled into Mr. Bannen's office and given the same ultimatum. That same week a decision was made to expel me from the student council and pull the National Honor Society nomination.

My father set up an appointment with Mr. Bannen to discuss the situation. Both my parents believed in justice and fairness. My father was not one to antagonize nor was he the sort to take ultimatums. After spending ten minutes with Mr. Bannen and hearing him say that unless I cut my hair I would be suspended, my father asked bluntly, "Mr. Bannen, specifically what does the length of hair have to do with learning?" After he got a lame non-answer, my father stated that I would not be cutting my hair and if necessary he would seek legal action against the school. He then stood up and said to Mr. Bannen, "I hear that you conduct yourself as a tyrant. Many of us went to war to destroy tyrants. Do not underestimate me, Mr. Bannen." And he walked out.

I was indefinitely suspended pending my adhering to the school's dress code. The two other families joined forces with my parents. The local news media picked up the story quickly, calling us the Middletown 3, and small-town Middletown was thrust into the regional and national spotlight. Within two days, the ACLU contacted the parents, advising them that they would like to represent the families in a joint lawsuit against the school. We agreed to be represented and took the school to the Supreme Court of Pennsylvania alleging that we had not broken the dress code, and that the three of us were being mistreated under the Pennsylvania constitution. The case was tried quickly and the school was found at fault. The school dress code states, "Men's hair is to be worn at a moderate length." The lawyers representing asked whether a boy who shaves his head would be in violation under the dress code, since a shaved head could easily be interpreted as not conforming to a "moderate" hair length. Furthermore, "moderate length" is interpreted to mean different things by different people. We won the case and entered the school as heroes to some and evildoers to others. The student body was split, as were the teachers. The school administrators, however, were united in their belief that we were the lowest of low.

The school year was challenging; especially gym class, which was run by the football coach, Mr. Koons, a former Army Green Beret who was as venomous as a viper and whose preferred method of interaction was violence and intimidation. Coach Koons did everything he could with the exception of hitting me to break me down. He called me into his office during a regularly scheduled gym class to scream in my face, slam his desk, break chairs and call my father a "pussy."

My only retort during the thirty-minute tirade was, "Your breath stinks."

He exploded in rage, smashing a chair over his desk. I received a minus one in gym that year, the equivalent of an F.

The coach's teenage son committed suicide a couple years after my graduation.

In small town America in my generation, one requirement for a guy to be cool was owning a hot car. The second was a motorcycle and I eventually owned both. I bought, for $850 cash, a 1965 Pontiac GTO convertible, candy-apple red metal-flake, 389 cubic inch V8, four-speed manual transmission, Hurst shifter—and fast. I embodied seventeen-year-old cool. I garnered much attention from a host of young ladies who wanted to sit next to me in the white bucket seats as well as to grace the back seat at times. I spent the summer and fall of 1972 exploring the world of the opposite sex.

My mother would often say to me, "You change girlfriends like you change your underwear!"

I would just smile and say I was playing the field. Throughout college and into young adulthood, I dated women from different parts of the world with diverse cultural backgrounds and ethnicities, from Jamaica, Czechoslovakia, Russia, Vietnam and the Philippines.

"Why can't you find a nice Irish Catholic girl?" she would ask. Had she lived long enough, she would have gotten her wish with my second wife, a light-skinned Catholic of Irish descent and a high-powered psychologist at that.

The Passionate Student

An undercurrent of discontent and limitation ruled my adolescent years. I attended Middletown Area High School, in a small-town, narrow-minded community of around ten thousand largely right-wing Republicans, a microcosm of rural Pennsylvania. In the context of a changing social consciousness with the later years of the Vietnam war, counterculture protests, the emergence of rock 'n' roll, drugs and sexual liberation, my own sense of self was stirred and electrified by what I saw as a world full of possibilities and endless adventures. One thing certain for me was an inability to remain static, for the energy and inner impulse driving me was powerful. It overrode any fear that would hinder my exploring this new world. My mother, during this time, would refer to me as having wings on my feet. I was continually running from, running to and running, period. I knew that I needed to open my wings and fly. Just what direction I was running was uncertain. Yet, I had a consuming drive that compelled me to explore.

The era of my own awakening started in my junior year of high school.

The year was 1972, the latter half of my junior year. Carrie Stiles, a fifteen-year-old blond, blue-eyed vixen entered our school midyear. Carrie was not your average tenth grader. Moving to Middletown from San Diego when her father changed jobs, she brought with her what all of us boys saw as the quintessential southern California surfer-girl image. She stirred testosterone-fueled fantasies in the entire male student body. As either good luck or bad luck would have it, my best friend Mark Davis, an athletic, handsome and intelligent teen, made a quick move on Carrie. They became a couple within the first several weeks of her entering school, and as his best friend I, too, had ample connection time with Carrie. I never was the type to undermine my friends and certainly had no inclination to steal Carrie away from Mark. Carrie, on the other hand, found my company easy and enjoyable. There was a subliminal and energetic connection that both of us knew was there; however, with our frontal lobes still not developed sufficiently, understanding this current was challenging. And no doubt I was attracted to her.

Then, quite unexpectedly the news came that Carrie and her family would be leaving to return to San Diego. Her father had been called back to southern California to resume his previous position. Stunned and disappointed, Mark was emotionally shattered by the news that his love would be leaving him. He called me. He was devastated. Unbeknownst to him, I, too, was heartbroken by her departure.

A couple weeks before she was scheduled to leave, Carrie approached me between classes one Wednesday afternoon, saying she needed to talk privately. Until this point I had done everything in my power to restrain myself in supporting my best friend in his relationship with Carrie by concealing my feelings in both words and actions. Truth was, I was terrified by my feelings. I had no experience with such overwhelming sexual desires, nor had I ever kept such intense feelings hidden in the recesses of my heart. So the anticipation of meeting her as she had requested filled me with both anxiety and teenage hope of a reciprocal admission of her desire and love for me. We agreed to meet after school.

Our meeting place was the side entrance to the Performing Arts Center, a place that was a second home for me, having spent countless hours practicing, performing and living out my passions on stage. I had recommended this place in that I knew every inch of the area as well as the security it provided so that we could be protected. At 3:30 I rounded the corner into the hallway toward the backstage entrance, where I spied Carrie standing inside the doorway, with the door cracked open. As I approached, I thought my insides were going to explode in anticipation. Her smile instantly elicited a dreamlike state. She reached out and grabbed my hand, pulling me inside. The door closed behind us.

She said, "Michael, it's you that I think of everyday, that I want to be with." She put her arms around my shoulders and pulled me into her blue eyes with a passionate kiss that lasted what seemed hours. "I love you. I've loved you from the start and didn't think you felt the same for me. But I came to see it in your eyes and knew that you did, right?"

And all I could do was reply honestly. "Yes, I have from the first time I saw you."

After another passionate kiss, we departed, saying that we would remain quiet so as to not upset Mark. In the center of my spirit and heart, I was torn by the deceit, yet caught in the midst of the ecstasy of knowing of her shared feelings. I remained silent and started to imagine a plan to visit her in San Diego.

Over the course of the next couple months, between her departure in late April 1972 and the end of our school year in early June, letter after letter came and went between Carrie and me, speaking of our love and rapture for each other. That she was fifteen years old seemed incomprehensible to me. Her physical, emotional and sexual maturity was so much further along than any other teen I had ever met. Her Southern California natural style, clothing that accentuated her natural blond hair, her young supple unshaved body, braless and scented with patchouli oil—it was all too much to bear for a seventeen-year-old young man still a boy. Nothing was going to keep me from making my way across the US to be with Carrie. The master plan was in place.

School ended the second week in June and my plan was to leave the following Wednesday, June 14, aboard my 1970 Suzuki 350 cc motorcycle. I was seventeen, so the law was not on my side when it came to legally having the ability to up and leave my family. I knew in my heart that I could not possibly discuss my dilemma with my parents, for no matter how I would sell the story, it would be met with a definitive no. In light of this, I realized that I had no other choice but to pull a clandestine departure, leaving without my parents' knowledge or approval. I had to do what I had to do.[6]

I filled a backpack with a smattering of clothes and supplies needed for the journey. I fired up my motorcycle and headed out, traveling west on the Pennsylvania Turnpike. From Harrisburg to western Pennsylvania is more than two hundred miles winding through the Allegheny Mountains, a challenging daylight trip in good weather. On a 350 cc motorcycle with the afternoon rapidly approaching, the wind and rain starting to pelt me as tractor-trailers blew past me, I was struggling. As the skies darkened, I heard my motorcycle engine spit and sputter. One of the cylinders was failing, causing the bike to slow down and lurch erratically. I pulled over at a safe place and attempted to adjust what I thought could be the mechanical issue. It was to no avail. A sense of darkness swept over me. I realized that I was still in Pennsylvania, with another 2,500 miles left in my trek. After consulting the inner voice of reason and what I now have come to understand as the voice of the Divine, I decided I should turn around and rethink the mission. Traveling at a top speed of 50 mph, I made my way to the next exit and headed east. Luckily, I returned prior to my mother coming home, so I was successful in grabbing my note.

Dejected and feeling a sense of failure, I decided to sleep on it. During a restless night, I came to the conclusion that I would resort to plan B; I was not going to let this first attempt shatter my dream.

Funny how love will find a way. I may have been down, but I wasn't out. I had almost $65 saved, which at the time felt like enough money to make a getaway. I would go to the Greyhound Bus Terminal the next morning in Harrisburg and buy a ticket as far as I could get on $40, saving the rest for any other unforeseen expenses, like eating. So on Friday morning, after my mother left for work at Penn State, I gathered my backpack, checked to see that I had all I needed, rewrote the letter to my parents, placed it on the table at the top of the landing and left for the bus terminal. By nine, I was on the road traveling west on I-90, the Pennsylvania Turnpike, my old friend. I knew that once my mother found my letter she would immediately worry and put into motion any and all methods to find me and return me home. I realized that making it to San Diego would require careful planning and thoughtful moves. At that time, it wasn't necessary to show identification to purchase a bus ticket, so I could not be traced from the bus station; however, I knew that this would be an obvious point of investigation. The ticket got me to St. Louis, Missouri, by the next morning, after twenty-two hours of travel with intermittent stops. In St. Louis I made a collect phone call to my Mother. I could hear the anxiety and stress in her voice when she asked if I was okay. I assured her that I was fine. I said that I was doing this not to hurt them, but because it was something I needed to do. If I had come to them asking for their blessing the answer would have been a definitive no. I told my mother I loved her and that I would contact her again in two days. She pleaded for me to tell her where I was and what I was doing. I told her, "No, I need to do this. I will call you in two days." And I hung up the phone.

I had $33 dollars in my pocket and now was in a rundown section of St. Louis not far from the railroad station. I walked several miles to the freight yard, where I stealthily moved between cars to a protected area where I could overhear conversations of railway workers preparing freight cars for travel to various cities. I knew I needed to go west and identified a series of cars that were heading to Oklahoma City and beyond. Waiting for the right moment, now midday on Saturday, I scurried to a partially empty car with the door slightly ajar. Making sure that no one was watching, I climbed up the side through the small opening and into the interior of the car. There were wooden crates carrying what appeared to be machinery of some sort in the back of the car and dirty wooden slats on the floor boards where I sat, back against the wall, mind racing and heart pounding. Seventeen and catching rail to Oklahoma City from St. Louis, the material that songs are made of. Yet, I also had an appropriate level of fear of what was to come. After about an hour, the train started to move, and off we went, heading southwest across the plains. There were several stops along the journey and I catnapped during the many hours of tapping and clacking on the tracks. It was early Sunday morning when the train pulled into Oklahoma City.

I did not know where the freight car would be heading next, so I exited to find another way further west. Someone saw me moving between cars, and the next thing I knew, three big men snuck up on me from the opposite side of the train and jumped out in front of me. They looked like lions about to come in for the kill. I saw a road adjacent to where we were, but just out of sight. Fearing for my life, I ran toward the road. I wanted to at least be visible to oncoming vehicles. But one of the men grabbed me and spun me around while another punched me hard in the head. The third punched me in the stomach, knocking the wind out of me, as he tried to rip the pack off my back. As I fell to the ground, one of the thugs jumped on top of me, flailing punches at my head until blood flowed from a gash on the side of my face and from my nose.

Just then I heard a car horn and heard the car approaching. The three men ran off into the freight yard. Lying on the dirt shoulder, I heard the car door open. A woman in her thirties reached down to help me sit up. She asked if I was okay and said, "Let's get you in my car and away from this place. Those guys are likely to come back." I got into the passenger seat and threw my pack in the back. The woman reached for a rag and placed it against the cut on my face. She told me to hold it tight to stop the bleeding. As she drove away, I managed to say, "Thank you for saving me back there. I don't know what I would have done if you hadn't come along." She said she was just finishing her shift and was leaving to go home.

"What were you doing out there?"

I told her that I had just traveled from St. Louis in one of the freight cars and was trying to make my way to another car so that I could get further west. "I'm trying to get to San Diego," I said.

"Why San Diego and why are you catching rail?"

Feeling the sting of the gash on my cheek I answered, "There's a girl that I need to see."

"Oh," she said. "Is this a girl you love?"

I told her it was and she asked if I was hungry. "Yes, very."

"I will take you to my place and make you some food. It's no problem."

My life experiences have shown that angels come in different forms at different times. That angel's name was Marci. She was unmarried, slightly overweight, with red hair, blue eyes and a big smile. Her timing was perfect in saving me from untold harm, and her generosity was overwhelming. Not only did Marci not judge me or treat me like a child, but she opened her small home to me, providing food and a place to sleep and shower before continuing my trek. Marci's shift began at seven the next

37

morning. Early Monday morning, after a cup of coffee and toast, Marci gave me $20 on the condition that I would take a bus the rest of the way. I nodded my consent and thanked her with a kiss and a warm smile.

After dropping me at the bus station, Marci sped away as quickly as she appeared. I bought a one-way ticket to San Diego on the next bus, leaving in forty-five minutes. I proceeded to a pay phone and dialed my home number collect. My mother was waiting for my call.

She accepted the collect call from the operator and said, "Where are you?"

I said I was safe and doing fine.

She said, "Well, I am not doing fine. I want you to know that we have contacted the police and they have an APB out to find you. Why are you doing this to us?"

"I'm not trying to do anything to you. I know I've hurt you and that you are very concerned. I will call you when I get where I'm going. I am fine." I hung up the phone. I felt bad for my mother.

The loudspeaker announced that the 9am bus to San Diego via Amarillo, Albuquerque and Phoenix was ready for boarding at gate 7. I climbed aboard and on Wednesday morning I arrived at the bus station in San Diego.

Carrie's mother answered the phone. I told her who I was and she said she was happy that I was visiting. Carrie came to the phone, excited, and asked me where I was. She told me to wait at the bus station and that they would come get me within twenty minutes.

I came clean both to my parents and to the Stileses. I told my parents where I was; and I told the Stileses that I had traveled across country without permission, causing my parents a great deal of stress and worry.

After two days with Carrie, I was shipped home via Greyhound bus, traveling from San Diego to Harrisburg. I arrived at the height and fury of Hurricane Agnes as it decimated central Pennsylvania with, at that time, the costliest tropical storm disaster in US history. There was no time to ground me for my actions, since all able-bodied men were called to work around-the-clock to support families ravaged by the effects of the hurricane.[7]

A Summer to Remember

Much to my chagrin, my brother took out my GTO one afternoon in late 1972 and blew the transmission, destroying my beautiful home on wheels. His explanation: "I forgot to shift!" I almost forgot to restrain myself. That wasn't the only car my brother destroyed. After the demise of my Pontiac, he drove my father's Olds 88 into a light pole. And he accidentally backed my mother's 1968 Olds Cutlass into a stream, submerging the engine and destroying another family vehicle.

Later in his life he drove an eighteen-wheel tractor-trailer for a small trucking company in western Ohio. He loved to drive. We learned not to lend our vehicles to Danny.

My senior year of high school was fairly easy, with half-day classes and a full-time dishwashing job at the Gimbels retail store restaurant in the new mall outside of Harrisburg.

Large malls were in their infancy in the 1970s, and procuring a job at Gimbels was considered a win. Earning enough money during my senior year allowed me to realize my plan of spending most of the summer on the West Coast.

In the summer of 1973, after graduating from Middletown, I continued running. I traveled across country again, in my new 1973 Chevy Vega, to meet Carrie Stiles and spend the summer living at the beach, Mission Beach specifically.

I found a one-room apartment in a rundown building two blocks from the beach where I lived for seven weeks that summer, before entering Harrisburg Area Community College (HACC) as a freshman in

September. Carrie's mother equipped me with a hotplate and a can opener, so I could heat up canned soup, beans and other assorted edibles. Elegant it was not.

Carrie had moved on in her romantic escapades, dating Vernon, a Hawaiian surfer dude three years my senior with rugged good looks and a proclivity for young surfer girls. The initial disappointment of confirming that Carrie was no longer interested in me wore off quickly, as Vernon and I became friends—or at least drug-sharing, surfing acquaintances—joining in two months of adventures that took me much further along in my drug-using career.

My summer in San Diego was consumed with expanding my acumen in drug use, guitar playing, surfing and learning a culture much different than small-town Pennsylvania provided. By this time my hair was well below my shoulders and my daily dress code involved surfer shorts, a T-shirt and sandals. Vernon and several of his Hawaiian drug surfer buddies lived not far from me between Mission and Pacific Beaches. Their connection to Island drug trafficking brought in pot, meth, heroin, Quaaludes and everything in between. We would get together early mornings, take some meth to ratchet up our bodies to an electric tempo and then head out to surf. Sometimes we would travel up or down the coast to find the best conditions. At times, to cut the edge off the meth, we would smoke a joint or two, which left us feeling energized, yet mellow, a combination that enhanced the surfing experience.

One time early in the summer as I was learning to surf, gaining confidence and becoming more adept, we swam out further into the ocean than usual, as the waves were breaking out along a ridge. Sitting on my Hobie board, gauging the waves as they were making their way across the ridge and building, I spotted a dorsal fin in the water about twenty feet from where I was stationed. My first reaction was terror. *A shark*, I thought. I was four hundred yards out in the ocean; I was sure we would be attacked.

Vernon and Josie were adjacent to me off my left shoulder, sitting on their boards when I yelled, "Shark!"

They both started screaming at me, "Paddle your board, go, go!" As I feverishly started paddling, I could hear them both chortling out loud, laughing hysterically. I stopped and turned to look and what was one dorsal fin became many. It was a school of dolphin coming through and looking to play. I sat up on my board, relieved yet embarrassed, and right next to my right leg appeared a seven-foot dolphin rubbing his body next to mine. The relief was profound in knowing I wasn't going to die.

Vernon called over to me. "They want to play." I saw him holding onto the fin of a dolphin, being pulled through the water. Josie, too, had joined in the fun. The dolphin cuddling up to me circled. I slipped off the board, grabbed his dorsal, and off we went, shooting through the water. The power and force was exhilarating. Our friends joined us for playtime more than once. I loved their joyful spirits and natural inclination to connect with us in their environment.

Over the weeks in San Diego, I went from one high to the next. The electric high of the daytime would turn to the all-consuming mellow rush of heroin, downers, alcohol and other assorted nighttime drugs. At first the idea of shooting heroin into my veins was abhorrent. But over time, I was convinced to give it a try. The immediate full-body experience was nothing I had ever encountered. To this day, in a safe audience, I will attest to the fact that heroin is the absolute best high. Days turned to nights and each rotation of the earth brought with it new adventures, some of which were not only terrifying, but dangerous. The Hawaiian drug cartel was in Vernon's family blood, so we seemed to have an endless supply and array of drugs.

The visit to Tijuana, Mexico, on a mid-July Tuesday brought me to an all-time high that took a week to undo. After our typical day of surfing, drinking and playing, Josie turned to us and said, "Hey dudes, let's do a road trip to Tijuana and find us some dirty senoritas!" To which all replied, "Totally," and off we went. Crossing the border was a bit risky in that Vernon was carrying enough heroin to keep all of us high for a month. Playing the good US citizens, we easily passed through customs and made our way into the dirt-bag of a town. In the early 1970s, Tijuana was starting to become a tourist town, with a smattering of trinket stores selling cheap useless figurines, coarse Mexican blankets, sombreros, and bottles of authentic mescal, worm and all. In the seedy part of town—which was most of it—drug pushers lined the streets hanging in the shadows, but we had no need for drugs. We came well stocked. Into the bars we strolled, a few beers here and then onto the next saloon, where beers turned to shots of 100 proof tequila. Over the next several hours we reinforced ourselves with meth on top of the heroin we had shot. The high was best described as frenetic warmth with enough capacity to continue drinking heavily. There were many young senoritas entertaining us, and at one point Josie was seen in a corner fully engaged with a young dark-haired girl who looked like she was sixteen. She was undressed, with her legs up in the air, lying on top of a table, screaming with either pleasure or pain. I wondered if her parents knew where she was—a curious question I remember asking myself, but even in my high it struck me as sad and wrong.

Somewhere in late afternoon, after many shots of tequila and more uppers and downers, I went into a blackout. Oh, I was still partying and participating, but I had no memory of what occurred. The next thing I remembered was waking up in my small apartment in Mission Beach. Although, waking up would not aptly describe my reemergence into conscious reality. Opening my eyes brought into opaque focus a world of complete distortion. I could not focus with any clarity and I was experiencing what can best be described as hallucinations. The porous wall in front of me appeared to have thousands of small bugs crawling across the surface; the sunlight diffused through the one window in my apartment shone jagged particles of light cascading as if being poured from a container into the room. I managed to sit up eventually, making my way to the bathroom, where the mirror showed a face completely out of proportion, bruised, intoxicated, sick and punished.

When I was able to regain a semblance of reality, I determined that it was two days later than when we started our Mexican journey. I had been out for an extended time. I had no recollection of anything that happened from midday Tuesday until waking in my dingy hole of a room, late Thursday afternoon. The effects of this abuse lasted for the better part of a week. Vernon and Josie were nowhere to be found. It took me until Saturday, two days later to be able to leave my apartment and find food. When I finally connected with Vernon the following Wednesday late morning, he found me sitting on the cement rail along the beach boardwalk. He called, "Michael," from a distance and rode up to me on his bike.

I greeted him with a question. "What happened?"

He climbed off his bike and sat beside me. For the next hour he told me that we had continued partying through the early morning hours on Wednesday.

We all ate the worms from empty bottles of mescal, continued to dope it up and ended up in a brothel with twice as many women as ourselves. Kinky things ensued and we ended up getting a room in a small hotel to gain enough clear head to make our way back to the US. I told him I couldn't remember anything.

He laughed heartily and said he was surprised, since he thought I was perfectly lucid and participating the whole time.

I asked him how we made it back through customs.

He said Aaron, the soberest of all of us, drove. He collected our IDs and we came through just before sunlight, all of us pretending to be asleep. Aaron told the US Customs officer that it was a tough night in Tijuana. He smiled at the agent, who smirked and told him to get some rest. When we pulled up to my apartment building off the beach, I opened the car door and was last seen going into the building. That was last Wednesday morning, a week ago. Vernon smiled and laughed out loud, slapping me on the back and saying, "Let's go dude. We have places to go and people to see." And off we went; I sat on his handlebars as he pedaled north up the boardwalk. The drugs started again immediately. The warm liquid flowing into my arm quickly brought on the nausea associated with the heroin high, but melted moments later into the best feeling I had experienced over the previous week. We were off to the races again.

The time had come for me to return to Pennsylvania and attend college. As punishing and exciting as the summer had been, leaving was necessary for more reasons than one. In truth, I was no closer to filling the hole inside me following my summer visit to San Diego, but the primary target for me was school. I never had to be told that higher education was important. It was always something I greatly valued, a goal to be sought, a destiny worthy of my time and energy. Being a jack-of-all-trades and master of none, I had no idea what educational path to pursue. All I knew was that I was getting my bachelor's degree, one way or another. While I had dreamed of attending NYU, Columbia, Berkeley or Cornell, knowing of the superlative quality of education along with their liberal progressive student culture, I simply was not prepared academically or financially to have applied, so Harrisburg Area Community College, HACC, as it's called, became my institution of higher learning for the next two years. I earned an Associate of Arts degree and was able to transfer all my credits to Syracuse University, a college I researched to find that had an outstanding theatre arts program.

The Lie

November 4, 1995, standing at the altar of Holy Names Catholic Church in Albany, New York, I turned to see the woman I would marry entering the church adorned in lace and white silk faille. Her fairytale wedding had commenced and I, her trophy husband to be, stood in the silent realization that what I was embarking on was in fact a lie. I was about to marry a woman who quite clearly suffered from a blend of colloquial myopia and an inability to understand what marriage, love and true union required. Looking back on this defining moment, I realize how incapable she was of having any meaningful intimate relationship, let alone a marriage. I knew, as I stood there, that what I was entering into was a sham. And how incredibly sad it was to know that I had gotten this far in my life, at age forty, unmarried, without children and trying desperately to attain some degree of normalcy, and that I was making a huge mistake, one that would haunt me for decades. The prospect of having a home, a family and a life worth living, all combined in my settling for this woman now walking down the aisle in a church, surrounded by local family, small town bigotry and the false hope of realizing a dream. What I had felt emotionally and spiritually in this realization became a reality.

The next five years were challenging. My mother was stricken with the slow deterioration of dementia, which finally took her in April 1996. Our son, James Mitchell Splann, was born in September 1996. We built a new home in Raymertown, New York. And these years saw incredible verbal and psychological abuse, eventually ending in a long, drawn-out divorce proceeding.

I had done more than marry into a blue-collar working-class family. I had unwittingly entered into a family where anger, bigotry, hatred and profound ignorance ruled. It was insane to try to be a good father to the son I had so desperately wanted under the onslaught of attacks I knew I was in for.

James's birth ripped me deeply. Until then, I had never known a blood relative, never had someone that I resembled and never experienced a truly connected family. I learned that my wife was pregnant in early 1996. After a few months, I knew I had made a colossal mistake. Her loud, accusatorial attacks confirmed the risk I took in marrying her.

I had pleaded in prayer and petition to the God of my understanding to not allow her to become pregnant. I knew at my core that parenting with her would be disastrous and would result in a lifetime of pain and hardship. My prayers were not answered and the result was what I had anticipated.[8]

The Second Time Not the Charm

After my first marriage, I found a partner who was a successful published author and an internationally recognized expert in her field, with an amazing track record of dramatically improving the lives of so many. She seemed too good to be true.

Divorce in New York State is preceded by a separation agreement. Once the agreement is in place for one year, the divorce becomes final. This process was painfully long and filled with unreasonable demands. When my first wife and I discussed our separation agreement and child custody, the starting point for her was that I could come by and see my son occasionally. For a deadbeat father, this might sound like a terrific deal, but for a dedicated loving father like me, this offer as a starting point to negotiations was not only insulting, but infuriating. And it only got worse over time.

For the last four years of my first marriage, from 1996 to 2000, while we both lived in our Raymertown home, we slept in different bedrooms. That she would not put our son into his crib over the weeks and months after his birth, wanting him to sleep with her instead, added to the perpetual verbal abuse, the incessant attacks and increasingly hostile home life.

She also insisted that her Jack Russell terrier, Butch, the most vicious and willful animal I had ever known, be in bed or on the couch or at the table with James and her. And I was the fool who purchased the dog after the loss of her seventeen-year-old beagle during her pregnancy. Of course, I did that out of love and concern for her losing the dog. That purchase ranks in the top ten bad decisions I've made, for this dog was a nightmare. When it was around my wife the dog would terrorize me, snapping, barking and goading me. There were many nights where I dreamed of taking the dog out in the backyard, grabbing my imaginary .357 Magnum with the eight-inch barrel and blasting the dog into a million pieces. Ah, how pleasant that dream! And I am a dog lover to boot.

There is a thin line between humiliation and humility, as my failed marriages have taught me. My first marriage was a life-altering mistake. My second marriage, however, takes on a more complex and powerful meaning. I was hung out like red meat, only to be psychologically thrashed, emasculated and duped by my own desire for sanity and love.

We had both experienced the anguish of divorce, hers after many years of marriage, three great children, a cranking private practice and a husband who wanted out. My first marriage, on the other hand, was much shorter, only five years, but nonetheless with a son, a bitter fight over custody and a lifetime of antagonism to follow. My divorce was not yet final when I met the doctor. Yes, she was an internationally recognized Ph.D. clinical psychologist, who, by her eager admission, would let anyone and everyone know that she was only twenty-five years old when she achieved her advanced degree and badge of honor. For her, title, class and the recognition of her personal and professional acquaintances were her prizes, her circle of influence.

I was coming out of a dreadful marriage. I needed time to process through the damage and not rebound too quickly into a new relationship. But after five years of a dead marriage with no affection, love or connection, I was so lonely and battered that once the divorce proceedings were underway, I wanted, needed sane companionship. During the years of my first marriage, I did not cheat or look for an extramarital affair. The thought crossed my mind often, but I chose to live true to some semblance of integrity, albeit a brutal existence.

In late 2000, Internet dating seemed the logical choice. I was busy in my work and I was a recovering alcoholic. Where was I to meet this sane companion? In a grocery store? At church? Certainly not in my work environment. So Match.com became the method for my reemergence into the dating scene.

In the first couple of months, I met some nice women, but none I had further interest in.

Then I saw her profile, an outgoing, attractive, professional, a parent of three children, with what appeared to be an intelligent, even humorous personality. I was interested. Having just come out of a horrendous marriage with a woman I believed was unstable, what I was initially reading in her profile seemed incredibly attractive. I wanted to find a partner who would embrace me as a whole person, a woman of stability and sanity, alive and thriving. The damage associated with my first marriage was pervasive and I desperately wanted someone that I could actually have intimacy, warmth and deep connection with. Ms. Psychologist had captured my interest in a big way.

We shared personal information over the Internet initially, getting to know each other and gaining additional comfort and confidence to actually connect. Our first conversation took place over the phone. I was sitting in a Walmart parking lot in Rensselaer, New York. Walmart was the anchor store off Route 4, adjacent to the Radio Shack where I had just purchased a cord for my computer. I decided it was time to call.

Her voice was rich and expressive. She told me about her life, family and first marriage. She shared details about what she was looking for in a partner. She was cogent, grown up and decisive about what she wanted. I told her about my life, its ups and downs, the abysmal failure of my marriage and the insanity of living a nightmare.

She claimed later on that I had not been forthcoming in letting her know that I was not officially divorced, although I remember differently. Of course, we spoke about our children and each of us being dedicated to them despite the challenges we both faced in our relationships. I was completely empathetic to her situation and she to mine.

Our first date was at a small Mediterranean bistro in Delmar, New York, on a cold late fall evening. While I had seen a few pictures of her, when we met I could see that she was stylish and quite put together. There was a bright energy that I could sense through her exterior. She was obviously intelligent, extroverted and accomplished. Her affect was both exhilarating and intimidating, for she was very direct in talking about her years of specialty practice and that her patients traveled in some cases by plane to take advantage of her expertise. She was in private practice and chose to not accept insurance; this impressed me, since her patients were all direct pay and clearly had the financial means to do so. She made it clear that she traveled with high-end professionals and was accustomed to a sophisticated lifestyle.

My initial meeting with her should have sounded the alarm to hightail it. I felt I was not in her league; my life had been nothing remotely close to hers, even given that we both suffered from our failed marriages. But I felt strongly attracted to her. The doctor in front of me was a welcome contrast to the woman I was divorcing. She offered a lifestyle and connection diametrically opposed to what I had just come from. Could this actually be a relationship where not only healing could take place, but one in which I would be fully supported in living an adult, intimate and enlivened life with a partner who wanted the same? That was my heartfelt desire.

We decided to combine our lives and move in together before our impending marriage in January 2002. She sold her family home of many years and we found a beautiful large home in Schenectady county. I had been renting after selling my Raymertown home in 2001, so I was able to move into the mansion before her. By this time, I had collected my own furniture along with pieces that I carried forward from my family. While my personal possessions were not ample enough to fill even a small portion of the house, I brought the items with me and moved in. Within the same month, her sale went through and she moved herself and her belongings into the house we would share. When she saw my furniture, she quickly decided that it would not work and was to be sold or given away.

What occurred was exactly that. And her unilateral decision to decorate and accessorize the house practically eliminated me from any decision making. I felt hurt, but unable to be truthful with her. She was determined and she always chose to dictate rather than engage me as her equal.

"Why don't you assert yourself? I always have to make the decisions," she would then say, after controlling any and all choices.

But wait, wasn't she the renowned psychotherapist? Wasn't she an expert? I was shattered and confused by the way she engaged with me. I was broken and unable to function in a healthy relationship. She was the expert. Who was I? If she thought that I was suffering from mental illness and incapacitated by psychological malady, then I must be sick, I thought.

One thing that I was hell-bent on achieving in any relationship following my first marriage was a partnership where honest and open intimacy along with sexual expression were cornerstones of the union. What I had originally thought possible with her became a nightmare of failed sexual connections; I was completely unable to function sexually with her. It wasn't until I realized how angry and abused I felt that I understood my physical rejection of her sexually.

It was as though she was the enemy, the hurt-mistress, the evil witch who on one hand wanted me desperately, but on the other did everything in her power to castrate me at every turn. And then I was expected to perform as her loving and intimate sexual partner.

I could not see the forest for the trees. I thought that surely it was my fault. Deep within I knew that she was vicious and controlling. It was as though I was the lost dog wandering in the pouring rain, chilled to the bone and looking for safe haven only to come to her back door, hearing her calling to me, "nice doggie, come here and I will give you food and warmth." But as I would come to the back door, she would stand up and kick me in the head.

We both realized early on that there were some issues between us, and we sought couples' therapy. We found a well-respected therapist who lived in the country on the border of New York and Massachusetts, near the Berkshires. We met with her at her home office. It didn't take very long before questions shifted to me. How did I feel about certain situations? I spoke my truth, indicating that I felt at times as though I was not being given a voice or a decision making opportunity in matters that affected both of us. The therapist homed in on what I was saying and asked my fiancée what her thought process was. She became angry and stopped the session, objecting to the therapist taking my side. It was awkward. It demonstrated her inability to see her own projection and dysfunction. Perhaps it was the hurt she carried from her first marriage breaking up. She was very clear that it was, for her, a happy marriage—three great kids and a husband that she loved. The breakup was hugely painful for her and the residual emotional carnage was still there. The unfortunate part was that I was the target of her anger and aggression. That would be the last time we sought couple's therapy.

What I had originally thought the sane choice, wasn't. I dreaded coming home at the end of my workday, only to sit at the dinner table with my doctor wife and her teenage son.

She would turn to me and ask, "What did you learn today?"

There were times when my day was filled with busywork, training development and a narrowly defined area of focus, and I answered, "Not much."

She would openly express disappointment, "So you didn't learn anything new today."

It got worse. She would chastise me for the way I chewed food, the way I ate ice cream, the way I held my fork, the color of my shirt, the way I walked, talked, drove, and on and on. She demanded that I do half the cooking. That was fine with me since I enjoyed cooking and was adept in the kitchen, or so I thought. But when I was cooking, she would intercede to ask why it was taking so long. What was my problem? Why was I cooking that dish the way I had chosen? She had a better way, of course.

There were dinner parties where she would invite her close friends and associates, usually doctors, authors, professors, artists and other elite and affluent souls who would banter about their newest success, book or medical breakthrough. She belonged to a book club that only took on classical or provocative novels, about which her circle of friends would opine with their deep revelations, one-upping each other, trying to sound the most intelligent and worldly. But I wasn't deemed worthy of an invitation. No loss there, I thought.

And she was the well-established psychologist. She insisted that I seek my own therapy to fix my issues. So I went to a series of therapists, one in Rochester, a six-hour round trip for a four-hour session with a female therapist trained in short-term intensive psychotherapy. The methodology was harsh and exhausting, resulting in no positive outcomes, just indignation and further castration. It wasn't until I worked with Robert, a psychiatrist who worked principally with children, out of the medical center, that I was able to find a nugget of sanity. Robert knew my wife fairly well, having had connections with her from the medical center. After several sessions, including prescriptions of various drugs that did nothing except make things worse, he provided me with advice and words that helped turn my life around. Robert listened to me tell the stories of my marriage, with its entangled, complex interactions. He paused, looked at me compassionately, and said, "It's not you, Michael. If my wife treated me half as badly as she is treating you, I would leave her quickly." This was the first time in what felt like an eternity that anyone had told me what was actually happening. He was absolutely correct. This was the start of our end, a short-lived relationship that I had had high hopes for.

I had thought that she and I were connected through past lives, for our energy together was combustible and electric. Even given the extreme duress of our relationship, I loved her and found her unique and desirable. But the dark side of this complex human being was so completely insidious and controlling that I could not find my way forward. There was an attraction between us that was visceral and powerful. It was challenging to relinquish my connection to her, because we were psychically connected beyond the mundane order of our visible world. Energetically, we remained connected for some time following our separation and divorce. It was only after undergoing deep past life regression work that I found out who she was in my past and how devastating her role had played out in that previous life. She was a force to be reckoned with.

But Irish Catholic she was.

I should have seen this freight train coming. I wasn't eighteen any more, torquing my testosterone driving a hot GTO.

CHAPTER 2 REFLECTIONS

[5] *Gladys was a young, intelligent and talented woman excelling in a male-driven, good-ole-boy construct. She needed to assert her power through arrogance and autocracy to succeed in that environment. The tactic may have been short-sighted and reprehensible, but it was understandable.*

Intimidating, accusing and beating up on direct reports provides no value and diminishes greatly a leader's ability to coalesce and unite those you lead and serve. Using the cattle prod technique may provide short-term results but will not sustain a loyal and trusting work group, nor will any semblance of integrity be maintained. In an environment where the manager leads with a stick, as Gladys did, those being led are forced to create a defense system to protect their own security.

[6] *I left my parents a note on the telephone table that attempted to explain the reasons for my leaving without their consent along with a sincere apology for what I knew would be severe heartache and concern. I tried to reassure my mother that I was capable and resourceful enough to take care of myself. This was a rite of passage for me. This was my wandering into the wilderness to kill the bear with my knife to prove myself a man.*

[7] *I would again travel across the country to visit Carrie after graduating in 1973, this time driving the new car purchased through all the hard work and money saved my senior year of high school.*

My relationship with Carrie had ended before it began. It was fun while it lasted, but it was an illusion of young love fueled by reckless risk-taking that characterized my youth.

Like other adolescents of my generation, I was willing to take on outdated patterns. My entrance into the drug world of the 1960s and 1970s was a natural transition for me, since my family history was replete with addiction to the most serious drug on the planet: alcohol. Of course even today, naysayers will argue that alcohol is an accepted part of a civilized society. Tell that to the many alcoholics unable to find the lifeboat to sanity.

[8] *It takes courage to take a risk. But discerning between reckless and prudent risk-taking requires learning from mistakes and embracing a level of conscious intention guided by a strong internal compass. While my marriages offer deep and relevant learning, there are other facets of my life that have also been guideposts for moving from recklessness to prudence. But no other aspect of one's life is more illuminating than relationships. My travels with the opposite sex provide a view of both my courage and my recklessness. I would gladly erase some adventures from my memory. And there are others that, despite the upheaval and challenge, I would repeat again and again.*

INSIGHTS AND TOOLS

Be a Risk-Taker - Life is not for the faint of heart! There is a difference between reckless and prudent risk-taking. Risk being real. Risk loving yourself and forgiving your imperfections, for perfection is highly over-rated and not a natural part of being human. Risk loving others, having compassion and seeking to understand the differences in others. Put aside your deeply held belief systems, strong biases and prejudices. Seek to understand those different than you to find commonality, for there is always some area to agree on and find connection.

3

BE A LOVE LEADER

From Constriction to Expansion

Among the internal firestorms that required my attention was my inability to be the real Michael and to be direct, open and honest in my connecting with others. When I started to embrace the love from within as a powerful gift offered to others, without fear of being seen as weak or as violating professional standards of etiquette, not only did my life improve greatly, but those I served responded in kind. The power attributed to genuine and honest expressions of love, compassion and understanding cannot be stressed enough in our troubled world. So where did I find my capacity to be loving and compassionate?

In the early years my family, particularly on my mother's side, was entrenched in the Catholic Church. It was not unusual to find a priest, several nuns and other church officials in the living room of my Aunt Bernadine's home, discussing church matters and drinking whiskey sours. There was even discussion early on that I would become a priest. I remember thinking it was a distinct possibility and imagining what that might feel like, having the collar and all. There was an overarching blind belief system in place among family members that Catholicism was the only path in life. God, of course, was a Catholic. Not only was *He* a Catholic, but He had white hair and a matching beard with an Irish complexion. That I would become an altar boy was a given.

My brother and I made our First Communion in the Philippines in 1961. My brother thought it would be a good idea if he gave himself a haircut, so the black and white pictures taken from our Brownie camera show a chunk of hair missing from the front of Danny's head. But his hands were folded appropriately, which is all that really mattered. Catechism and confirmation came next in the Catholic tradition. My father did not attend Mass. No surprise that Mom would tell us that he just didn't feel good on Sunday mornings. Somewhere in the late 1960s, after we made our "obligation" of confirmation, my brother and I convinced our mother to skip going to church every Sunday.

Kathleen Splann was a broken soul. Born on November 11, 1919, in Detroit, Michigan, to William and Catherine Eigo, she was the younger sister to James Michael Eigo. Following her first marriage to James Keenan at age 23, the young soldier was shipped off to the European front to fight against Nazi Germany. Kathleen gave birth to their daughter, Catherine, who at age eighteen months mysteriously died in the arms of my Great Aunt Bernadine, or so the story goes. If that was not tragic enough, within the same thirty-day period, her husband, Jim, was shot and killed in battle, and her father, William, dropped dead at the breakfast table.

Every time I imagine the magnitude of loss attached to this period for my mother, I am left in wonderment, with a sense of deep awe as to how she could possibly have managed through this pain. She never really got over the loss, for it carried in her eyes. I witnessed it during moments of reflection, in the subtle innuendos of sarcasm, in her laughter shadowed with hints of sadness. I felt her brokenness deeply as I got to know her. I always felt a strong compassion and love for Kathleen that even now brings me to tears. There was sadness in her that pulled at my heart. I often wondered why I felt as I did, as I do. The deep compassion for her pain comes from another source, of knowing pain and incredible loss, perhaps my own but carried forward from past lives. There is a touch point within my soul that resonates with the collective sadness of our human experience. [9]

As an adolescent or even a young adult I had no access to the understanding I have today. I am reminded of times when the *feeling* of difference—of inexplicable compassion and love—would sweep over me at random moments while observing others who were engaged in nondescript exchanges or when I encountered moving scenes in books or movies. Later in my adulthood, I would be completely enveloped by Divine grace while performing on stage, singing masterpieces such as Bach's Mass in B minor or the Brahms *Requiem*. During those moments, I was left in omnipresent wonderment. I did not know then what I know today.

Those experiences, while inexplicable, would draw me to a place of deep emotion, the same emotion I felt when I witnessed the pain and sadness of Kathleen, my adoptive mother.

We go through transitions in our lives, passing from birth into childhood; then on to the teenage years, where parents lose their children, becoming aliens of a sort; to again rejoining the human race as young adults. We go from parent–child to adult–adult relationships in the natural course of growing and evolving. My relationship with my mother changed over time: in my twenties, I became friends with my mother, especially following the death of my father in September 1982.

Growing Up

I brought into this life the capacity to have a curious mind, compassionate heart and also a resilient, flexible body. I had interests beyond the arts when I was growing up.

My mother always rued the day she left the Philippines. Housework, cooking, cleaning and maternal duties were not her forte, and she made no bones about it. Having a live-in maid, servants who did everything from making our clothes to climbing our coconut trees for fresh coconuts, not to mention having breakfast, lunch and dinner prepared each day and the accompanying clean up done by others—all this was a slice of paradise for my mother.

Rural Pennsylvania was about the worst place my mother could imagine moving to. She tended to be outspoken and it was not uncommon to hear her swear aloud multiple times in one thought process. Being from an Irish Catholic background, she was a die-hard Democrat. Keeping her opinions to herself was a challenge. Even when she was silent, her nonverbal communications screamed.

Sports became a natural outlet for me, with baseball, the American pastime, being my primary sport. The movie *Sandlot* captures both the correct period and the real-life impact summer baseball had on me. I prided myself on being an outstanding shortstop, able to easily turn a double play at age seven, able to bunt my way on base in a pinch. Our suburban home on Richard Avenue was just two blocks from the ball field, and lucky for my brother and me, we always had kids our own age to play with.

And play hard I did. One hot July afternoon, we took on the best team in our league. It was the bottom of the seventh inning, the score tied, one out with a runner on second, and I was up to bat. As the second man in the lineup, my job was to get on base. I earned that slot because of my ability to run and steal bases. I was a scrappy seven-year-old who took baseball seriously, so when the pitcher launched his fastball at me, I zeroed in on the sweet spot and fired the ball over the first baseman's head into right field. No doubt it was a hit and would advance the runner from second to third, but young Michael Splann was not satisfied with an easy single. No, I had to stretch this one out. My first base coach was yelling for me to stay on first as I rounded the base. But I had different plans. Off I ripped, heading to second, as the right fielder scooped up the ball and rocketed it toward the second baseman. I was two-thirds of the way from first to second when I saw the throw coming into second base. Knowing that I was likely to be tagged out, I decided to go in feet first, guns blazing.

I knocked the ball out of the second baseman's glove and was called safe, scoring the run from third to take a lead in the game. The only issue was that in my unorthodox slide, I caught my left arm under my body and badly broke my arm. That would be the last game of my season. But, we won the game and took first place that summer. Ah, baseball!

Our suburban community in Pennsylvania would be our home for twelve years. Danny and I had a slow time acclimating ourselves to this new environment. The kids were plentiful, as we lived in an ideal suburban community where families intentionally moved so that their children had a great place to grow up. This oasis suburban island was surrounded primarily by farms with a population best described as conservative, politically right and Republican, with a significant segment being Mennonite or Evangelicals.

Imagine for a moment two officer's kids growing up in a country-club lifestyle in the Philippines moving to an area of right-wing conservative religious values where sixty-five percent of the kids grew up in a rural environment without the advantages of diversity and exposure to progressive thinking. There was certainly a period of adjustment associated with the immersion into this new environment. But as kids will do—when in Rome do as the Romans do—we quickly assimilated into the pace and pulse of our new surroundings. In fact, beyond baseball, basketball and football, the three organized sporting venues available, there were outdoor activities that became a huge part of my extracurricular life. It was during the second half of the 1960s that I joined the Boy Scouts, learned to trap muskrat, raccoon and fox, became a proficient trout fisherman, was certified by the NRA as a Junior Expert Marksman, hunted small and large game and developed an appreciation for Mother Earth that I would carry with me to the present day. What I initially saw as a prison sentence of dull and limited living became rich and life-filling for me.

Astrologically, as a Taurus, my identification with earth was apparent and certainly came to fruition in our move to Pennsylvania. My two buddies, Skip and Freddy, and I formed the three amigos, going on periodic fishing sojourns into the mountains and wilderness above Harrisburg. My father would drop us off at the entrance to the expanse of state game lands for three-day periods. We would set up a fully functional camp next to a freshwater stream where we would keep select items cooled by the cold mountain stream at night. Equipped with hip waders, fishing creels, poles, backpacks, a cast iron skillet and a Marlin Model 90 20-gauge over and under combination shotgun and .22 magnum slung across my back, we would walk the streams all day catching trout and enjoying the wilderness with the confidence of Daniel Boone. Our agreement was that every time we caught three trout among us, we would stop, build a fire and panfry the fresh catch.

It was a natural environment for us as thirteen-year-olds in 1968. We were perfectly equipped and trained to live without adult supervision, protected by our knowledge of outdoor safety, proficiency with handguns and rifles, as well as the ability to catch delicious trout all day long. To change up our dinners, we would on occasion hunt and kill a couple rabbits to roast over the open fire. It was a slice of heaven on earth.

The three of us formed a trapping business that thrived for two years, operating from the fall through the springtime. We had 150 traps of various types and sizes primarily to trap muskrats along the banks of the Susquehanna River, which was a five-mile bike ride for us in the wee hours of the morning. We would get up at 3:30am, gather our backpacks, hip waders and handguns, jump on our spider bikes and meet at the ball field up the street. Riding in complete darkness through the countryside we would make our way into the small town of Highspire. Across the railroad tracks we would come to the banks of the mile-wide river.

Our trap line was about two miles long. Donning our waders to walk along the riverbank, we would go to our traps, many of which were under water just off the bank, embedded in channels carved out by the musk-rats as passageways into their homes. These traps would catch the animal swimming through the channel into the trap and snap their backs, drown-ing them. There were other trap sites set where we would see droppings or tracks. Occasionally, we would set up different trap configurations to catch raccoons and an infrequent fox. It was not uncommon for us to re-trieve up to ten muskrats in a morning.

Thursday nights we would go to a local farmers' market, where we would sell our muskrat pelts for eight dollars apiece. Raccoons would bring us twenty to twenty-five dollars. Gray fox brought in fifty dollars and red fox pelts were worth upwards of seventy-five dollars. We became little adolescent businessmen. A portion of our profit was reinvested into traps, oils and other related business gear. Our profits gave us all enough money in our pockets to buy albums, stereos, bikes and sporting gear.

Love for Golf

The game of golf carries with it many memories of weekends shared with my father in the late 1960s and early 1970s. When we lived in the Philippines my father introduced me to golf. He was an avid player as well as a fan of the sport. I remember sitting with him in front of the black and white television and watching PGA events that featured Arnold Palmer, Lee Trevino, Gary Player and young Jack Nicklaus.

From age six I immediately connected with the unique strategic na-ture of golf, the beauty of walking outside on manicured fairways and the rhythm of pace attached to hitting a small white ball with metal clubs into a dog-food-can-sized hole. In fact, by age ten, I had plugged the entire lawn surrounding our suburban home with eighteen dog-food cans to create a chipping and putting course where I would invest hours of time and energy to improving my short game. As a result, I became a very good golfer by the age of sixteen and a great companion player for my father.

For three years, 1969 through 1972, my father and I played golf every weekend at the New Cumberland Army Base golf course. Most of the memories I have of my father are harsh, angry and filled with ire. But our time together on the golf course allowed us to connect with each other, share thoughts and to have fun.

It was during this period that I acquired my driver's license. This made drinking beer in large quantities much easier for my father, since he had me to drive. And drink he would, packing his golf bag with iced cans of beer to consume throughout the eighteen holes. As much as I hated my father's drunkenness, playing golf was more important for me than the angst of watching him get drunk. It also made his game sloppy, which in my competitive spirit assured my besting him in scoring.

Mother's Helper

For several years while my father was still active military, my grandmother on my mother's side, Catherine, lived with us in our suburban home. Catherine was the oldest of eleven children, born in 1889 to James Michael and Catherine Anne O'Hearn. Unfortunately, she had suffered several strokes by the time she moved in with us, leaving her in a constant state of confusion, dementia and distress. What was more challenging though was her inability to walk. She had broken a hip before the strokes and she required constant aid to move from the bed to the chair, to the portable commode, to any other place in the house. My mother took this on, and of course I, being the good soldier, took on assisting and supporting my mother.

On many nights we were awakened by my grandmother's screaming, her shouting for people who were no longer alive, pleading for her husband to take her away, calling on her son, my Uncle Jim, to help her. And there was helping her onto the portable commode and cleaning her after she soiled the bed or missed the commode; all this was part of my childhood, living on Richard Avenue in the mid 1960s.

I insisted that my mom go to bingo with her girlfriend one night a week so that she could have some down time. "I'll look after Grandma. You go, Mom," I told her. And she did. I was eleven at the time. Danny was not capable of providing any help in caring for my grandmother. Danny was limited in many ways. I only ever loved him and felt enormous compassion, a protective emotional and physical connection that, at times, Danny would rebel against. [10]

For me, it was never that simple. As I came through my adolescent years I longed for something more, something undefined and nondescript, something missed, a love, a connection to something of definition and certainty. A hole always existed in the center of my being that I sought to fill. But with what? That was the question. And I searched in my own inexperienced and determined fashion. My search was complicated over the years by the distortion of not knowing if I was running from or running to the source. But running I was.

Formative Years

I entered high school in 1969, a formative period throughout which the perpetual running that characterized my life at age fourteen would continue. Psychically, I was a master defense artist, hiding my true feelings of separateness and fear from all I encountered. I was an enigma in many ways: a student who excelled academically; an athlete that even as a late bloomer could hold my own on the playing field; and an established actor, singer and artist recognized by the community as a real talent. Yet, for me, it was a time of great transition and turmoil, exacerbated by the counterculture forces of the late sixties, with the Vietnam War protests, the electric infusion of rock 'n' roll, drugs, the feminist movement and a strong urge to break away from conservative and limiting forces. I grew up on the tail end of Vietnam, missing the draft by two years, but seduced by the counterculture that offered more than my life was offering in Middletown, Pennsylvania.

In high school I earned the nickname Rebel, primarily due to my natural proclivity for the unorthodox—although I kept it within the lines, so as not to be caught or impugned in any way that might prevent future success.

About the time I entered Middletown Area High School, my mother decided after many years to reenter the workforce, a bold move on her part to find her own voice, to regain a semblance of balance in her life. She was happy to get a clerk position at Capital Campus, a satellite campus to Penn State. This job changed my mother in profound ways, allowing her access to the student body and the experiential interplay with young counterculture adults. My mother gained a bit of hip by working at Penn State, which was important not only for her own growth, but also as it related to my own jagged journey.

On to College

1973 through 1975 were years of further exploration on all fronts. Living at home mitigated expenses but placed some constraints on a free lifestyle, absent parental questioning and minor restrictions. My parents trusted me, due in large part to my independent strong will and proven experience of leaving, staying alive and returning to attend school.

Once during my freshman year, my mother asked me casually on a Saturday morning what I did the night before. I decided in that instant to not hold back, but rather tell her the details of what I had done the previous evening. The sentences that followed contained words such as drinking heavily, pot, sex and dancing, to name a few. After hearing of the night's activities, she said, "That is the last time I will ever ask you what you did!" And she never asked again.

While in San Diego, I became not only a junkie but a much better guitar player. I spent hours with a variety of musicians, some street performers and others classically trained. Playing every day, sometimes for hours, I developed a natural talent and became a very good guitarist. Being able to play and sing gave me a tremendous asset as I started my college career. Within a short time, I had connected with many other musicians attending HACC, some of whom were outstanding vocalists and instrumentalists.

At this time country rock, with bands primarily from the south—including the Doobie Brothers, Marshall Tucker and the Allman Brothers; and acoustic rock—with the Eagles, Poco, Loggins and Messina, Dan Fogelberg, Crosby, Stills & Nash, James Taylor and Jackson Browne— were branching off from rock 'n' roll. My interests, while strongly aligned to the rock genre, moved toward acoustic rock; it was more melodic and poetic in lyrics and images.

Early in my freshman year of college, a cute blonde in a Theatre Arts class caught my eye. She had a great smile and she exuded warmth. She walked up to me after class and said, "Hi, my name is Lee. Who are you?" She told me that her boyfriend, Ted, played guitar and she had recently taken up the banjo.

I said, "I'm a guitar player."

"Cool," she responded. I told Lee I was meeting up with my friend Dave after class at the student center. Would she like to join us?

Lee, Ted, Dave and I forged a friendship from that day forward taking us into adventure after adventure.

Ted and Lee were into country bluegrass, a style unknown to me at that point. I initially thought bluegrass was some farmer heehaw simplistic nonsense music designed for no-teeth, rural, uneducated country folk. What I found was nothing like that, but rather a music that transcended generations, was steeped in Americana and was incredibly fun to play.

With our instruments, we met later that week in the student center and began playing. Ted was a mechanical player, with a choppy, hard pick style. He played easy chord progressions and attempted to pluck bass notes with his pick, rolling between chords. Yet, the simplicity of the chord progression and the string picking emblematic of bluegrass guitar had an attractive element to it. I was fascinated by the flat-picking style and started practicing. It required a different touch and rhythm. Once I got the hang of the flat-picking, it became joyful to play, especially when we combined the banjo, mandolin, string bass and fiddle that eventually became our band composition. Wheatstraw was the name Ted chose. It seemed like a good bluegrass name and got no challenge from me.

Lee was a talented painter with a keen eye and a natural ability. She was extraordinary in many ways. She picked up the banjo and, practicing for hours, quickly became proficient. She was devoted to becoming a superb banjo picker. And that is exactly what she did.

Over the course of months, we developed a playlist of fifty-plus songs, some more contemporary and many others of the traditional bluegrass flavor. We secured a Friday night gig at a small country bar outside of York, Pennsylvania, where locals of all ages, from kids to seniors, would come, drink, dance, kiss and have a ball. I even had groupies that followed the band and me. On Saturdays we booked our band at other venues throughout central Pennsylvania and into Maryland as well. We were invited to play at bluegrass festivals over the summer. These were great entertainment and engendered many new friendships. Of all the music styles I undertook during these years, bluegrass offered the very best mix of friendly people, happy experiences and warm feelings, totally different than I had expected.

My love affair with drugs continued over the two years at HACC, but modified slightly in that I stopped doing heroin, continued on and off with crystal meth, smoked a lot of pot and started to drink a lot of beer. As a matter of course, we would gather at my parents' house, where there was a refrigerator full of beer that my father stocked for us. They preferred to have us there drinking rather than out somewhere else. Besides, my parents loved to listen to our playing. One thing unique and loving about my parents was their undying love for my music. In fact, there were times when both my mother and father independently would ask me to play something for them. My friends really liked my parents because of their interest in us and the beer in the refrigerator. Little did they know of the pain and dysfunction attached to years of alcoholic family abuse.

The band continued through the early summer of 1975, when we all were moving in different directions, me off to Syracuse University to continue my education and the others off on their own paths. Lee and Ted moved to State College, Pennsylvania, and Lee became a nationally recognized banjo player over the years.

The last time I saw Lee was in 1979. I had begun working with Eastern Airlines and was living on Park Avenue and 19th Street in Manhattan. My phone rang, and to my great surprise it was Lee. She was coming through the City and heard I was living there. She got my phone number from my mother. She thought it might be fun to get together and I, of course, acquiesced without hesitation. Lee and I were able to spend a couple days together, for as luck would have it, I had consecutive days off from flying. She stayed in my studio apartment and slept with me. She told me that she found our friendship to be a wonderful gift, but had always wanted to be my lover. From the first time she saw me in class she had an incredible desire for me. Lee was exceptionally honest, and when she shared herself openly it was done with deep emotion and truth. It was a challenge for her to be as close to me as she was for so many years and not be able to show her true feelings. This was the first time we had the opportunity to be alone with each other. We consummated our friendship with the passion of lost years. It was a time that I've always held close in my heart.

My life can be seen as a series of training adventures on the one hand, but on the other, it can be seen as a patched quilt of experiences that I survived to come out the other side, beat up, bruised and still running.

When I learned of my acceptance at Syracuse University in late spring 1975, I had a renewed sense of possibilities. But what should I pursue? I had ample passions from which to choose—acting and music, law, psychology, sociology, even geology, a scientific study that captured my interest in my sophomore year. What I should study as a chosen field was a perplexing and consuming question as I readied myself to attend a "real" university going into my junior year.

My parents always supported my decision to pursue higher education and knew I was destined to move in this direction. Yet their ability to provide me with meaningful coaching, support and clarification of the right path was limited. Interestingly, the anticipation of attending Syracuse brought with it a right-sized internal realization that I would need to find balance in my recreational partying, drinking and drug use to be able to measure up to what I imagined would be more challenging study. And more challenging it was, in a big way.

Since I had not attended the university for the first two years, I walked into my junior year completely alone, watching other students around me, 16,000 undergraduates, cajoling, reuniting and having in place circles of friends and acquaintances that I longed for. The loneliness and isolation during those first few weeks at Syracuse were unnerving and palpable. While it was not in my nature to call home out of desperation, I did so just to hear a loving voice, just to reconnect with someone who cared enough to talk with me.

My living situation was also challenging in that I lived off the main campus in alternative apartment housing, a mile from the center of student life, with two roommates from Long Island who were close friends. The three-bedroom apartment included small bedrooms, a shared kitchen, small dining area and living room. Chuck and Joe, while polite, did not invite any inclusion. They talked primarily between themselves and curtly dismissed any attempt on my part to connect, share or invite a warm exchange.

I recall thinking what assholes they were to treat me with such scorn and indifference.

As the weeks progressed in my new adventure in Syracuse, I realized that most of the student body was from downstate, mostly from Long Island. I learned firsthand how pervasive discrimination was, as I was excluded from certain groups of students, the Jewish students being the largest contingent.

Up until that time, my only experience with Jews was in my sophomore year at HACC, dating Roz Ross, a beauty with long dark hair and bright green eyes and a propensity for kissing, among other pleasurable attributes. We dated for a short while, and aside from her desire to talk endlessly, I found her to be delightful. Syracuse University presented a very different experience.

In my quest to connect with others to find friendship, I was able to make inroads with a small circle of friends after meeting Ted Boyle, a frumpy student I casually met one night while drinking at one of the watering holes off Marshall Street, the center of activity for entertainment just off campus. Ted was a film major from Ravena, New York, just south of Albany. Accompanying Ted was a small group of friends, Ginsberg—"Ginzo" as we called him—Rick, Stephie, Georgie and Pete. This offbeat cadre of new acquaintances provided an initial connection. On Sunday nights, the ritual was to smoke pot and watch *Monty Python and the Flying Circus*, a thirty-minute infusion of laughter and insane frivolity.

Ginzo was a math major with an extraordinary gift for theory. His childhood playground was the Upper East Side of Manhattan, specifically 92nd Street and Central Park. Ginzo's father was a renowned architect. They lived in a spacious fourteenth floor, four-bedroom corner home with their front windows overlooking Central Park. Ginzo was a city kid, with an innate sense of independence and confidence that separated him from others. He simply did not care what others thought of him. He was as comfortable in his skin as a lion in the African wilderness, and no one got under his skin, nor did he stress about anything except taking care of his cat. While he had the option as a junior to move from dorm life to a more independent life style, he opted to stay in the dorm together with his cat, Jinx, a sixteen-year-old gray tomcat that was his pet from childhood. Having animals in the dorms was strictly prohibited; remarkably, Ginzo found a way to have Jinx with him the entire duration of his undergraduate career. I learned after graduation from Stan that Jinx died shortly after leaving Syracuse. Ginzo took it hard.

Winters in Syracuse were brutal. My first winter delivered an endless amount of snow and bitter cold. I recall two days in January 1976 when the outside temperatures reached minus thirty-eight degrees Fahrenheit. Add thirty-five mile per hour winds and you have the surface of the moon right in upstate New York. Of course, people in Syracuse were used to this and never batted an eyelash, although the cold immediately froze your eyelashes and any other part of your exposed body. Being the explorer that I've always been, I looked forward to experiencing how different this type of cold felt. Wandering out to hitchhike the mile to the main campus was indeed a new adventure. The snow under foot creaked, followed by a high, whining screech, screech, screech as I walked. The power lines above hummed and buzzed from the intensity of the cold and wind.

My new friends loved to drink, smoke pot and ski. There was ample snow for Friday night expeditions to Song Mountain, forty-five minutes south on I-81, where their special was night skiing from 4pm to 4am, perfect for college students from Syracuse and Cornell, just down the road. I had never skied, but was definitely open to learning. What I didn't know was how rudimentary my training would be. My friends were eager for me to come with them and they were up for the task of training me. We rented skis from the lodge, and Ginzo and Rick took me to the T-bar lift at the bunny hill.

Ginzo said, "You don't need this bunny hill, do you?"

I replied, "If you say so, Ginz," not knowing whether that was the correct answer or not.

"Nah, you come with us," Ginzo and Rick agreed. So inch by inch, alongside my two trainers, I worked my way to the three-person chair lift. Just getting to the chair lift was a major success, I thought. With the help of my two assassins, I was able to actually get on the lift, sitting in the middle. Getting off was another story altogether.

It was twelve degrees, with westerly winds blowing harder as we climbed. Rick turned to me and said that getting off the chair was tricky.

I said, "Now you tell me!"

"Keep your ski tips up at a forty-five-degree angle as the chair brings us to the snow and then feel the snow beneath your skis, adjusting your body to then bend at the knees and come off the chair," he said.

I could see the destination fifty yards ahead. The best laid plans of mice and crazy students! Tips up and the snow on the bottoms of my skis, I proceeded to do as instructed. What I did not know was how much balance skiing required, not to mention the basics of getting off a chair lift. Down I went. Both skis popped off, and I twisted into a ball. Ginzo and Rick came to my rescue, propping me up, finally, and securing both skis. The incline immediately to the left of the chair lift was not as sharp, with a gentle slow grade, so we proceeded to ease our way down. I felt completely awkward and unbalanced. What was apparent to me immediately was that I did not know how to turn or, more importantly, to stop.

"Just bring your knees inward to form a pizza slice," Rick said.

And moving slowly, I did as instructed. This seemed to work! Ok, I was now feeling a bit more confident knowing that I could at least stop—or so I thought. My surge of confidence convinced my two instructors that I was good to go. Wrong! Ginzo and Rick both wanted to jump on the slopes and enjoy the packed snow, making the conditions excellent.

Before I could express my reservations, Ginzo turned to me, lifted his goggles, and said, "We'll leave you now. Follow the left-hand side of the mountain. It's marked as easy and will give you the best chance to learn. Have fun! We will come back on the next run to find you." Off they both went in a blur of snow, out of sight almost instantly. "Stay on the left," I said out loud. Planting my first pole, I moved from my stopped position and started to move. And move I did, for the gentle slope wasn't as gentle as it appeared. I started to move much faster very quickly and panicked. But I remembered to lean in with my knees, doing the pizza slice to stop. It was not working and I was again moving faster than I expected. What to do? I simply sat back and tried to fall to the side, but caught a ski in the hardened snow. That flipped me completely around in a 360-degree circle, now airborne and hitting the snow in a hard spinning motion and a thud. When I finally stopped, I was covered with snow and had again lost both skis. Needless to say, my first skiing expedition was unnerving and painful.

I eventually made my way down the mountain, but not until I had fallen countless times. Rick and Ginzo were not to be found after leaving me on my first ski run. It took me two hours to make it to the bottom of Song Mountain. Bruised and battered, I unclipped the skis and sat on a bench at the base of the main chair lift waiting to see if the two amigos would show up. The night lights showed two figures swooshing down the center trail, carving out perfect curves. I recognized them to be Rick and Ginzo. They tried to convince me that they were looking for me. I looked at both of them in disbelief. "Sure you were. You obviously knew that I would be on that black diamond run you just skied."

This time they agreed to take me up and spend the next run supporting me. Before we attempted to get back on the ski lift, Ginzo reached in his ski jacket and pulled out a covered flask, twisting off the top, which hung by a metal chain. "Kentucky bourbon," he said, taking a swig and offering it to me. By this time, I had grapefruit-size bruises on both knees, hips, elbows and God knows where else. I gladly took the flask and downed a few healthy jolts. I am unsure whether the booze helped or not, but it seemed that the falls became easier to take. So much for my first skiing adventure. I would eventually learn to ski and become proficient enough to ski black diamonds myself.

There was a clear separation during those years between students who joined fraternities and sororities and those of us who refrained. Even clearer was the distinction between Jewish, primarily downstate, students and Gentile students like me. Early on, Stan told me of a huge party taking place on Friday night at one of the Jewish fraternity houses on campus. Stan and I decided to go.

Students were streaming in and out of the front door. A couple of male students with yarmulkes were the doorkeepers. When we approached, they asked if we were Jewish, to which we replied no. They said we could not enter. Stan and I were caught off guard. We slowly backed away without saying anything. We saw several dolled up young women enter without challenge, the two doorkeepers smiling like Cheshire cats. [11]

Choosing a Path

I had enrolled to pursue pre-law, but a sudden urge had come over me to change my course of study to geology, moving from social science to physical science, and so I did.

I spoke with my father and did a pulse check as to which direction felt more aligned to my true self. The answer was evidenced by my personal history. Was I more inclined to be social, among people, or consumed by a passion for extensive lonely lab work, mathematics and a preponderance of chemistry, biology and physics. The answer was easy. I shifted on a dime and reinstated my course work to pursue pre-law.

One of the primary courses for the junior year, a course that had a profound influence on me and changed my life at age twenty, was Constitutional Law, a two-semester study that others referred to as the counterpart of Comparative Anatomy in pre-med study. And hard it was, with a textbook weighing pounds and being inches thick. I did the rest of my undergraduate work at the Maxwell School of Citizenship and Public Affairs.

I entered Maxwell School through one of the many doors opening onto the foyer in front of a large amphitheater. The room was a piece of history, a place where prominent and influential scholars had forged for the school a reputation as one of the leading universities in the country for public affairs and international relations. I felt like a fish out of water, but I remained composed. Dr. Michael Sawyer entered the room to a standing ovation that lasted for several minutes. Clearly this professor was held in high esteem by his students. I wondered whether this was a Syracuse tradition or whether Dr. Sawyer was considered an exceptional man. I watched as he humbly placed his small portfolio on the lecture stand, cleared his throat and looked up from his thick glasses with a smile to greet the students. I knew that I was in for a ride. I was not clear on where the ride was taking me, but I was willing to go, nonetheless.

After the applause stopped, Dr. Sawyer posed a question to the class. He seemed to pick up in the middle of a sentence, continuing his thoughts centered on a pivotal constitutional point based on several cases that had established precedent, but short of concise clarity as applied to the facts of the case. In other words, I had zero understanding of any part of the question posed. Double-digit hands went up. I was stunned to see that anyone had comprehended the question let alone been courageous enough to attempt a response.

From the lectern, Dr. Sawyer gazed upward, moving his eyes to the right, and said, "Mr. Cooper, you have something to elucidate?"

To which, Mr. Cooper—dressed in his New York City fashionable late 1970s slacks, dress shirt, herringbone jacket, slicked back hair, wire-rimmed glasses—stood confidently and quoted from some obscure constitutional dissenting opinion from the 1920s. Mr. Cooper proceeded to provide a cogent summary of information that sounded more like Mandarin than English to me.

Dr. Sawyer smiled and said, "Perhaps, Mr. Cooper. But what is missing?"

Again hands flew up in the lecture hall. This time, Sawyer looked to the upper left of the amphitheater, calling on Mr. Goldstein.

Once more the student purposefully rose to address the question intelligently, and the discussion continued. Student after student added to the discussion, and for twenty minutes the juridical analysis continued, leaving me in a pool of quiet despair, uncertainty and shock. In those moments I realized how ill-prepared I was to compete with this caliber of student. My 3.85 average from HACC was vaporous, worth nothing when viewed against the incredible passion, talent and dynamic force experienced that day in Maxwell. It was jarring to see so clearly what I was dealing with in terms of the level of intelligence, preparedness and competition of these lawyers-to-be. I was overwhelmed and disillusioned, but not defeated.

Seeing how well prepared and engaged these students were in their studies reinforced the isolation I felt. That the predominant feature of my legal competition was again downstate Jewish was simply a fact. These same pretentious young lawyers-to-be had been rejected by Yale, Harvard and Cornell—down the road in Ithaca. Syracuse was their safe school.

Several weeks into Con Law I discovered that a core group of the brightest students, mostly men, met weekly in a study group designed to collegially support learning, understanding and ultimately each other's success. This seemed like a wonderful method to gain the edge in such a complex study as law.

After class one early October morning, I approached Evan Stein, one of the class superstars, to inquire about joining their study group. Catching his attention prior to walking out of the hall, I commented on his terrific insights and knowledge, thinking a genuine compliment the right choice in broaching the subject of an invite. "I understand you and several others get together weekly as a study group to improve your learning. I would be interested in joining you if possible."

Stein looked at me with a tinge of condescension and asked, "What is your name?"

I replied, "Michael Splann."

His glare quickly went cold. "No, we are not accepting any more students." He turned abruptly to leave.

Standing there watching as he walked away I again felt a harsh darkness sweep over me like a winter wind cutting through an overcoat. My name became the decider of advantages others were reaping; however, Splann was not the right name.

That night I drank too many beers. I was fuzzy the next morning in my classes, nauseated indeed. All I knew from these experiences was being an outsider, a non-Jew at Syracuse University, was a distinct disadvantage. It was the mid 1970s, only thirty years from the Holocaust, and these were children and grandchildren of survivors of Nazi atrocities in some cases. To me, that did not explain their protective and separatist practices. It felt like exclusion, discrimination and unfair treatment. All the more reason, then, for me to lean toward the rights of the underserved and the international protection of human rights, which ultimately became a strong passion of mine as I worked toward my degree in international relations.

I didn't make the connection then, but in hindsight I can tie the feeling of being discriminated against at Syracuse to the abandonment and loss I felt as a young child given up for adoption. The hole in the center of my being was widened by non-acceptance and rejection at that time and in the years to follow. My incessant running was fueled by a search for love and a connection to a mother lost at birth. My struggles with being alone, although I had the emotional wherewithal to create an elaborate defense system to shield my inner child from pain and sorrow, continued as I entered into young adulthood. I had wings on my feet, as my mother said often, as she watched me leave on one adventure after another. I ran again. Toward the end of my junior year, I petitioned the university, working with my advisor, to do an independent study program in Strasbourg, France.

Larry Splann, Bigger Than Life

My Father, Lawrence John Splann, born in Binghamton, New York, June 24, 1918, was the product of a physically abusive father and a mother of strong will and determination. The Splann grandparents died before I was born. I was told little about my paternal grandfather and only slightly more about my grandmother.

Mrs. Splann, as others referred to her, was loved by all my family, including Kathleen. I remember occasions as a child hearing her speak fondly about Mrs. Splann.

To my father, as for other men of his generation, the news of the United States declaring war on Germany meant enlistment. At age twenty-two, he signed up and was sent to South Carolina to train with the Army Air Corps. The early years of WWII found the allied forces being decimated by the German war machine, especially with their superior air power and ground defenses, which became the backdrop for my father flying twenty-nine bombing missions in 1942. My father's younger brother, Daniel, lied about his age and enlisted to fight in the Pacific theater. Uncle Danny was killed in the South Pacific.

Kids of my generation, especially those of us growing up in military families, were interested in World War II. After all, it was only a decade after the end of the war when I was born. That my father was a B-17 captain at age twenty-three instilled in me as a young boy a real sense of curiosity and deep respect. My brother and I would on occasion, particularly after my father had a few scotches, ask him about the war. We usually began by asking, "Weren't you scared?" to which my father might reply, "We were too busy to be scared." But we pressed the issue, asking him, "What was it like?" There were a few times when Larry would give us some additional information, but his reticence to share this part of his life clearly denoted the harsh realities of war, specifically his. He told us that for each mission his chances of dying were far greater than his chances of living. After flying three missions, his crew was given a three-day pass to go into London and do what it is that soldiers do during time away from fighting. There were occasions when he would return from London to find that a large portion of his squadron had been shot down. One story stuck with Danny and me. He had successfully bombed factories in the Stuttgart area of Germany and was making his way in the company of his beleaguered squadron back across the German–French border when Messerschmitts— what my father referred to as bumble bee aircraft—intercepted them.

This particular evening the Messerschmitts were relentlessly encircling the B-17s as they made their way across western France. As they were approaching the area where the aircraft would turn and retreat back to Germany, several of the German planes made a turn to pass them one last time. Wing and tail gunners could be heard swearing loudly as they prepared for the onslaught. As they came through the formation of B-17 Fortresses, my father remembered his cockpit window being strafed by several of the nine-inch bullets. They missed him by inches. As he turned to Joe, his copilot, he saw that he had been decapitated by the shots, his headless body still strapped in the copilot seat. I felt a sense of horror as he told the story and imagined how incredibly challenging it must have been to experience such tremendous brutality. If there was any semblance of understanding or forgiveness on my part as to my father's alcoholism and the dysfunction it created, it was in knowing that he had lived through such terror and loss. His was a generation of men that did not show their emotions, nor did they feel compelled to acknowledge the inner ravages and destruction they carried with them as they lived on in their lives. Therapy was not a concept that existed for this generation. I often reflect on the tragedy of my father's life. He died on September 26, 1982, after spending five years in the Albany VA hospital. The last several years of his life were indelible for me.

Perhaps the most poignant memory I have of my father was in 1978, a year after I graduated from Syracuse University, where I had made a name for myself on stage. I was tending bar at Sutter's Mill Bar and Restaurant, near the Syracuse campus, and living a life of heavy cocaine and alcohol intake, early morning escapades and dangerous—yes, destructive—irrational, behavior.

After his retirement from the military in the late 1960s, my father had worked for the Social Security Administration, first in Baltimore and then in Philadelphia. In late 1977, my family made the transition back to Schenectady, New York, their original hometown, settling in the Hamilton Hill area, a quintessential blue-collar neighborhood that arose during the 1920s and filled up with the thousands of workers who built large steam turbine generators at the Schenectady GE plant. But GE had pared back its headquarter manufacturing operation from the 40,000 employed in the early 1960s to several thousand workers in a limited manufacturing area. The neighborhood had deteriorated significantly over the past decade with drugs, prostitution and the associated violence that accompanied this urban decay.

At this point I had been living apart from my parents, in Syracuse, for years, with the occasional visits home on holidays, special events and breaks.

The phone rang in my small apartment on Lancaster Avenue in Syracuse. I answered. My mother's voice sounded concerned and uncharacteristically serious. "Your father's sick."

"What's wrong with Dad?"

She then proceeded to tell me that he had been struggling to walk, his varicose veins were taking a toll on him, he was increasingly out of breath and coughing incessantly.

I asked if he had been examined.

My mother told me that he had gone to the doctor, who recommended tests to determine the nature of his illness. Keep in mind that by this point in my life, Larry Splann had undergone major lung surgery, nearly died from an auto accident, suffered from cirrhosis of the liver and been fortunate enough not to have killed himself and others while driving drunk for years.

Kathleen stopped for a moment and then said, "Your dad has been diagnosed with throat cancer and they are recommending surgery within the next ten days."

Numbness swept over me as I became attuned to the meaning of the words. "Are they sure, Mom?"

Her response confirmed the certainty of the diagnosis.

I felt so sad to hear this news. I recalled how much compassion I felt for him, even though he had been such a force of darkness in my family at times. I did not want my father to be in pain or to suffer, but what was ahead was nothing except torture and brutality.

It was a Tuesday night around seven when the phone rang. I was expecting the call, for my mother had arranged with my father that I would be available to speak with him at that time. It was to be the last time I spoke to my father, and I knew it.

I picked up the phone and said, "Hi Dad."

"Hi Bumper, how are you?" He had nicknamed me Bumper as a baby, because when I crawled I would do so with my rear up in the air.

I told him that I was doing great, lying through my teeth. Time slowed down. I remember hearing him tell me that he was going into Temple University Medical Center in two days for the surgery. The doctors felt confident that they would be able to get all the cancer, but more than likely he would lose his voice box and have a portion of his throat removed. It was the first time in my life I heard fear in my father's voice.

All I could do while listening was try to remain strong and reassuring, but inside I was dying. I wanted to tell him how much I loved him and that I forgave him for all that he had done, but all I could do was remain composed, still the good soldier trying to be there emotionally for him. We spoke for fifteen minutes or so and then he told me, "This may be the last time you hear my voice. So I want to tell you that I love you."

I swallowed and gained enough resource to answer him back, "I love you too, Dad. I will see you soon." We hung up.

I broke down completely and wept for hours.

It was a ten-hour surgery. The surgeons cut my father's throat from ear to ear under his chin, removing his voice box along with the cancerous tissue surrounding the mass. My mother and aunt traveled together from Schenectady to Philadelphia for the surgery, calling me several hours after it was completed to inform me that he had lived through the operation. The anesthesia required for such a long surgery left my father barely living. He had lost a lot of blood, as well, and was in intensive care, listed as critical. What my mother didn't tell me was that when she was allowed to see him, his head appeared to be twice its normal size and looked as if it been put through a meat grinder.

It was seven days after the surgery when I arrived in Philadelphia, my mother having insisted there was nothing I could do by being there. Later I would realize that she was trying to protect me. My mom and aunt both looked shell-shocked and exhausted when I arrived.

Temple University Medical Center was a blur of activity. The anticipation of seeing my father for the first time was palpable. My heart raced and I could feel adrenalin pumping courage into my cells, bracing me for an unknown reaction. I rounded the corner of the seventh floor, walking slightly ahead of my mother and aunt. I caught sight of my father standing outside his room holding onto an IV pole. He turned and saw us coming. He looked into my eyes, a look I will never forget. The terror I saw in his eyes can only be described as from a nightmare. He looked lost, frightened and ravaged by a scalpel. For good or for bad, my father's voice was not only his means of communication, but more than anything else his tool, his weapon and the external manifestation of his manhood. He had been a commanding officer in the Air Force, strong, in control and intelligent. His words were his armament, the means for his defining himself.

Now he was sliced up, wounded and emasculated; I saw the horror of it all in an instant. His head was still enlarged as he recuperated from the trauma of surgery, but the incision stapled together from ear to ear, spotting with blood seeping through, was almost too much to bear. I was speechless and in shock. But I quelled the tears in my eyes and softly embraced him. "Hi Dad." I couldn't ask him how he was doing; I could see for myself.

My mother and aunt made small talk about the doctors, his care and his progress.

As I write this passage the memory of that day in 1979 is as real as it was in those precious and horrible moments, and it brings me to tears today.

I knew that my father's life was over and so did he. He survived for three more years.

Danny

In the spring of 2005 I learned in a phone call one Saturday morning that my older brother, Danny, had been diagnosed with skin cancer. He was 50 years old, living modestly in Wilmington, Ohio, the town where his best childhood friend, Bobby and his older brother, Bill, had settled. In June of the same year, I traveled to visit Danny, who by this time was undergoing chemotherapy. The toxic therapy made him perpetually nauseated and unable to eat. There were days when he wasn't able to do much more than get out of bed and sit in a comfortable chair.

His spirit and health improved enough during my visit to allow for outings. We spent a couple days together, meeting with his friends, his girlfriend, Karla, as well as his boss, who treated Danny with great love and friendship. I was uplifted to see that he had built a life for himself that was filled with people who loved and cared for him. He had achieved something his younger brother had not found, a circle of friends that gladly surrounded him and were there during his time of illness. I remain haunted by the last time I saw Danny. I had just said goodbye to him as

I was about to get in my rental car and drive back to Columbus for my return trip to Albany.

I hugged him and looked into his eyes. I realized that this would be the last time I saw him alive. And although we had drawn apart over the past many years, he was still my brother, and I still loved him. My heart broke for Danny throughout his entire life, but this time his image cemented in my memory, as I turned the car around from the parking space. A wave, a smile and I proceeded to drive out of his driveway. Looking in my rearview mirror, with him standing there following me as I drove off, I remember him turning slowly to walk back into the house. Tears flooded my eyes as I drove away, recalling all the mean and incredibly brutal abuse he endured throughout his young years. It was horrible how badly kids treated him.

From my earliest recollection, I carried Danny with great love and care. Being so close in age, we grew up in the Splann family sharing our early childhood experiences together as close siblings. I came into this life with a deep appreciation for those of lesser means and my brother pulled at my heartstrings from the first to the last encounter.

I traveled to Wilmington, Ohio, in August 2005, to bury Danny, who had succumbed to his skin cancer. I had lost my entire family with Danny's death. And now with two divorces behind me, I knew my fair share of disappointment and loss.

A Hard Life

Daniel William Splann, born November 22, 1954, in Bellevue Women's Hospital, on Troy–Schenectady Road, was also adopted. Danny's background was always in the shadows, for we never really knew anything more than that he was given up for adoption by a woman of meager means. We were six months apart. Danny was my older brother. Since the Splanns never spoke of our adoption, we were treated like fraternal twins, especially in the younger years. Later I would simply state that I was born prematurely. As a boy I wasn't even sure what *prematurely* meant, but it sounded like a truth that I could go with, so I did.

Danny's life was challenging right from the start, though the Splanns loved and provided for him in every way they could. We grew up together, playmates and friends sharing in similar activities through our younger years. Active military life with the many moves, making new friends, leaving new friends and adjusting was just the way life went. We knew no different. After settling in our suburban Pennsylvania home on Richard Avenue, Danny and I made friends with another pair of brothers, Bill and Bobby, whose father was also military. The four of us on summer breaks would ride our little spider bikes all over the country roads, exploring different forests, fields and playgrounds.

I learned very early how desperately mean and hostile children could be as I watched my brother get brutally attacked. First and second graders verbally abused him, calling him retarded, slow, a moron, weird and so many other negative labels. The awful pain inflicted on Danny was unbearable for me to witness. He was bigger than me, yet for being a smaller kid, I was fierce and would not hesitate to physically attack more than one kid who dared hurt my brother. Danny, on the other hand, resented to the day he died my getting involved in his fights, even those where he was being beaten to a pulp.

When Danny started to speak as a child he had a speech impediment. He couldn't produce certain sounds, such as *th* and *s*. Kids would taunt him by calling him names and go as far as punching him. Danny had a badge of courage that to this day I don't quite understand; yet, he would take it from kids. He wouldn't retaliate but rather tried to stand his ground, even as a young boy. I think watching him, as I did, made it that much worse for me to tolerate anyone hurting him. It was impossible for me to stand aside and not protect my brother, impossible! Then there was the time in junior high school, eighth grade to be precise.

The school day had ended, and I was walking from the gymnasium building toward the south side of our school and the side exit where kids were picked up by the buses. From the back of the building I rounded the corner and looked up toward the covered platform area just outside the school doors, where there were several kids gathered around what appeared to be some sort of fight going on. As I got closer I saw that Randy Hicks, the school bully whose reputation was just short of being a felon, was viciously punching my brother in the face once, twice and a third time. Danny was just taking the punches, trying to defend himself, but completely unable to escape each devastating blow. I immediately reacted, running toward the attack. As I got closer I heard Danny telling Randy that he couldn't hurt him.

Within seconds I motored up the cement steps and proceeded to pummel Randy with a series of rights and lefts until he fell to the ground covered in blood, completely dazed by what must have been ten to fifteen punches to the head, all of which landed. Danny kept screaming at me. "This is my fight! I can handle myself!"

I looked at him and said, "No Danny, he was beating you badly! I can't stand back and let that happen!"

Danny turned and left the scene. Randy, getting to his feet, attempted to threaten me and I quickly threw one right hand and knocked him to the ground again, saying, "If you ever touch my brother again, I will kill you!" I turned and left leaving him on the ground and leaving a group of kids in awe as to what had just transpired. Randy never spoke to my brother or me again. Four months later we learned that he had committed an armed robbery and was sent away to the juvenile system.

Eventually my parents moved Danny to a private school and then later in high school to a vocational technical school where he took an interest in auto mechanics. My brother had an aptitude for putting things together. At times he was sloppy, but his innate ability to understand puzzles, put together models without instructions, build Lego structures was an indication of a strength my parents noticed and supported in his education as well as in preparing him for the real world. Where I excelled in being a social butterfly, in educational pursuits, the arts and athletics as in most endeavors, Danny barely made it through the educational system. He was physically uncoordinated in sports, awkward in social situations, particularly around girls, and less inclined to pursue anything other than mechanics, cars, trucks and motors. That was his niche. Danny told me that what he really wanted was a new Chevy Camaro. I always admired him for knowing exactly what he wanted, plain and simple: a Camaro.

I, on the other hand, possessed a perpetual longing, not to be filled with possessions or the simplicity of anything materialistic. Mine was a spiritual longing, the desire to find love, pure and fulfilling.

This would turn out to be elusive, until I found my soulmate.

My Soulmate

Janeen and I had joined our lives together in the summer of 2006. Janeen and her two boys transitioned to upstate New York, moving into our newly purchased four-bedroom home in Niskayuna. I was cemented to upstate New York because of the custody arrangements with my son, James. So the only way to combine our lives was for Janeen and the boys to relocate.

The timing could not have been more challenging for the boys and for Janeen. While she never complained, it was a huge undertaking to leave her prized position. She had been the eleventh-grade English teacher at the prestigious Port Jefferson High School. She had also built a thriving tutoring business, leveraging her teaching position as an incentive for eager parents to send their kids to her for dramatic improvements in their SAT verbal scores. And dramatic her tutoring was, for there were students she coached that advanced their verbal scores by two hundred or more points, with a couple students achieving perfect scores.

Marty and Matt were eleven months apart in age. Janeen enrolled them in school the same year. Matt was the youngest student in his class. Experts on teenage years concur that moving kids in their high school years is the hardest time. And it was hard for both kids.

At the same time Janeen and the boys moved to Niskayuna, I was given a prestigious assignment with the bank that meant my leaving home each week for four days, traveling to a campus in Rhode Island. So just as we combined our lives, I exited, leaving them alone in a strange place without friends or even knowing where to go for basic needs. And as if that wasn't enough, I would often pick up my son, James, on the way back from Rhode Island and bring him into the house.

Combining our families was challenging. By this time, my son's mother and her parents had pulled me into family court countless times, for infractions such as letting James watch movies they didn't approve of or giving him permission to walk five blocks to the CVS with my landlord's two boys, ages nine and twelve. Each time they dragged me to court, a perturbed judge advised my ex-wife and her controlling mother to get out of his court and stop bringing such insignificant issues to the bench.

Sam

Matt had a passion for animals, specifically lizards and other exotic creatures. But most of all during this time, he wanted a dog. Matt was not one to let things lie dormant, nor was he afraid to ask for what he wanted in special cases. Getting a dog became his mantra during this transitional time. For me, having a dog as a single professional was completely out of the question. But I was no longer alone, for I had constructed an extended family, a blended family, with a woman that I adored.

"Maybe we could consider a dog," I said to Janeen. We decided to tell Matt that if he wanted a dog, he would need to do the research. We agreed on the type of dog we would pursue. Labrador retrievers were great dogs, right? Matt was on a mission.

Days later, after extensive research on the Internet, Matt found a breeder in North Carolina that had champion line yellow labs available. Thus began the Sam adventure. There was a litter of dogs available from which to choose. Online pictures portrayed puppies that melted hearts— cute, furry balls of love impossible not to want. $2,500 later, arrangements were made to ship via airfreight the male puppy we selected from the website. The day arrived, we jumped into my Mercedes S500 and made our way to the Albany Airport freight office to pick up the dog we had named Sam. Oh, he was a beautiful eight-week-old yellow lab! We brought him home, following the instructions to get him crated immediately. We expected the initial getting used to the crate and new family, but what followed was a nightmare.

Sam grew quickly and was ravenous at every meal, nearly uncontrollable when his food was being placed in the bowl. He had boundless energy, perpetually jumping, eating, and terrorizing our home. The dog was out of control, despite following all the instructions, adhering to prescribed diet and trying to maintain patience.

Nighttime was insane, for even the slightest movement and noise from our bedroom at the far end of the house would result in nonstop barking and howling. Nothing we did made a difference. Our home had become a place of terror. After two months and many calls to the breeder, it just so happened that he would be flying his plane into the upstate New York area. He came to our home to inspect our situation. We convinced him that it would be a great idea to take the dog with him to see if he could make progress with the dog's lack of obedience. He stayed at a local hotel that night. The next day he told us that Sam had chewed through the bed frame overnight. The breeder wanted to return the dog to us. We said, "No way!"

Sometime after this experience, we watched the movie *Marley and Me*. As bad as Marley was in the movie, Sam would have made Marley look like a saint.

A year later, Matt still wanted a dog. Maybe the past problem, we thought, was that Sam was left by himself during the daytime, with both Janeen and me working and with the boys at school. "Let's get two, a brother and sister, to keep each other company." Great idea! Yes, not one dog, but two.

We found a breeder of labradoodles, two hours from our home, outside of Oneonta. It turned out that the dogs, named Mercedes and Ben, were misrepresented as Labradoodles, for they both possessed pigeon-sized brains and would do incredibly weird things, such as eating the bark of trees, rocks and even their own excrement. Within six months, Ben developed a twisted stomach, requiring that we make a compassionate decision. Mercedes suffered the same malady as her brother, but this time, the veterinarian would keep her.

So much for dogs, we thought.

Blending Family- A Jagged Edge

After our divorce, my first ex-wife challenged everything I did, irrationally, unrealistically and unnecessarily. James carried with him an extraordinary amount of internalized anger, resentment, confusion and conflict. He became a trouble-making insidious entity in our house, being contrite and obedient with me, but stirring up ill will and conflict with Janeen, Martin and Matt. It was a difficult time in our young blended family, leading to arguments, great tension and the internal threats of breaking up our relationship.

What was more disorienting were the weekends where James would not join us. Janeen and I wrapped ourselves in a cocoon of love and sharing, a warm pleasurable union of ecstasy and bonding that was life-filling and healing. The jagged edge of our blended family was almost too much to bear.

But I had experienced so much duress in my life up to this point. And I was not one to easily let discouragement and pain rule my world. Giving up was never my choice!

A Milestone

Standing outside Proctors Theatre, a landmark in downtown Schenectady, once a vaudeville theatre and a gem of the town, Janeen and I took a long deep breath. We had gotten our oldest son, Martin, to his high school graduation on that sunny day in June, 2009. His younger brother, Matthew, had graduated a week previously from Darrow School, a private boarding facility in the Berkshires on the border between New York and Massachusetts. Martin Dufner, the oldest of our three blended family kids, was an enigma. He was one of the brightest kids I had ever met, yet his writing disability crippled his success in the mainstream educational process. So getting him to graduation was a monumental success.

Loving

I was once told by a male coworker after the birth of his son that being a parent had given him a love he otherwise would not have known. This is true! In the context of being a love leader, nothing has supported my leadership delivery more than being a parent and living true to its calling. Furthermore, the challenges of my life, while heartbreaking and painful, have been gifts of the soul, pathways to expansion and a continued journey of enlightenment. Resilience, fortitude and redemption characterize my life, all emblematic of the power of choice. The divine seed within provided me with enough light to choose love over fear, compassion rather than resentment and seeking to understand as opposed to self-serving fulfillment. For this, I am grateful.

CHAPTER 3 REFLECTIONS

[9] *Are we endowed as human beings with the divine capacity to love? The jury is out as to whether it is a natural human attribute to feel something intangible like love. After all, you can't touch it, right? But most of us, to some degree, would admit its existence. How do we embrace qualities of love, compassion and understanding to effectively connect with others? And what keeps us locked inside our heads as thinking, intelligent beings while denying a place for squishy, mushy heart-centered feelings in our professional lives?*

This is a fallacy of grave proportion, in that the heart–mind connection frees us from the bonds of fear and anxiety and from our chatterbox false-self egos that chide us to adhere to the limiting structures of a corporate playbook or a neatly organized dogma. These and other foundational structures not only constrain our behavior, but also instruct us to separate our humanness from our leadership role.

Being a love leader, as a key principle of conscious leadership, invites you to imagine a holistic self, one of unison between the mind—with its unlimited potential—and the heart—beating, feeling and directing us to a higher order. Both can thrive in unity when you are able to relinquish the fears that prevent authentic connection with those you lead and serve. My work since 2006 has been an exploration of bringing genuine caring and honest support to those I lead. As a baby-boomer, I was taught to separate personal from professional; this was an accepted protocol for living successfully. Consider for a moment how damaging this practice is to our individual and collective humanness.

Years ago, I observed how limiting this view of reality is when I noted the common practice of going to work and hanging up one's personality on a hook, to become a banker or doctor or teacher or some other professional title. I watched good people go to work and intentionally decide to shelve their most precious and valuable human quality, to set it aside and denote it as unimportant. Especially in businesses with face-to-face customer interaction, we become robotic, scripted, conformist professionals, touting the corporate lingo and reducing our essential nature to secondary or tertiary importance. Human beings want to connect from a point of integrity and honesty, not from an automated and contrived construct. This is where love and compassion come into the mix. If a customer feels the sincerity of an employee's care and concern for them, there is a human connection that ignites positive energetic flow. This is true with conscious leaders when they are unafraid to actually love and care for their associates. Human beings seek meaningful connection and respond favorably to leaders who are truly interested in their wellbeing, their aspirations and their unique desires to live fully.

Perhaps the most complimentary statement I can hear from someone I lead is, "Michael, I know that you care about me." Small things make a difference in our lives—smiles, genuine eye contact, actually meaning it when you say to another, "How's it going?" It takes a small amount of time and energy to start off a business conversation by connecting with your employee in a human statement that bridges you to the other person; it simply requires being present and aware that we are more than our title or our position in life. True human connection builds loyalty and trust, priceless gifts that any leader would relish.

[10] *Glimpses of the true Michael were evident in the those touching moments of loving my brother in spite of his shortcomings and limitations; the deeply held compassion felt for those of lesser means and circumstances; all the inner workings of the heart–mind connection speaking to the Divine in our collective experience. My history is replete with quiet, compelling sparks of profound emotional love and connection that earlier in my life were but passing touch points of disjointed events and people moving in my line of encounter. I have come to know now that none*

of my experiences happened in a vacuum of coincidence; rather they have been the thread of Divine intervention moving me to a greater purpose. There were many challenges to face and perhaps the greatest was the self-destruction attached to my alcoholism. After all, it was the family tradition.

[11] *This was the first time that I had been discriminated against. The feeling of less-than or not-worthy was a harsh reality. The memory of that rebuke stayed with me and allowed me a visceral compassion and empathy for others being cast away, hated, threatened and unfairly treated based on color, religion, sexual orientation or place in society.*

INSIGHTS AND TOOLS

Be a Love Leader - Nothing is more important than leading from the heart. Allow yourself to lead from the heart. Of course, a strong durable intellect is essential for living a whole life, but relying solely on the mind is very limiting. On the continuum of life, we operate either from fear or from love. When we let fear orchestrate our behaviors, we shut the door to genuine caring, compassion and love. This is true in our personal lives, but equally relevant in our professional lives. Whether a corporate leader, a small business owner, a teacher, minister, non-profit professional, medical provider, parent, grandparent or neighbor, leadership demands more than a rote, scripted and non-personal delivery. Leadership in any form requires a connection between heart and mind.

4

BE A TRANSFORMATIVE COMMUNICATOR

From Words to Broader Understanding

A conscious leader is a transformative communicator. Conscious leaders examine the human connection from an understanding that words are a small part of effective communication. When we move beyond the constraints of our 3-D world and consider alternative methods of listening to others to hear their true meaning, we elevate ourselves into a higher realm of humanness, one of transformation.

It was early morning, September 20, 1996, a Friday.

"I think it's time. My water just broke."

Off we sped in my red Chevy Blazer to Albany Medical Center. Twenty-seven hours in labor ended in a caesarian section and James Mitchell Splann was born. It was mid-morning, September 21, 1996, a Saturday.

My first wife was never more even-tempered and happy than during her pregnancy.

The birth of my son was a defining moment in my life. I realized that not only was my first marriage a sham, but there never was any real love between us. I was the vehicle, the trophy husband for giving my wife a child, plain and simple. How deeply I had wanted a child, wanted to be a father, wanted an intimate loving partner, wanted a secure family; only to find myself embroiled in a no-win situation where my wife, buttressed by her parents' complete hatred and scorn toward me, formed the world I had created. No words can capture how wounded and misunderstood I felt during the early years of parenthood and marriage. I was rocked to my core.

After the birth of James Mitchell, I became the resident enemy, targeted with a continual barrage of barbs, complaints and nonsensical tirades, always directed at some aspect of my behavior. It didn't matter what I said or did; it was grounds for attack and rebuke. I wanted to hold the baby days after his birth, only to be scolded and chided as not being capable of doing so correctly. My mother-in-law, constantly by her daughter's side, directed the show, loading the weapons with her angry and hateful venom, spitting toxic barbs. The two of them did as much damage as possible. I was their antichrist figure, their demon at which they felt completely comfortable and justified in directing any and all problems or challenges; I was the source and scourge of their shared discontent. It was maddening. I did not know it at the time, but this failure would be the springboard from which I would garner life-affirming knowledge and an expanded life, despite the pain and loss of my aspirations.

Being a father to my son has been one of the greatest challenges of my life. I had so wanted to have my own opportunity to bring a child into the world. But without the love and sharing of a partner who actually wanted to co-parent and who did everything within her power to prevent and diminish my involvement, I was dead in the water.

Movin' On Up

In 1997, Computer Science Corporation (now CSC) was a Fortune 500 multinational technology company with eleven divisions, healthcare being one. The company formed an outsourcing arm that provided complete technology solutions for startup healthcare organizations, particularly companies set up to manage state Medicaid programs. Several clients were being courted when I was hired. My job was to lead the project teams in establishing customized technology packages along with developing customer service platforms to provide support for anticipated members, providers and insurance companies.

My first week at CSC, I flew to Orlando, Florida, accompanied by several technical support personnel and lead project managers. We were to meet with the CEO and her direct reports to present our strategies for providing the outsourcing technology and our proposed customer service plans. What I did not know was that the CEO and her team were scheduled to meet with Florida state regulators to communicate their overarching plans for building their health plan and gaining the needed approvals from the state. For me, this was initiation by fire.

I had only generic talking points and a vague understanding of the agreement structure with our client. We met with Florida regulators for four hours. I represented CSC as the primary director and elaborated on how CSC would be contracting with the health plan. I do not have a clue as to how I was able to pull off representing CSC and our client during what can only be described as a harrowing meeting. But it worked and the health plan was given intermediate approval to move forward. The CEO and her team were thrilled and I quickly made a name for myself, bridging the outsourcing relationship nicely.

My success in representing CSC resulted in a quick promotion to national accounts manager, working directly with executive teams in health plans in Kentucky and Washington, DC.

This position afforded me a newfound confidence. I learned that I was quick on my feet and able to communicate effectively, even without experience and exposure in an area. I began to advance within organizations and take on greater authority and capacity. My work at CSC connected me with executive-level professionals, CEOs, CFOs and movers and shakers in their respective fields. I became aware that high-level executives put their pants on just as I did, experienced similar trials and tribulations and were, in fact, human beings. I gained comfort and confidence in being able to communicate with anyone at any time and any place. [12]

In January 1999, my employer, Computer Sciences Corporation (CSC), in Latham, New York, announced that the division failed to make their revenue targets and the department was being shut down. I was out of a job after two years working as a national accounts manager and concurrently managing the customer service departments at two client sites.

Unemployment was accompanied by the realization that I now had a two-year-old son, a new house, bills to pay and a marriage that was anything but good.

My wife was working for the phone company, as had her mother for over thirty years. When we married, she insisted on contributing only a small portion of her salary to the shared household expenses so that she would have enough money to buy things, meet with friends and have a social life. When my income became unemployment checks, significantly less than my regular pay, she refused to take on any additional financial responsibility. We separated less than a year later.

New Industry, New Career

The 11:15am time slot to review my 1999 performance appraisal with Sam Stein, the division president and my direct report manager, was in five minutes. I took a deep breath, gathered up my self-assessment and made my way to Sarah Caldwell, Sam's administrative assistant.

"Hi Michael. Sam will be with you right after his call."

"Great, thanks Sarah."

I was the division training director, my first career assignment in financial services. This would be the first performance appraisal I would attend as my future continued to open up in banking. Standing outside the bank president's office, I wondered how I would be assessed in my new position. I had been onboard only since April 1999.

Through the glass panel, I watched as Sam hung up the phone, pushed his leather chair back to stand up and came to his door. His hand extended to shake mine. Sam smiled.

"Michael, come in. Good to see you."

"Same here Sam. How are you?"

During the next hour, we moved through the formatted performance appraisal with Sam having positive and affirming observations, all of which were superlative. But when it came to the competency "communicating with impact," Sam's whole disposition perked up. After a thoughtful pause, he told me exuberantly that of all his direct reports over time, I was one of the most effective communicators he had had. I was surprised by his praise and grateful for it.

In my position as director of training, I collaborated with several nationally recognized training organizations to become master certified. I delivered high-impact sales and service leadership training programs across the company. I was the principal executive training facilitator not just in my division, but across the entire footprint. Sam was a raving fan.

I was able to rise to that position in less than a year because of good timing combined with my inner strength and resilience. At Eastern Airlines in the mid 1980s, I briefly trained flight attendants. This introduction to corporate training gave me enough background to step into my leadership position. Another key element was my desire to be my own boss, not be under the thumb of a micromanager.

Sam had joined the bank just two weeks before me. His leadership style was collaborative and hands-off. Sam and I connected immediately. He made me his right-hand man in the field, his eyes and ears as we did our due diligence as to how to build the divisional retail bank.

Starting from scratch in my position allowed me great latitude in hiring my own team of trainers, aligning with the business line executives and rapidly inserting myself into the core of the decision making machinery. It also gave me the opportunity to install my voice, my intentional style and my passionate perspective within the organization.

Reporting directly to the president had its perks, no doubt. Not only did I build the training department to serve three states, but I also created my own job. Over the first year I wrote training programs for various job families, while becoming more of a performance consultant to the ten regional sales managers with whom I collaborated.

Where did this ability of mine come from and how did I find my way to understanding how to communicate beyond words?

It started with a French kiss.

Adventure en Français

Midsummer 1976, in between my junior and senior year at Syracuse, I was invited to an annual party held at a friend's farm outside Hershey, in the green rolling hills of south-central Pennsylvania. The party featured live bands, unlimited beer on tap, chicken barbeque, fresh farm-grown vegetables, pot, meth, heroin and more. Partygoers brought tents to set up for the entire weekend.

Bill, the owner, brought in a flatbed semitrailer and set it up against the side of his barn to use as a stage. The surrounding hills formed a perfect amphitheater in the middle of the large farm, so noise was not an issue for the neighboring farmers, all of whom contributed to the event every year. It was the perfect setting for a party of grand proportion.

Music was scheduled throughout the weekend. Bill provided high-end sound equipment and lighting, including amplifiers, soundboards, microphones and everything necessary to just plug and play. My band—Ted, Lee, John, Shorty and me—were slotted to perform at four Saturday afternoon.

Several hours into the Saturday festivities, I saw Kimberly, a student I had casually befriended at HACC during my sophomore year. Kim was a stunning five-foot-ten brunette with long curls and deep green eyes. I had always been attracted to her and, voilà, there she stood drinking a beer and chatting with friends. My friend Dave knew of my attraction and jabbed me in the shoulder.

"Michael, check it out! There's Kim. Go talk to her."

It was midafternoon and the fourth beer had done its job in lessening my inhibitions. I responded in an instant. I walked over to Kim and greeted her with a warm smile. She responded with a hug and a kiss on my cheek. She was braless under her T-shirt, further accelerating young male testosterone. Several of her friends and mine collected together during the rest of the day, drinking, smoking pot and later splitting a Quaalude to really solidify the high.

At 4:15pm we were summoned to take the stage. It was an exuberant reunion for all of us, since we had not played together for well over a year at that point. The songs came naturally and we were quickly unified in our melding of instruments and vocals. Lee's banjo picking was tight and much better than when we were together performing.

The party was a blast and for the most part a lovefest. I saw Kim, along with several other friends, off to the left of the stage, clapping and having a terrific time while we played. After we finished our set, I joined Kim. Dave, Lee and Ted backed off intentionally, letting me have the time with her. By early evening we were intoxicated and buzzed, as were the other hundreds of partygoers. By this time, we were lip-locked, hands moving into each other's intimate anatomy. She leaned over and said, "let's go back to my tent." [13]

I eagerly assented. Yes, it was a terrific party. Several hours later, we emerged back into the party, stating our intentions to get together in the days to come. The summer wasn't over yet!

After the weekend, Kim became a focus of my attention. She lived in Palmyra, Pennsylvania, a small conservative town to the east of Hershey. Her parents were right-wing Christians closed to the shift in generational attitudes and practices; it was a challenge for me to get close to her.

My first encounter with Kim's parents was memorable. Early on a Saturday evening, Kim and I had a date to go to the movies. I arrived at her small, well-maintained home and I was greeted at the door by a large bald man in his late forties. He was slightly overweight, but at least sixty pounds above my 175 pounds. He looked me up and down, and scowled in disapproval at my shoulder-length hair. I extended my hand to greet him and he reluctantly reached back to shake mine.

"What are your plans for this evening with Kim?" he asked.

"We are planning on going to the movies and then getting some late dinner."

"What time will Kim be returning?" he snapped, now with Kim's mother standing meekly in the background.

"What time would you like me to have her home, sir?"

"Before midnight!" he barked.

At this point Kim showed up, dressed appropriately, this time with her breasts encased in a bra. We hurried out.

We met several times after the weekend love tryst, mostly at bars and for an occasional bite to eat, but never forming a substantial connection. We were quite different in our thinking and aspirations, she being more parochial as a product of her environment and I, an activist of sorts, ready and willing to take on the next adventure, the next exploration, and viewing life from a vantage point of questioning, wanting to know and learn. What connected us was sex, plain and simple. My attraction to her was similar to a dog chasing a bitch in heat.

On a Friday evening in mid August, Kim and I had arranged to meet at one of our watering holes on the outskirts of Hershey, ten miles from Palmyra. I arrived at the bar around 5:30 and ordered a beer. Kim was to meet me at 6:30. At seven, several beers downed and no Kim, I went to the pay phone to call her house. I dreaded doing so because her parents clearly did not approve of me.

The phone just rang and rang, no answer and no answering machines, for they were not yet commonplace. Old-fashioned communications of picking up a landline phone and calling someone were the norm. I waited and continued drinking. I knew I would be leaving for an extended time with no plans for return to Pennsylvania, and I wanted the evening to be special; so I borrowed my friend Brian's Porsche for the evening's entertainment. It was now ten o'clock, no Kim, and I was inebriated and angry. Leaving the bar, I made the stupid decision to drive to her house to find her, a choice that I ultimately regretted. Pulling up in front of her house I could see that no lights were on. Everyone was either gone or asleep. In my drunken state, I made a good choice in not knocking on the door to find out.

I pulled away from her house, now increasingly upset. I came to a stop sign at one of the small town intersections. I did not stop completely, but cruised through the intersection. Just as I was speeding up, I saw flashing lights turn on in the Porsche's rear view mirror. A police patrol car turned onto the street behind me. My heart instantly raced. I was drunk and I knew that if I pulled over I would be arrested. *Wait a minute, I'm in a Porsche*, I thought. I decided to gun it and run. Downshifting into second gear, I accelerated onto the main road, gaining speed as I saw the patrol car do the same. There was one main road between Palmyra and Hershey.

From second to third, now moving well over ninety, I flew down Route 422 into Hershey, where I decided to take a left turn into a more rural exit. By this time, however, the officer had called for backup. As I turned to make my way on the south side of Hershey, a police blockade was ahead. Police ahead and behind, I slowed the vehicle down, pulled off the side of the road and came to a stop in front of the two local police cruisers. It was a bad scene, for sure. With their guns drawn, one officer told me to get out of the car. I did so and the second officer handcuffed me, guiding me to the back of his patrol car. Into the station I went.

I was drunk, but having a gun pointed at me had a rapid sobering effect. What was I going to do to get out of this? I was supposed to leave for France in less than a week for a French immersion program. Getting arrested would surely put an end to my journey abroad. At the station there were two officers from the Palmyra police force, young and strutting their power. It was after midnight at this point. I told them about Kim not showing up, how hurt I was. Then I told them I was scheduled to go to Europe in a week and arresting me would prevent this from happening. They seemed completely unmoved and uninterested in any excuse until I told them about my father.

Somewhere in my unconscious, a voice pushed me to say that arresting me would surely kill my father, a Second World War hero, a retired colonel in the Air Force, a man of honor. One of the officers looked interested when I mentioned how much I loved my father and how deeply wounded he would be by my actions. The officer asked me where my father served in the war. I told him that he flew twenty-nine B-17 missions over Germany in 1942. He then told me that his father was also in the war, an aircraft machinist who worked on B-17s. I told him that it was possible that our fathers knew each other. A soft spot opened in the police officer's heart and I knew he was empathetic.

By now it was after two in the morning and the conversation changed. In a last-ditch effort, I pleaded with the two young officers. "Please don't arrest me for my actions tonight! I am asking you as the son of an Air Force officer and a World War II veteran." They then went into another office, where I could see them conversing. Several minutes went by and they returned. "We are going to let you go. However, you will need to have someone pick you up and are not to touch the vehicle until tomorrow."

I was incredibly relieved.

They continued, "We are citing you with a moving violation, speeding of fifteen miles over the limit and you will need to pay the fines."

My appreciation was apparent. I said, "Thank you so much!"

I called my friend Dave, waking him from a sound sleep, and told him that he needed to get up and come to the Palmyra Police station and pick me up now.

"What are you talking about?" he said.

I replied, "Don't ask. Just get up and drive to Palmyra, right now."

An hour later Dave arrived and I left the station. I avoided incarceration and paid $125 for the violation.

Au Revoir

Saying goodbye to my family and friends, I boarded a flight from Harrisburg Airport to JFK to meet with several other foreign exchange students joining me in Strasbourg, France. Nine credits of my undergraduate bachelor's degree were approved through the dean of Syracuse Law School on the condition that I would deliver a thesis upon completion of my study abroad.

Syracuse University offered international study programs to cities throughout the world.

The dean had asked me whether I spoke French or not. No, I told him. It never occurred to me to be concerned about my not speaking the language of the country where I would be living. I have often wondered why such an important detail never worried me or gave me pause. But it was never a deterrent for my choice.

Aboard an Air France B-747, along with six other students from various colleges and universities, I departed JFK in the early evening for our overnight flight to Paris.

Arriving at Charles De Gaulle airport early the next morning, we were met by one of our French mentors, Mme. Dubois, and bused into the City of Lights, Paris, France. In the distance I saw the Eiffel Tower as we journeyed along the route. The newness and excitement of actually being in France, knowing that I was to spend enough time in a culture that helped define civilized society, to learn and to grow, was enthralling.

We were to spend two days in Paris, most of the time left to our own devices to explore and take in the Parisian sights, sounds and attractions. A couple of us bonded quickly. Nick was from Ohio and Rob was from Buffalo. Nick attended Rollins School in Orlando and Rob was a fellow Orangeman from Syracuse. We three formed a friendship during our time in France that would lead to many adventures, from staying in a brothel in Nice, to spending a drunken week in Munich during Oktoberfest, to traveling on the Orient Express to Vienna, to downhill skiing on Halloween in the Austrian Alps.

Paris was wonderful. I fell in love with the city immediately. Perhaps my desire to be in France was predestined: I learned during a past-life regression many years later of a former life as a French peasant fighting during the French Revolution. Nonetheless, my spirit coalesced around being in France. It would not be the last time I visited Paris.

On the afternoon of my second day in Paris, I was strolling toward the Seine River. I rounded a corner, my gaze was fixed in a different direction, and was not paying attention to what was ahead of me. I bumped into a young man around my age, staggering him to the side. I was caught off guard by the collision. I said, "I'm so sorry!"

Gathering himself up the young man said, "That's okay, nothing broken."

That he spoke English was at first surprising, but then a welcome contrast to my inability to communicate at all with the French, who seemed to take it upon themselves to simply not speak English at all. He had dropped a bag he was carrying in the collision, so I moved to assist in picking up the items that had strewn on the sidewalk. I said again how sorry I was for not paying any attention to where I was walking. He assured me that he understood. I told him that I had just arrived the day before for an extended study in Strasbourg. "Today is my last day before we leave," I told him.

He, too, was studying in Paris, spending a semester abroad from Penn State University. This led to my telling him that I lived in Pennsylvania, Middletown to be exact. He stated that he lived in New Cumberland, just across the Susquehanna River from my hometown. I then mentioned to him that I lived in New Cumberland from 1963 to 1964. One thing led to another and we soon realized that we lived on the same street, at the same time, and were playmates and friends. We both just shook our heads at the coincidence. Afterwards, we strolled together along the quai and ended up at a small bistro, drinking several beers and telling stories of our lives thus far. We shook hands, knowing we were unlikely to meet again. We wished each other a great life and departed.[14]

Our group boarded a bus to Strasbourg the next morning. The green countryside was dotted with quaint towns, steeped in history older than any towns I knew in the United States. I saw thatched roofs, fields planted with late summer crops, women in sun dresses and men in slacks, not jeans. I quietly took in the sights along the ride. The textures and colors seemed more vivid and deeper for some reason. My senses were alive with a greater openness and appreciation. I particularly noticed the quality of light as we rode along, a luminosity I had not witnessed in the States. Years later, touring with a choral group, I noticed that same light in certain parts of France, especially the Loire valley.

Part of my stay in Strasbourg was arranged with a French host family that consisted of a husband, wife and four children ages four to ten. There was a tinge of trepidation in learning that I would be living with young children, for I had no experience up until that point in my life with children. But I kept an open mind and chalked it up as something new to experience.

There were four men and eight women enrolled in the study abroad program from various colleges and universities. The group I traveled with was the JFK contingent. The others traveled from different locations. We introduced ourselves and shared some of our travel stories. First impressions are not always true, but with this group it quickly became clear that some of the students were uptight, smug, standoffish or just unfriendly. The good news was that most of the students were likeable and open to the experience. One of the women seemed to be there because Mommy and Daddy made her come, which instantly drew my compassion for her.

Another of the women was a fish out of water—introverted, quiet and frightened. Smiling at her, I walked up and grabbed her hand, shaking it as I told her my name and asked for hers. She seemed shocked at my being as forward as I was, but it felt like the right thing to do at that moment.

"Debbie," she said.

I said, "I'm happy to meet you. Where are you from?"

She loosened up noticeably. We never became close friends, but she always understood, without it being said, that I was there for her. Over the months that followed I would check in with her periodically to see how she was doing.

Around five o'clock, shortly after our gathering, the host parents started arriving. After several students were paired up with their parents, most of whom arrived as couples, a lone gentleman entered the room wearing a black leather jacket. He was approximately six feet tall, with dark hair, a thin mustache and what I would call a suave French look about him. He had a smart, charismatic attitude and looked confident and well put together. Roland was his name and he was there to pick me up.

Roland was a middle-level executive for a lumber company outside of Strasbourg. Roland's wife, Christine, was a registered nurse at a major hospital in Strasbourg. She worked the overnight shift when I arrived. I later discovered that Christine had just undergone surgery on her hand due to an injury received at work.

I immediately liked Roland and he instantly took a liking to me as well. The only issue was language. Neither of us spoke the other's language, which prompted Roland to stop at the supermarché to purchase a French–English Dictionary on the way back to Illkirch-Graffenstaden, the town where I would reside for my first four months in France.

As luck and destiny would have it, Roland enjoyed drinking. In addition to the dictionary, we got a bottle of Chivas Regal scotch, Roland's drink of choice. Scotch turned my stomach; the stench from my father's excessive scotch drinking has stayed with me my whole life. But when in France, do as the French would do. So who was I to let my own psychology and history ruin this important meeting? Besides, if I couldn't understand French, at least I could get drunk with my new French host.

When we arrived at Roland and Christine's middle-class suburban four-bedroom home, I was greeted by four children running up to me, the youngest of which jumped into my arms, to welcome me to their home. That evening Roland and I listened to Elvis Presley records and drank nearly an entire bottle of scotch. Roland and Christine were huge Elvis fans, having gone to Paris years previously to see him perform. "Hound Dog," slightly off center and with a French accent, lifted our time together into loud laughter and cemented the start of a great relationship with

Roland. The evening remains a blur and the degree to which we learned each other's language was questionable, yet we bonded over music and booze, a common theme that emerged repeatedly in my life.

The next morning, I awoke to a headache of monumental proportion. I felt like someone had taken a baseball bat to my head; my vision was obscured and my balance was off center. It was in that state that I met Christine, who had returned early that morning. She was in her mid-thirties, slightly overweight, with a huge warm smile and an immediate sensitivity that I felt viscerally. Even with my hangover, I felt her warmth and loving spirit. Christine was open and real. She wasn't made up or dressed up, yet she had a natural beauty I had not encountered before. A free spirit shone in her essence and I could feel it. My embarrassment and uncoordinated movement coupled with not being able to speak the language were eased by Christine's style, for she had been there before. She and Roland were drinkers, Roland a much heavier and daily drinker. A kiss on both cheeks and a "Bonjour Michel," and our relationship began. And for our time together, as I began to learn and communicate in French, our friendship grew.

This was a world very different from the one I had been living in. It was 1976, with the women's liberation movement underway in the States as well as cultural change occurring at all levels. I thought I had been on the cutting edge of social experimentation as a twenty-one-year-old college student. But Strasbourg was a much more liberated and uninhibited culture, with a true progressive freedom among the people, especially in my generation.

The young French women possessed a natural beauty that transcended the usual teenage insecurities, social trappings and repressive societal norms I was used to encountering in the United States. Early on, it became apparent to me that many French women were attracted to me sexually and were not in the least bit afraid of expressing their desire. There was a unique and entirely consuming sexual aura that distinguished French women from their American counterparts. And they were not afraid to express their most erotic and sensual selves. They gave no attention to shaving underarms, legs or any other parts of their bodies. That the French bathed once a week initially caused me to question body odor and hygiene, but in a matter of days that became a non-issue especially when around the female students, whose feminine odor I found incredibly alluring and sexually exciting. My French experience brought with it a sexual immersion that ultimately changed my life.

Roland and Christine had taken on American students in the past, but this time they requested a male student. They found the American women to be unhappy, unwilling to embrace their host country's culture and arrogant, not to mention requiring special accommodations of daily baths and American-style food. Knowing that most Americans take showers daily, Christine told me that it would be okay with Roland and her to take two baths a week. In broken French and lots of sign language I said "Merci beaucoup, Christine."

The Kraft home did not have a stall shower, just a bathtub with a handheld sprayer that could be used as a shower while sitting or standing in the tub.

Sharing the bathtub was a common practice in their home. A couple weeks into my stay, two of the children bounced around the corner into the bathroom and plunged into the tub with me. My initial surprise dissolved into laughter and I washed their backs, legs and bodies as I would have with my own children. This was just another enlivening cultural difference that I found so freeing. A week later, I was bathing when Christine walked into the bathroom completely naked, excused herself politely and retrieved some curlers for her hair. Whether she was trying to excite me or just living her uninhibited life, either way my twenty-one-year old body responded, forcing me to cover the protuberance standing out of the water with a washcloth. Grabbing the hair rollers, she then turned to have a small conversation with me. She stood above the tub while I struggled to keep my eyes on hers and not on the large breasts with protruding nipples staring me in the face. She smiled and casually walked out of the bathroom. I clearly was not in Kansas.

The Kraft home was approximately twelve miles outside the city of Strasbourg. Getting into town each day meant a bus ride of thirty minutes. I usually stood because of the large number of people who commuted each day. I learned very quickly that the European culture was to walk everywhere. Auto transport was not the rule, but rather for weekly trips to attend to errands, holidays and special outings. And for me, walking made perfect sense and aligned to my true nature.

Strasbourg is a historic city in Alsace, a region of France. It is on the Rhine, which forms the border between France and Germany in this region. Over the centuries, this area was by turns part of Germany and France as the two nations conducted wars along their border. The Nazis took over Strasbourg before the Second World War. Marching across the Rhine into the city, the German army quickly took control of the Office of Ministry and Records, which contained the personal records of all men in Strasbourg between the ages of eighteen and thirty-five. These men were forcibly conscripted into the German army and sent off to the Russian front to fight for Germany. Stories still haunted the seniors I met during my time there of over the more than 100,000 Alsatians who were sent off to war never to return.

Coming out of WWII and as part of the treaty forming the union of European nations that would thwart the rise of another Nazi takeover, Strasbourg became the seat of the Council of Europe, and the European Commission of Human Rights and the European Court of Human Rights. This semi-juridical body was designed to entertain human rights violations of abuse, mistreatment and harm.

My international relations degree program at Syracuse University inspired my passion for the protection of human rights. The Carter administration was vocal in their support of protecting basic human rights, focusing on the imprisonment of Nelson Mandela by the apartheid regime in South Africa. At Syracuse, my personal interest in this field of study was what led to my petitioning the dean of the law school to support an independent study program in Strasbourg, where an international study program was already established.

While I was immersing myself in social and cultural experiences, I was also studying and developing a first-hand understanding of the European bodies headquartered in the city. My European adventures had just begun.

When I landed in Paris, I realized I had underestimated the challenges attached to not speaking the language. Simple but important phrases such as, "Where is the bathroom?" or "My name is Michael" or "Where is the train station?" were not in my vocabulary. And even if they were, I would not have been able to understand the answers. So the early part of my French experience was hampered by my not being able to communicate on the most basic level. Learning French was an imperative for sure. The four Kraft children were patient teachers. They would come to me in the evenings after finishing their own schoolwork to teach me. Holding up pencils, paper and anything they could get their hands on, they would instruct me on the noun, correcting my pronunciation with unabashed glee.

Before I arrived in Strasbourg, I was convinced that I would not bring more children into an overpopulated world. But the four Kraft children melted away my commitment. What I found in them was a gift of innocence and purity of spirit. I saw their unfiltered love and exuberance. They embodied for me the essence of living in the moment, finding joy in the simplest of activities, where laughter and love flowed with ease. The experience changed my life.

I often awoke in the early hours of the morning to one or more of the children climbing into bed with me. No, there were no nightmares, just the childlike desire to sleep next to me. It was not the only time where surprises came to the bed I slept in. Sundays were feast days at the Kraft home. Friends, family and neighbors would gather to eat, drink, sing, dance, eat and drink more. The first Sunday fête I attended was my second week in France. I was the attraction, a twenty-one-year-old male student with shoulder-length hair, warm, curious and American. I was a novelty that Roland and Christine were happy to show off. Despite not understanding much of the conversation, I ascertained that I was the topic of much attention. The afternoon proceeded with heightened adult inebriation and diminished inhibitions as the women would touch and kiss me. Kissing in France was just a way of life. Women kissed men, women kissed women and men kissed men. And if you were close friends, kissing on the mouth was routine for both men and women.

Several people were trying to converse with me as I struggled to understand and find the right words. I had planned a trip with my friends to the French Riviera and worked to find the translation to be able to say how excited I was to be traveling to the south of France. It was the middle of the afternoon, following many bottles of wine and two courses of great food. Twelve of us sat around the dining room table smoking, laughing and enjoying the frivolity. I told Roland that I had something to say to the group. He hushed the guests to listen to what the American had to say. After all, I had carefully constructed the sentence to show my progress in French and now was my time to let everyone know about my trip. The room came to a hush as I cleared my voice and proceeded to say, "Je suis excité de voyage vers la cote d'azure." Feeling a sense of accomplishment, I looked out at the men and women who just hung in silence for what felt like an eternity. Then, in an instant, the room exploded in laughter. What had just happened? It appeared that I had said something hilariously outrageous. It wasn't until weeks later that I learned that in French there were different verbs for excitement. The one I had chosen indeed implied excitement, but not in the sense of my upcoming travel. The light bulb finally came on that I had stated I was *sexually* excited to go to the French Riviera. While there was truth in this, I had not intended to say so. Christine was the person who finally explained what had happened and we both laughed until we cried.

It was during this Sunday grand fête that I was introduced to the next door neighbors, close friends of Christine and Roland. Charles and Maria shared a wonderful, loving relationship with each other. They were both at ease among their friends, touching hands frequently, smiling and sharing a kiss from time to time. They had two children, Pierre, who was attending his first year of college, and Bridget, a stunning seventeen-year-old with bright green eyes, white even teeth that sparkled when she smiled and a slender body. And she smiled in my direction frequently on that Sunday. She was dressed in a simple and elegant pale yellow sundress with a spattering of aqua and pink flowers. I could see that she wore no bra, as the curves of her pert breasts and protruding nipples were in my line of sight.

I had not paid much attention to Bridget; although, she was a beauty. She was seventeen and too young to consider for anything other than a nice friend. But Christine poked me a couple times nodding her head in Bridget's direction, seemingly indicating that I should be interested. I didn't know how to ask why Christine was egging me on as she was. Didn't she know that I was twenty-one and Bridget was seventeen? It was confusing and frustrating at the same time, because the truth was I would have been brain dead to not be attracted to Bridget. But she was jail bait and I knew it.

What I had held as clear lines of demarcation in terms of right and wrong, acceptable and unacceptable, were being questioned early in my

French immersion. And most complicating was that the adults were eager to have me cross those lines. *These crazy French*, I thought.

On a Wednesday evening I got back to the Kraft home around ten, having spent several hours with friends at the local café, drinking wine and discussing important matters of politics, sex and music. The kids were already asleep and Roland was going to bed. "Bonne nuit, Michel," he said.

I walked down the hallway at the top of the stairs, trying to be quiet as I entered my bedroom. I undressed in the dark, in silence. As I pulled the covers back and climbed into bed, I found someone was waiting there for me. Yes, Bridget, with Roland's approval, lay naked and wanting upon my arrival. Now, in my bed, was a beautiful girl, yet inside I knew that to be with her would ruin my life forever. A kiss on her cheek and off she went.

What I didn't know then was that Bridget had just turned 18, having celebrated her birthday the week prior. C'est la vie!

The French Riviera

Early in the fall semester, we were given one week as fall break. Among the American students, my two traveling buddies, Nick and Rob and I, *les trois amis*, had wings on our feet, as my mother would say. We intended to see as much of Europe as we could. We had purchased Eurail passes for months of travel on the train system, to take advantage of traveling when we had free time. And travel we did. The sojourn on the French Riviera was the first of many travels. Only a few weeks into our academic semester, we were off to explore the Mediterranean and experience what we had heard was glamorous high society. The train ride from Strasbourg to Nice took several hours. I gazed out from our coach compartment. The countryside was not much different from rural Pennsylvania, with rolling hills, green farmland and the occasional cow pasture. Yet there was a more radiant texture to the sunlight as it filtered through the trees, as though permeating a longer history of past lives, a rich fabric of visual beauty that enlivened my spirit. Perhaps it was the novelty of the experience, but nonetheless, I was enthralled by the elegant simplicity of the countryside. Rob and Nick were characters. They noticed every pretty mademoiselle and commented on their sexual fantasies. I joined in with great zeal.

At the Nice train station, we gathered our packs and made our way into town. Getting to the sea was our initial goal. Just as I had wanted to get to the Pacific Ocean my first time in California, here was a chance to see the Mediterranean. I had studied enough history to know that this sea had been the major waterway for the rise and fall of many civilizations, and I felt compelled to honor the water for its historical impact and natural beauty. Eventually, we made our way to the coastline and found a moped rental store where we secured three 90cc mopeds for the three days we would be visiting. Now we had transportation. Next was to find lodging where we could set up base camp for our exploration. The Internet didn't exist in 1976, so research was through reading material either found in the library or purchased in a bookstore. We had enough combined knowledge to know that inns or brothels were cheap with adequate rooming, something that college students could afford. We located a small bar and restaurant just off the main street parallel to the coastline. We went inside, had a glass of beer and inquired about a room. The proprietor answered, "Oui" to our inquiry and guided us upstairs to a room with two twin beds and a couch. The room was in the corner of the building; one window had an obstructed view of the coastline to the east. Perfect, we thought. And it was well within our budget. Off we went to explore.

On the first night of our stay, after we had eaten dinner and retired to our room, there was a knock at the door. Standing in front me, was Monique, a woman of nineteen wearing a French maid outfit with her breasts exposed to the top of her nipples. Rob, who spoke the best French, interpreted for us.

She asked, in French, "Would you like some entertainment?"

Nick jumped up from the couch. Rob asked her what entertainment she was referring to. Monique said she was available to us for "cent francs."

Although the US dollar was worth four francs, we were operating on a tight budget. So, much to Nick's displeasure, we told Monique we did not have enough to have her entertain all of us.

She told us that the inn was a brothel and optional sex was available to its guests. This was a common practice. Monique smiled and told Rob if we changed our minds, she would gladly make us all very happy. During the rest of our stay in Nice we caught glimpses of her working the streets below and making arrangements with different men. Yes, we were not in Syracuse.

Not only did I learn to drink wine during my time in Europe, but I immediately fell prey to the taste of French bread. Never before had I tasted bread like those baguettes. The Wonder Bread I had been brought up on felt like a sham to me after my first bite of this amazing food. How was it that the bread in France tasted so much better than in America? My indignation was apparent. I could not get enough of this manna from heaven. There was one problem. Consuming all that bread eventually led to my being as constipated as I had ever been, ten days without a bowel movement. Here I was in Nice and in a grave state of constipation that required action of some sort. Rob and Nick found my dilemma to be a point of hilarity, but soon realized that it was something I needed help with. It was Nick who would come to my rescue. "No problem, Michel," he said.

Nick was a jokester, always with a sly smile, carefree and at times recklessly uninhibited and direct. He stood no more than five-foot-six. His stocky and sturdy frame was not what I thought women would find attractive. But he was charismatic and charming at times, with no filter of shyness or discomfort around people, especially women. I could not count the times he simply walked up to a beautiful woman and introduced himself, followed by smiling and telling her how lovely she was. Enough women succumbed to his charms, ending up in a sexual interlude, that Rob and I, without any similar outcomes of our own, stood in wonder. Nick was unique and unpredictable. Sometimes we had to keep an eye on his antics, lest he be inappropriate—particularly when we were all inebriated, which we were with some frequency.

We found a pharmacy and proceeded to the back, where we found an attractive mademoiselle behind the counter. She was in her mid-twenties, with light brown hair, beautiful brown eyes, long lashes and a body that immediately spurned young enthusiasm. Nick smiled at me and said, "Leave it to me." I am sure that Nick was trying to reassure me in his own inimitable manner, but knowing Nick I became even more concerned. What was he going to say to the beautiful druggist? Rob and I stood behind Nick as he proceeded to catch the young woman's attention.

"Monsieur, s'il vous plait."

Nick responded, "Bonjour, mademoiselle, mon ami est CONSTIPATED, non poop!"

If that wasn't embarrassing enough, he immediately followed this with a huge mouth fart. I remember recoiling in complete shock that he would do this. The woman began laughing uncontrollably.

Nick, feeling quite proud of himself, smiled like a Cheshire cat as she guided us to the remedy for my problem. After two days of taking the strong laxative, I was able to unblock the block and get on with my life.

The Riviera was stunning. On our mopeds we traveled along the hilly coastline from Monaco, twenty kilometers to the northeast, to many kilometers southeast of Nice, passing through quaint towns and affluent estates and viewing a lifestyle very different from that where we had traveled from. We found a fourteenth-century fortress and graveyards with tombstones dating back hundreds of years. We stopped into cafés for glasses of beer, *jambon et fromage* sandwiches and dark chocolate.

My French Tutor

Strasbourg was the home of Kronenbourg Brewery, one of Europe's largest and finest beer manufacturers. Beer, like the wine from this region, was delicious and flowed freely for us college students. We spent our afternoons in cafes around the university, drinking beer and wine while we discussed politics and social injustice, engaging in anti-government blasphemy. I became friendly with several French students, including a wild-haired beauty by the name of Allie. She was of Moroccan heritage, with almond skin, dark thick curly hair well down her back and deep dark eyes. She dressed in jeans and long-sleeve cotton pullovers, and her unshaven body was curvy.

My French was improving slowly. I was starting to understand sentences and colloquialisms more and more. I met Allie in early October at Café Grande. She was with several other students attending the University of Strasbourg, where she was in her senior year. As I sat with my friends, I looked across the large gathering and saw her staring at me. She smiled easily, not losing eye contact, as though to say *I like you and am not in the least afraid or shy about my feelings.* I realized early on that the French did not have the same inhibitions as Americans when it came to their attractions.

She came to where I was sitting and put out her hand to introduce herself. I took it, taking note of her slender, but strong fingers. As I shook her hand I responded in as proper French as I could, "Bonjour Allie, mon nom est Michel. Je suis Americain." Allie smiled, holding onto my handshake for what felt like minutes and proceeded to sit next to me. She immediately started to teach me more French, providing translation from English to French. There were many phrases in English that could not be translated into French. The trick was to start thinking in French. We drank beer and continued getting to know each other for a couple more hours until she asked if I would walk her to her apartment. Of course I would. She had captured me and I was a willing, young participant.

Allie lived in Strasbourg on the outskirts of Old Town along the canals, in a building constructed several hundred years earlier. As we walked along the narrow streets, her arm intertwined with mine, she continued to work with me in strengthening my French. Her English, while elementary, was much better than my French; so she was able to assist me in making myself understood. We arrived at her apartment building. She turned to me, smiling, pressed her open mouth to mine and inserted her tongue to give me a kiss that was unlike any I'd experienced before. There was nothing held back or reserved for a more passionate moment. It was erotic and sensual, a kiss that left me stupefied and erect as I stood outside in the darkening evening.

Taking my hand without any words, she opened the door and led me up three flights of stairs and into her one-bedroom apartment. It was adorned with beads, Moroccan artisan pottery, lamps and tapestries. Lighting a couple large candles, she threw her jacket across a chair and disappeared into the kitchen, bringing back two glasses of dark red wine. Handing me a glass, she took a sip from her own and came to me once again, mouth pressed to mine. Her lips against mine, she opened her mouth, letting the dark wine flow into my mouth as her tongue probed mine. She continued to kiss me as though she wanted to taste the wine from my tongue. Putting down her glass, she stepped back, lifted her cotton shirt over her head to expose her hairy armpits and her huge breasts with their long dark nipples. She then dropped her jeans to expose her curvaceous lower body, unshaven, with a dark pubic area that accompanied hair from her navel to her ankles. As she came towards me her feminine scent swept over me like magic elixir. There was something extraordinary about French women who bathed once a week and let their natural body odor free. I found her to be the most sexually arousing woman I had ever imagined. She proceeded to undress me as she worked herself up into frenetic passion, kissing me and licking places on my body I'd never dreamt of. With Allie, nothing was off limits. I not only learned to speak French with her, but moved from uncoordinated, unfulfilling juvenile sex to raw, deeply passionate and mutually satisfying, full body, everything goes sexual fulfillment. She and I would continue to have these encounters for several months until she decided to move to Paris, pursuing an underground communist political agenda with others who were trying to infiltrate the political establishment. So far, my French journey had been quite illuminating.

Party-Time

Drinking was the culture in France, and I was at home with the pace and style of living. There were afternoon beers followed by evening glasses of wine with Roland and Christine. Occasionally Roland would break out the Russian or Polish schnapps for several shots each. My past experience with peppermint schnapps did not prepare me for the real deal. The potency of this beverage was powerful; after three or four shots, I was completely inebriated. But this was the culture. I later learned from Christine that Roland wanted a male student so that he had a drinking buddy. And I was just that. My upbringing was perfectly aligned with my being a drinking buddy, someone to get drunk with. Every day in France was a day of drinking, some more than others, and alcohol was an integral part of my European experience. There were more alcoholic adventures ahead.

For years I had heard great tales about the Oktoberfest in Germany. Living on the Rhine just a walk across the bridge to Germany, *les trois amis* decided we were going to make a trek to the party. Several days before Oktoberfest, while drinking with a group of students, some others decided to join us. One of the students attending a different university offered to drive. Rob was among the group that accepted the offer and broke ranks with Nick and me. We had previous plans to get together with other students coming into town. Nick looked at me and said, "Let's hitchhike to Munich."

I said, "Why not?"

Nick's friends from the Midwest arrived in Strasbourg early in the afternoon en route to Vienna, the day before the start of Oktoberfest. The first place they wanted to see was the Kronenbourg Brewery. We had been through the tour many times, but gladly escorted the four students, all women, through the tour to the beer tasting at the end. The beer was potent and fresh, and there were ample amounts to leave the six of us tipsy by midafternoon. Walking around town, we of course ended up at one of our watering holes and had several more beers. We then found our way to a local restaurant to feast on some authentic Alsatian food along with several bottles of Gewürztraminer wine and multiple shots of Polish schnapps. I lost track of the evening's events shortly after dinner. The last thing I remember is one of the women throwing up on a back street from all the alcohol. Off the four women went to their hotel as Nick and I stumbled back to his place in town, where I was staying the night in preparation for our hitchhiking trip the next day.

The next morning Nick prodded me to peel my eyes open and get up so that we could get on the road. I had a huge hangover. When I sat up from the couch where I had passed out the night before, the room moved and my vision felt permanently distorted. My head pounded. But Nick and I committed to our friends that we would meet them at five in the Hofbräuhaus in downtown Munich. It was now eight in the morning and we needed to get on the road.

So we loaded up our packs with enough clothes to last us a few days along with our passports and assorted necessities, and headed out to hitchhike across half of Germany to Munich. Our first ride came from a gentleman in a Citroën sedan who was traveling to just outside Stuttgart. It was my first time on the autobahn, and with the average speed around 160 kilometers per hour and a huge hangover, the ride felt like a Space Mountain

Disney ride. Our driver turned off the motorway, left us on the exit ramp and bid us farewell and good luck.

We walked over to the onramp and there we stood for several hours. We were still well over 150 kilometers from Munich. All we could hear from where we stood were the buzzing sounds of Porsches, Mercedes and other finely tuned sports cars racing along the speedway. It sounded like the Daytona 500, engines whining at a high pitch as blurs of vehicles whizzed by. We worried that we were going to remain on this entrance ramp for days. Meanwhile, my head continued to pound.

Then I saw a 1960s-style painted van coming our way. It looked completely out of place with its hippie-style chrome wheels and flower power psychedelic paint on the exterior. Nick and I just held out our thumbs. The van came to a stop off the shoulder. The male driver had long hair and wire-rimmed glasses. The side door opened and we were greeted by two gorgeous blonde women in their early twenties asking if we'd like a ride. They sounded British at first, but with a few more phrases we could tell they were Australian. And beauties they were. We jumped into the shag-carpeted van. The women helped us with our packs and asked us where we were heading.

"Munich, for the Oktoberfest," I said.

Debra, the thinner of the two, smiled at me. "Great luck, mates. We are heading there ourselves."

There were angels on earth, I thought.

Mary, the other woman, looked at me and asked, "Are you in pain?"

I said, "Is it that apparent?" I then told her that I had a very bad headache.

Debra motioned me to the back of the van where there was a platform bed. "Lie down. I have some aspirin and I will rub your head."

Within ten minutes I had gone from hell to heaven. The aspirin was helpful, but Debra's head rub lasted a good twenty minutes and that arrested all pain and brought me back to earth. It was remarkable.

As fortune would have it, the van pulled into the city of Munich at 4:30pm. The three angels from Australia advised that they were staying with some friends during the fest. Debra said to me that she hoped we could find each other. "Look for me at the Heineken beer hall." She gave me a warm kiss. A kiss on Mary's cheek and a great hug for George, our driver, and we departed to make our way to the Hofbräuhaus to meet our friends as planned. We entered the landmark beer hall at 4:53pm, seven minutes ahead of our planned meeting, to find the group gathered at a large table, being served by a Fräulein carrying several liters of beer.

The next days were a blur of drunkenness. The city of Munich was alive with thousands of visitors from all over the world coming together for one big beer drinking party filled with German oompah bands, line dancing—sometimes with drunken nudity—and complete abandon.

Before the official start of the event several of us wandered to Theresienwiese, the area of Munich where the beer halls were being set up for the five million visitors who would be passing through Munich. I had a sense of awe at the grandeur and I wondered what it must have been like during the rise of Adolph Hitler. Being in Germany carried with it an uncomfortable omnipresence of historical emotion left behind lingering in the ethers, a palpable energy of past lives, turmoil and oppression. Yet I found the Germans to be hospitable and gracious, tempered with a collective efficiency and order unlike that of the French. Their neighbors to the west were romantics, less interested in timeliness and regimen, but more concerned with relationships, pleasure and the righteousness of being French. Language, food and culture were the strength of the French, for they were certain that God was a Frenchman.

The emotional resonance of Munich was quickly thwarted by beer consumption. I spent each night with a different Fräulein, for we had not given any thought to where we would be staying during the party. It was just something for which we had no concern. Nick, being Captain Avant Garde, the poster boy for "what-ever-happens," was not concerned with details such as where to sleep. Given my alcohol-saturated young brain, I didn't give any worry to where I would be staying or with whom, either. Each night *les trois amis* split up with women we met, finding our way to their pensione, apartment or hotel. Nationality did not make a difference, nor did color of skin, language spoken or religious affiliation. We were simply there to experience the party. And party we did! On the evening before our last day of festivities, we were drinking among thousands in the Heineken House, sitting with several of our original friends along with a large group of young foreigners. As I was returning from using the restroom yet again, who should I run into but Debra, my Aussie angel in the van. She saw me walking in the crowd and bolted toward me from my right side, grabbing my arm. I said, "What were the chances that we would run into each other?"

She said, "I knew I'd find you!"

Mary and George were seated across the hall with several others they had accumulated. Debra pulled me with her, hand in hand, and roused up her mates. We all gathered at our table. Several more hours of beer drinking, dancing and sheer intoxicated frivolity later, we left the hall and made our way through the streets of Munich.

By this time, it was into the early hours of the morning. Debra insisted that I come with her. She had booked a small hotel room in the old section of town, not far from where we were walking. Leaving the others behind, we proceeded to her room and spent the next couple hours entwined in lewd drunken sex. After four hours of sleep, we arose to say goodbye. The Aussie friends were on their way out of Munich to their next travel destination, Vienna. We shared addresses and said we would stay in contact, but knew that we wouldn't. A kiss, a smile and a last touch of her hand, and I was off.

The fifth and last day of our stay culminated in meeting the other *deux amis* at Marienplatz, home of the Rathaus-Glockenspiel clock, at the stroke of eleven. I stood still and watched as the figurines marched in a circle atop the historical clock. By this time a constant alcoholic dullness had set in, so finding Nick and Rob in the busy square was a challenge. After twenty minutes of wandering, I spied the two ragged-looking guys through the crowd. Their late-evening escapades had turned out different from mine. No sexy Aussie to play with, no bed to sleep in and no shower to be had for them. But they accepted the evening's outcomes and the three of us planned our last day.

We were traveling light. The fashion in Europe at the time was that men carried a large shoulder bag or a male purse. This was highly practical. Why did men travel with only a wallet? That never made much sense to me, even at the age of twenty-one. So I carried both a small backpack and a shoulder bag that was safe haven for our three passports and what little money we carried. Nick knew he'd have trouble keeping track of his passport, which was the most important document a foreigner had, even in Western Europe in the mid-1970s.

Time for us was nebulous and transparent. The hours flew by. We went to three different beer halls, Löwenbräu, Kronenbourg and finally back to Heineken, where we imbibed to the point of saturation. The only issue was to make sure we were on the 10:05pm train back to Strasbourg. Rob, ever focused on the details, kept close track with his watch as the time drew near for us to leave. We knew it would take us at least thirty minutes to negotiate the walk from the fest to the train station. Getting Nick to leave was a challenge. By this time he was quite intoxicated and did not want to leave the fun. With some physical persuasion, I pulled him out of the hall and onto the street, and we stumbled to the station.

Nick was not a belligerent drunk; he was an uninhibited friendly drunk, sexually forward with any and all women. This created some tension when the woman was with her husband or a large boyfriend. More than a couple of times on our way to the station, we saved Nick from a whipping.

We somehow managed to find our way onto the right train. Rob pulled us together and cautioned us in parental fashion that we had a train change in some small town in northern Germany. He said that the stop was only four minutes, so we needed to be prepared to get off the train.

European trains have enclosed coach cabins with half-windows to see inside from the corridor. There are curtains in the interior that can be drawn to provide semi-privacy. As we entered the car, Nick, Rob and I walked along the corridor to find an empty cabin. Somehow Nick kept walking when Rob and I discovered an open compartment. There were two bench seats, one forward and one aft in the compartment. Rob took the back seat and I took the forward one. Even in our drunken state, we realized that Nick was not with us. Where had he gone? I left the cabin and started yelling "Nick, Nick!" It was after 10:00pm, and many other passengers were now on the train. I heard several German voices trying to stop my yelling, but I needed to find Nick. After several minutes the train jolted forward and we were off on our return to Strasbourg. Coming back to the compartment, Rob inquired if I found Nick. The answer was negative. "I hope he remembers our stop around midnight," Rob muttered.

The next thing I remember was the feeling of coming to a stop. I awoke disoriented.

I heard Rob jump up to gather his bag. He said, with some urgency, "It's time to get off the train. Where's Nick?"

We had four minutes to get off the train, and both Rob and I started yelling, "Nick, Nick! Get off the train!" After a few loud rebukes from other passengers, Rob pulled me to the exit door and we climbed down onto the platform. We ran up and down the platform yelling for Nick at the top of our lungs, but he wasn't there. In an instant the train blew its whistle and off it went. As we waited for the next connection to Strasbourg, arriving in twenty-seven minutes, it occurred to me that Nick's passport was in my shoulder bag. And Nick had no money either, because I was holding the money for all of us. An expletive followed as I brought Rob into this reality. "Now what?" I said.

We were very concerned. The train arrived right on schedule, as the German trains do. After we found our way to a compartment, we pondered what, if anything, we could do. But it was Nick. And while the situation seemed urgent, we consoled ourselves knowing fully well that with Nick anything was possible. With his sense of confidence and creativity, he'd figure something out. We wondered where his train would end up.

Ours ended up in Strasbourg.

Rob and I were caught between alerting someone from the university to Nick's situation and just hoping that he would find his way back. We chose to be silent rather than stir the pot and risk disciplinary action. After the second day without hearing from Nick, we began to question our silence, but agreed to wait till the next day, a Wednesday.

I was sitting with Allie and several others at a café for lunch. I lifted a glass of beer to my lips when I saw a figure strolling along l'Avenue de la Forêt Noire, carefree and smiling. It was Nick. I jumped up from my seat, exited the café and ran up to him, arms extended, to give him a big hug. "Where have you been? What happened?"

Smiling the wry Nick smile, he said, "I ended up in Poland." The words came out as though the phrase was as commonplace as, "I woke up and brushed my teeth."

Nick was carrying a small, dark leather satchel that he did not have when I last saw him. I motioned to the bag asking what it was. Nick told me that the farm girl who took him in gave him some money and food for the travel home. I brought him back to the café to eat lunch and tell the story.

"All I remember was feeling the train come to a stop," he began. Being disoriented at first, he got up from the cushions where he had been sleeping and looked out his window to see what appeared to be a station with other passenger cars lined along the tracks. Quickly gathering himself, he opened the door of the compartment and walked down the train corridor only to hear from behind a gruff voice spewing words in an unfamiliar language. Turning to the man, Nick gestured that he didn't understand. What he did hear was the word, passport. The problem was that Nick did not have his passport.

Nick wasn't sure what to do. "Just then," he said, "there was some noise and commotion occurring in the opposite end of the car. The man turned from me and moved toward the noise on the other end. I bolted out the door ahead of me and hightailed it through the station area and out into a village."

"Then what happened?" I asked.

Nick started walking and walking. The small town, Brody, was typically old European, with small, thatched-roofed homes, an assortment of local shops, churches and parks. After walking through the town, he decided to sit for a few minutes to collect himself. He was sitting on a park bench watching parents and grandparents playing with their children when he spotted a young woman. "Hallo Fräulein. Sprichst du Englisch?" Nick spoke enough German to be dangerous, but still wasn't quite sure where he was.

The young woman turned and smiled. She said, "Yes, but we speak Polish here," in broken, but understandable English. Nick smiled his smile and I immediately knew where the story was going.

Nick befriended the young Polish woman and convinced her to take him back to her apartment, not far from where they met.

Nick gulped down his first beer and flagged the mademoiselle down for another. Then he continued his tale.

The young Polish woman took him in, like a lost puppy, fed him, bathed him and took care of his other male needs. A day later, kissing his Polish princess goodbye, throwing the shoulder bag over his shoulder, now with money and a few sandwiches, he left again on foot. She provided him not only shelter, food, drink and sex, but also an escape route.

Walking out of Brody, he made his way southwest through a wooded expanse, crossed over various property lines that were usually marked by stone walls constructed hundreds of years before. At one point, he had to negotiate a small lake by circling through a village with small houses, goats, sheep and a few old horses. Onward he went. The map showed that he was less than twenty-five kilometers from the German border. A particularly rural route allowed him to simply walk through the woods into Germany. In Germany, he was more at home because he could communicate more effectively. He found his way to a well-traveled route and he stuck out his thumb. A lucky thumb it was, for the driver of an Audi who picked him up was traveling all the way to Stuttgart, only a hop, skip and a jump from Strasbourg.

I lost touch with Nick after my time in France, but I was blessed to know him at that point in my life. I was entirely enriched by him. And what fun we had together, *les trois amis*, Rob, Nick and I, twenty-one, free-spirited and living fully engaged. Memories occasionally surface that remind me of another time, another place, when we just didn't take it so seriously.

Looking into the Crystal Ball

The escapades of my early adulthood, while enmeshed with wild abandon and adventurous risk-taking, provided me with life-enriching experiences, all of which opened my heart to hear beyond differences in language and culture. These were transformational times, moments of exploration and wonder, that fueled my passions and sparked my internal curiosity and desire for more. I carry these experiences with me as guideposts of an expanded reality, one that has greatly impacted my ability to communicate, listen and relate to others.

CHAPTER 4 REFLECTIONS

[12] *I developed resiliency and nonverbal ways of communicating early in life. I learned to appreciate the connections between music, dance, and the silent artworks of the masters. I grew up with an aptitude for contemplation, prayer and Zen-like immersion in nature. I have always felt a visceral communication in nature, surrounded by trees, flowers, animals and all that our planet brings to us. My spirit soars in the presence of beauty, soaking in connective sharing that comes from acknowledging our divine unity with others and the greater universe. If we listen, we can hear a whole world of communication taking place around us without any words being spoken.*

[13] *The mid-1970s was a time of discovery and experimentation in so many areas of life. Sex, drugs, music, literature, global causes as well as questions of the meaning of existence all captivated my generation at that time.*

[14] *This would be one of many coincidences that involved running into acquaintances from the past. As I have grown spiritually over the years, I have come to understand the power and connectivity existing among all of us in the collective unconscious, or more accurately, the real world.*

INSIGHTS AND TOOLS

Be a Transformative Communicator - develop the eyes to see and the ears to hear beyond the words, beyond the obvious. Put down the smartphone, turn off the television, set aside your work and quiet your mind, to actually feel the presence of another human being. Effective communication requires focus, attention and an openness to listening to the whole person, the whole message with its subtleties, nuances and feelings. Each day, make it your intention to be present to those you interact with beyond the casual nod, gesture or autopilot responses.

5

BE A PEACE-BUILDER

Quelling the Fires Within

To become an effective conscious leader, you must peel back the layers of self-justification to expose the internal firestorms that rage, eating at your divine essence, pulling you away from love and into the many facets of fear. You cannot expect to be a peace builder without first quelling those internal flames that sometimes smolder and sometimes rage. Our deeply held belief systems, largely the product of congenital and environmental factors, direct and guide us in our everyday affairs. We hold on to these beliefs as certainties, cemented into our thoughts, intentions and ultimately the choices we make in our lives. These choices create our reality. Conscious leadership requires us to wake up.

Sutter's Mill Bar and Restaurant was a cranking evening hot spot adjacent to SUNY Albany. It was also a center of drug distribution and use. The bar was a fixture in the Capital District for college students and those underage drinkers—including me—who were able to fake their way into the bar. I became familiar with Sutter's Mill following my graduation from high school when I visited my family in the Schenectady area. My cousins would get together with their friends and invite me to join them on their escapades of weekend bar hopping. Sutter's Mill was high on the list, since it attracted mostly college-age students attending the State University. There was always fun to be had at Sutter's.

After graduation from Syracuse in 1977, money was becoming an issue. When I learned that Sutter's Mill planned to expand into the Syracuse University area, I decided it was time for a change. I applied for a bartender job before the grand opening and I was hired.

Sutter's instantly became a huge success, with lines of people waiting to get in from Thursday through Saturday night. Five male bartenders worked the bar and I quickly became not only a proficient bartender, but well liked among the clientele, primarily students, and the employees. Early on, a disc jockey was hired to spin music from nine at night until closing at two in the morning. Keith Bornstein, a Syracuse native, had long dark hair, a big smile and an insatiable appetite for women. Keith and I became fast friends. We developed a symbiotic toxic relationship: I provided him with drinks and he supplied me with nonstop drugs. Keith was always generous with the cocaine. In return, I attracted many women who were eager to please, given a taste of white rock, Quaaludes or meth. Keith was always ready to take a woman or several women to his place for after-hours playtime.

It was through my association with Keith that I met Scotty A. and Scotty B., two mavericks in their early twenties whose territory was Syracuse University. Not your typical salesmen, no, the Scottys were high-volume drug dealers, lieutenants in mob drug trafficking, selling cocaine, Quaaludes, pot and methamphetamines to the tune of between $50,000 and $200,000 a week. The drugs were being brought into the area through Canada, bypassing more visible ports. I befriended both of them and acted as a conduit at the bar in setting up deals, scheduling meetings and assisting them in their trade. My reward: free drugs.... lots of them.

There were many nights that flowed well into the next morning, nights when I did not know if I was up or down. I would cut my meth or cocaine buzz with more alcohol and a Quaalude or vice versa.

It was a scary time in my life, a time where running felt necessary. Interestingly enough, it was during this time that I took up the sport of running. My lifestyle was so dramatically destructive that I needed some way to offset the terror, the complete dysfunction ruling my world. Running was penitential and it was one way to find a mustard seed of balance. I had a sports background and the ability to physically exert myself was life-saving.

A Life on the Run

My addiction, more specifically my alcoholism, developed over time; occasional drinks, catching a buzz and easing the tension were starting points. Between my life, my girlfriend, my parents and my job, I needed to have a few drinks to take away the edge, right?

I have always pondered whether there is a genetic predisposition to alcoholism or addiction or whether it is entirely environmental, behavioral and the result of circumstances. Either way, how you get there really does not matter. Finding your way back is the path that so often eludes people.

I attribute much of my reliance on alcohol and drugs to a central theme of running away, hiding, remaining defensive and not living truthfully to my real and genuine self, that divine *I am* that is my soul.

I was twenty-three, and I had been running my entire life in one way or another, beginning with little Michael unable to speak directly to my father's destructive drinking, kept silent by my mother's incessant pleadings and the unconscious attempts not to be abandoned again. I ran inside, putting up defense systems that were impenetrable and guarded. The repression I felt as a young child gave way to finding expression through my pursuit of music and acting. However, as I would later learn, it was a Band-Aid on a cauldron of anger and sadness that festered over time into self-destructive behavior and sickness. All my energy was bottled up inside and I dealt with it by throwing water on a raging fire within. Unfortunately, the water was alcohol and drugs that stoked the fire rather than quelling it.

Syracuse had become toxic and dangerous. The FBI infiltrated the huge drug distribution ring. It was only a matter of time before those around me, including me, would be discovered and charged. I decided to leave town and pursue my acting career. That meant moving to the center of it all, New York City. The use of drugs—including cocaine, heroin and crack—skyrocketed in New York City in the 1980s. I was an active participant in this trend; I became deeply attached to cocaine as a supplement to my escalating alcoholism.

Having tasted success and notoriety from a variety of performances in the upstate New York theatre scene, I wanted more. But, I wanted to at least be employed. I did not want to be the stereotypic starving actor working long hours as a waiter, hanging on for the big break.[15]

While working at Sutter's, I had also been working part-time, along with some friends, at Hancock Airport in Syracuse doing charter flight cargo work; and I met airline personnel who told me about a surge in hiring flight attendants for many of the major carriers. I put one and one together and concluded that I could escape the FBI, get a job as a flight attendant, move to the City and become a superstar. So, I applied to many airlines, TWA, Pan AM, Braniff, Delta, American and Eastern among them.

The airlines at that time were selective. Applicants needed to be at least twenty-one, have an associate's degree and have experience in customer service. They also had to meet rigid physical standards of weight, height and looks.

My first interview was with American Airlines. I was flown first-class on a DC-10 from Syracuse to Dallas. American's Learning Center felt more like a brainwashing center than any learning environment I'd experienced. I joined about fifty others from various parts of the country. I did not make the cut with American, an outcome that did not upset me.

I was turned down on paper by other airlines, but I received a positive reply from Eastern Airlines in December 1978. My invitation was to travel to Rochester, New York, to the Airport Sheraton Hotel for an interview. The day of the interview I was fighting a chest cold, and the forecast was for blowing snow and temperatures in the twenties. For Syracuse, this was a typical day in paradise, warmer than most. My beat-up 1974 Plymouth Fury had no heat or reverse gear. Inches of snow fell as I drove west on the New York Thruway and my cold raged. But I was determined to get to the interview. I arrived to find myself one of ninety recruits. We assembled in a large conference area, seated in a horseshoe around three Eastern Airlines recruiters, who started asking questions. I was the first to stand up. I smiled and told the audience, with conviction and confidence, of my passion for travel, that I always had wings on my feet, that I was the son of an Air Force pilot, that I traveled extensively early on as well as lived in France for a year as an undergraduate, and that my passion for travel was superseded only by my interest in people and their cultures.

After the group session, we were herded into breakout groups, where each recruit was called into a one-on-one interview and then released. I didn't feel well, but I gave it my best shot. Six days later I received notification in the mail from Eastern Airlines that I had been selected for the next interview process in Miami.

Just after New Year's 1979, I flew from Syracuse to Miami aboard a Lockheed L-1011, first class, to my interview at the corporate headquarters of Eastern Airlines, a company that had been around for forty-plus years and that was now under the leadership of CEO Frank Borman, who was the commander of Apollo 8 on the second mission to the moon. Eastern had more than 50,000 employees, 7,000 of whom were flight attendants.

I was impressed both by the size of the company and the formality of their headquarters. I met with three interviewers, each of whom assessed me up and down and then advanced me to the next level. This was my first formal interview process. It would not be my last.

Leaving sunny Miami and returning to Syracuse, I was excited at the possibility of changing my world. There never was a time, even during my quest to work in the airlines, that I had wanted to be a flight attendant. It was a means to an end. But pursuing acting was not the only reason why I needed to change my life, to leave Syracuse. My drug use and drug associations were at a critical juncture. The FBI and local authorities were scrutinizing the Scottys, and I needed to extricate myself from people, places and things that would certainly bring me down. I had to get out of town and this was my chance.[16]

A week after returning from Miami, I received a letter welcoming me to Eastern Airlines. Furthermore, my request to be based in New York City was approved. I was to report to the Miami Flight Attendant Training School the first week in February. Another chapter was opening up, yet another way to run away.

In Miami I found my way to Miami Springs, where the training facility was located, not far from the airport and corporate offices. I was paired with another young man, Bill Cassels, from Decatur, Georgia, who was friendly and excited to start a new career. Eight of the twenty-eight trainees were male. This was the first of many new hire classes in 1979, as the push was on to expand flight operations domestically and internationally. Being in this first class meant we had seniority over the rest of the new hires who would be trained that year. Seniority meant we would more rapidly secure a regular flight schedule; I would have some control over my life.

I learned quickly that work was measured and scheduled in months, not weeks. Time seemed to pass by faster this way.

The attention to appearance during the eight weeks of training was rigid and non-negotiable. Four female trainees were released because they had gained too much weight. The all-you-can-eat cafeteria got the best of them.

The first week of training we were bused to Saks Fifth Avenue in a local mall, where we were taken to the beauty salon to have our hair properly cut and our nails manicured, and we were given lessons on skin care. Yes, in 1979, we men were being pampered and shown the intricacies of personal care. I was open to learning and certainly have always been an aficionado of the finer things in life, which I later came to understand by discovering that I lived one of my previous lifetimes during the Renaissance.

Our training schedules were full days with the primary schooling around emergency equipment, evacuations and various service standards and workflows. We were required to know many aircraft in great detail. The largest aircraft being flown by Eastern at that time was the Lockheed L-1011 which was the second-largest commercial aircraft after the Boeing 747. There were also the Airbus A300, Boeing 727 Stretch, Boeing 727 (Baby, we called it), and the McDonnell Douglas DC-9 (all three models). Later I would be trained on the Boeing 757 and the DC-10 for transatlantic routes. I thought being an in-flight trainer would be a cool job.

I was consciously trying to clean myself up. I realized how lucky I was to have dodged a bullet in Syracuse. The newness of the experience carried me along without having a strong desire for drinking and drugging. I continued the running I had started in Syracuse during the eight-week training program, taking an early morning run through the Coral Gables area before starting my day.

I was voted by my training class as the most likely to succeed, which earned me recognition and a personal commendation from Winnie Gilbert, the senior vice-president in charge of in-flight services.

After graduation, the twenty-four of us needed to decide where we would live in New York City. Most of the class were from areas outside of the City, many from small southern towns, so the anticipation of moving to New York City was overwhelming and terrifying for them. I, on the other hand, was absolutely determined to live in Manhattan; after all, my reason for taking on this job was to follow my passion for theatre.

During the training, I was thrilled at the prospect of moving to New York City, starting a career where my office was onboard an aircraft flying at 39,000 feet going to locations from small town North Carolina to Acapulco, Mexico.

Most of the flight attendants from my class decided to move to Long Beach or Atlantic Beach, a haven for airline personnel and a party environment within close proximity to Kennedy Airport, yet more affordable than living in Manhattan. Brooklyn was still in its genesis of gentrification and Queens was a viable option for many.

After a chaotic search, I found a small studio apartment on the corner of Park Avenue and 19th Street, adjacent to Gramercy Park. I roomed with Preston Lawless, an affable artist turned flight attendant, whose southern drawl masked his dark, double-edged, Bible-thumping right-wing personality that eventually made its way to the surface, causing tension that ultimately resulted in our separating as roommates.

Living in Manhattan on a flight attendant salary of $16,500 a year did not provide extra money to enjoy this incredible city. I scraped enough funds together, at times, to get a six-pack of beer or a cheap bottle of wine.

I became close with three flight attendants who lived in the Murray Hill area off Third Avenue not far from my Gramercy Park studio. They knew how to use their looks to advantage. As their friend, I would be casually included in their invitations to parties at Upper East Side, West Side, and Central Park penthouses, where celebrities gathered, drinking and drugging. I, of course, would join in the fun.

In the summer of 1979, I worked a trip with Eileen Brandeis from Chicago and we had developed a friendship. Eileen was funny, self-effacing and delightful in every way. I really liked Eileen. Her roommate, Eileen Mansfield—yes, two Eileens—and I hit it off in a grand fashion. Both Eileens were fun and loving women with whom I found a strong connection. Blonde Eileen, as I called her, was from Long Island and wanted to relocate from Long Beach to the North Shore. The Eileens found a house to rent in Locust Valley, right on the bay, and needed another roommate. I was their target. Since my relationship with Preston had deteriorated, I decided reluctantly to accept the Eileens' offer. The TV series *Three's Company* became the reality for us. I left Manhattan and made the move to Locust Valley. We shared a three-bedroom house at the end of a dead-end street with the yard ending right at the bay. Across the street was a marina that stored boats of various sizes. The neighborhood was picturesque and quaint. It was a great location.[17]

After living with the Eileens for a few months, I met Helen Santos Montez, while flying a four-day trip. Helen was of Dominican heritage, exotic, almond-skinned, with long black hair, deep penetrating eyes and a fun spirit. She quickly captured my twenty-four-year-old's heart.

Within a couple months, Helen asked me to move into her three-and-a-half-room apartment in Flushing, Queens. I lived with her for the next eight years.

Our relationship initially centered on drinking, for she also had a love for wine and beer. In our first years together, we traveled to New Orleans, Key West, the Chesapeake Bay, and the Adriatic coast of Yugoslavia. One of our travel adventures took us to Tuscany for great food and wine. We also went to Hong Kong on several occasions, one being to rescue her younger sister, who had been placed in a psychiatric ward pending permanent placement in a mainland Chinese mental hospital.

One of the advantages of working for a major airline at that time was the interline travel benefit available to airline employees. We took full advantage of this benefit. I was reading the *New York Times* travel section one Sunday and came across an article about Chester, Maryland, a small town on the Chesapeake Bay. Chester had a restored Victorian hotel that predated the Civil War. A few blocks from the hotel were no-frills eateries with newspaper-covered tables where seasonal visitors could dine on soft-shell crabs—oiled, baked, fried, any way you could possibly imagine. We had to go, and we did.

The summer of 1980, we traveled to upstate New York to visit my mother for the first time. It was July 4th weekend and the annual jazz festival was playing at Saratoga Performing Arts Center. Our plan was to attend the Saturday program and make our way back to Scotia, thirty miles from the venue. We did just that. We had both been drinking all day when we arrived for the introductions. As being drunk was a family tradition, this did not seem to make the situation worse.

The next day, my mother said to me, "Why can't you ever meet a nice Irish Catholic girl?"

I responded indignantly that my choices were my choices.

Helen and I shared many drunken episodes during the first half decade, some filled with laughter and delight, but many turning out to be horrendous explosions of temper, throwing things, the destruction of my dramatic portfolio materials, public arguments and embarrassing tirades. I drank daily, often at the local watering holes.

In the early 1980s, Lynn's Bar on Main Street in Flushing was a favorite. There were twenty-five cent glasses of beer, a colorful selection of misfits as patrons and Johnny McGriskin, a big red-haired Irishman who worked seven days a week and took a liking to me. Johnny was from

Northern Ireland with a thick brogue that was hard to understand at times. Johnny was Lynn's Bar, for he was bigger than life, with story after story and a heart of gold. He would take on anyone who tried to misbehave.

One night I had returned from a trip and was still dressed in my flight attendant uniform. I watched Johnny jump across the bar and physically take down two perpetrators who came into the bar looking to cause trouble. Johnny was in his fifties, upwards of 300 pounds and well over six feet tall. He moved with the agility of a gazelle, hopping over the wooden bar and hustling the two men out in a flash.

Johnny also cared about others, even given the toxic environment; he would insist that patrons who had tippled too much take taxis. He would take their keys as well as call and pay for them to get home safe. There were a couple occasions where he extended this mandate to me.

Lynn's was sold in late 1984 and downtown Flushing was changing rapidly. Asian investors came into the area with large sums of cash and bought up local businesses.

My dry cleaner was one of these purchases. Henry, my dry cleaner, originally from Colombia, informed me one Saturday in 1985 that he had sold his small strip mall business. When I asked what happened, he told me that a South Korean man came in and offered him a million dollars in cash. "What could I say except sold?"

The Big Stage

I did not give up my dream of an acting career, although it took me the better part of two years to find a schedule that allowed me to pursue it. I followed *Billboard* magazine as well as AFTRA and Equity publications to keep up with auditions, both on Broadway and off Broadway.

I realized I needed an agent. In 1981, I was flying a three-day trip on a Boeing 727 with a crew of four. One of the flight attendants was Connie Fitzpatrick, a delightfully attractive blonde from the panhandle of Florida.

She had a southern drawl right out of *Fried Green Tomatoes*. It turned out that she was involved in her own acting career. She had made a couple of small television commercials, and she auditioned with some regularity for TV and stage productions.

I was flabbergasted by the fact that she was able to switch her southern drawl off at will. She said she'd been taking voice lessons for over a year to rid her of the cute, but unsellable accent. She also told me that her husband, Tom Fitzpatrick, a former NYC cop, had landed several regional TV commercials in addition to small roles in daytime soap operas. The offer was made to meet up with them in Soho to discuss show business and possibly share resources. I was all-in on this.

Tom, Connie and I met at a bar on 17th Street on the West Side in Flatiron. After lots of drinks and laughs, Tom shared with me his photographer, several leads on agents and the recommendation that I attend the Weist-Barron School for Acting, a proving ground where agents watched for talent and careers were started.

The decision was made. I enrolled in Weist-Barron School, on West 45th Street. I signed up for an eight-week television commercial class. I felt both excitement and trepidation at stepping up to the big leagues. It was now over two years since I had performed, and while I knew that I had strong talent, the others I came in contact with were your exceptional talents, deeply committed to their futures. It was intimidating, yet deep inside I felt confident of my innate ability.

It took courage to overcome my fear and to step forward in the various classroom activities. There were sample readings that were videotaped as well as impromptu scenes that pulled at all of my acting reserves. I completed several courses at Weist-Barron, making friends with a number of students, teachers and actors actually working in the business and making money.

It was during a class on voice-overs that I met Lionel Wilson, a character voice-over genius who brought to life the cartoon character Tom Terrific on the children's show *Captain Kangaroo*, which I watched religiously as a child growing up in the 1960s. Lionel took an interest in me. He offered me his recording studio in Midtown, along with its producer and engineer, to produce my voice-over tape. The demo tape, headshot and résumé were an actor's professional calling card. In the commercial and cartoon industry, having a unique tape could mean landing an audition.

Auditions for television voice-over usually had between 150 and 250 people show up. This was in stark contrast to on-screen commercial auditions and casting calls for Broadway and off Broadway, where 400 to 600 might show up. So the chances were much better with voice-over. The other advantage was that with voice-over, your face did not appear on screen, attached to a particular product, should an opportunity arise to land a big commercial for a different product. It was not as much a problem to be associated with selling Chanel as it would to be known for selling Phillips' Milk of Magnesia.

Artists aligned one of three commercial groupings based on the overall quality, tone, range and sound of your voice. There were voice-over artists whose voices were tailored to the companies that needed big, rough, deep and gravelly voices—advertisers selling automobiles, beer or military enlistment, for example. There were companies looking for artists to make training and corporate messaging videos that required straightforward, unemotional and clean vocal talents. And then there was the middle market voice-over segment that my voice fell into, where a myriad of companies and products were being sold via TV and radio voice-over. Products from diapers to Hershey's chocolate syrup, from Quaker oatmeal to Tide laundry detergent; all were fair game in my search for voice-over stardom. Landing a national voice-over commercial would be a huge financial gain. Companies such as Ford, GM, Anheuser-Busch and Proctor and Gamble invested tens of millions of dollars in advertising, which meant a tremendous payout to the agencies and the talent.

My relationship with Lionel came to a screeching halt one evening. He invited me to his penthouse in Midtown, where after many drinks he proceeded to make sexual advances toward me. I was not interested and while trading sex for favors in the business was commonplace, I did not have the stomach or desire to prostitute myself.

I had a great demo tape and I had gained huge experience along the way. All I needed now was continued courage and the ability to accept constant rejection. I had the courage, but rejection played into the deep-seeded unconscious layers of abandonment and rejection that I held from my birth, a realization I came to understand later in life.

A couple of agents took me on for six months, principally for TV commercial and soap opera jobs. I also got a callback for a cartoon show being produced in Los Angeles. After I flew to LA for the audition, I was beat out for the job.

My routine when I left an audition was to stop at the first deli or bodega I saw to get a large cold beer to drink on my way back to the subway. Cutting the edge was routine, a natural process with which I had years of experience.

While I pursued my acting career in late 1984 and 1985, I was recognized by my in-flight supervisor, Jim Mullaney, as one of the top-rated flight attendants from the New York base. While I had never envisioned myself working as a flight attendant, my natural ability to relate to people, good manners, a sparkling three-piece tailored suit, a sense of humor and impeccable service skills combined to earn the recognition.

This was before deregulation; airline travelers were different than our modern-day everyone-travels-by-air society. During the early 1980s, air travel was a luxury service for the well-to-do. The masses traveled by bus or train. The texture of air travel changed rapidly with deregulation opening the door to competitive market forces. On Eastern Airlines and other legacy carriers, flight attendants were seen as attractive, elegant and friendly jet-setters. People gave us envious, inquisitive looks as we moved through public places; they saw us as attractive and glamorous.

Nine months into my new job, I attended a senior flight attendant training program that certified me to be in charge of in-flight operations. Along with the added authority, I was able to select trips to better locations and arrange my schedule for better time off. I had some seniority as a flight attendant, but senior flight attendant status gave me distinct advantages in holding better lines. Most flight attendants did not want the extra responsibility.

Jim, my supervisor, had documented my performance over the previous four-plus years as exceptional. And my personnel file held many letters of commendation that customers had forwarded to corporate. As a consequence, I was a strong candidate for being promoted into management. There was some security in knowing that I was doing well with the airline, so I decided to go with the flow and apply for a management position. After all, it would mean additional income. Living in New York City was expensive and there was little left over beyond what I would find for drinking money.

Applying for a management position at Eastern Airlines was a long process that included going through an Assessment Center in Miami. After a four-hour battery of challenging scenarios that required quick thinking, aptitude and dexterity in interpersonal skills, as well as organizational competencies necessary for supervision, I went before an interview tribunal of sorts. I took the elevator to the eighteenth floor, sharing the ride with the former astronaut and now CEO of Eastern, Frank Borman himself; he just happened to be on the elevator as I entered from the fourth floor. After a cordial quick good luck from Mr. Borman, I exited to room 1802.

The executive conference room was official-looking, with a long table at one end of the rectangular room and a single chair at the other. Seated behind the table were three men and two women. Introductions were made, and it was clear to me that Eastern Airlines meant business when it came to ensuring that their front line supervisors were qualified and duly certified by officers from various corporate functions. The questions felt more like interrogation than interview repartee. After forty-five minutes of grilling, in which I stood my ground, I was thanked for my time and sent on my way back to New York. By the time I boarded my first class seat, I had already achieved an intoxicated glow.

Within a week the decision came down that I was to be promoted to in-flight supervisor, reporting to John Scully at LaGuardia Airport. The next phase begins.

Stepping into Leadership

My management position in the in-flight services division of Eastern Airlines lasted three years. I had little time to pursue my acting, for I now was managing more than a hundred flight attendants. Several months into my position I was given a special assignment to work with a team of nine other in-flight supervisors from across the company to train and acculturate South American personnel. We had acquired them through the purchase of former Pan Am routes in South and Central America. This assignment took me to Columbia, Brazil, Argentina and Panama for extended periods.

I enjoyed the collaboration with my peers, and learned and grew through the experience. The people and culture of the countries I visited expanded my view of how connected we are as a human family. I knew this despite my lack of internal compass and depth of soul, yet the experiences illuminated my being. It was a time that took me away from my own destructive behavior, lessening the chains that continued to tighten around me. It was a reprieve from my running. I look back on that time and those experiences with great love and appreciation.

But all good things eventually come to an end and my special assignment came to a close in early 1986. It was back to life in New York, back to the world that seemed to be slowly, but surely closing in. My relationship with Helen was tepid; we became more like roommates than lovers. She had formed her own circle of friends and was traveling on her own to visit family and others with some frequency. It was, on the one hand, threatening to me to know that I was somehow losing her, but freeing on the other hand, because it gave me opportunities to drink and drug without having to answer to her. Confusion, angst and deterioration followed my return home.

John Scully forged our team of six in-flight supervisors into a working family at LaGuardia. We had ample work to do, including operating the lucrative Eastern Airlines Shuttle between Washington, D.C., New York and Boston, but we also managed to build strong friendships.

John was born south of Madrid to a Spanish mother and an Irishman; he moved from Spain to New Jersey when he was ten years old. He spoke with a Castilian accent and his Spanish good looks were outshone only by his charisma and charm.

John was good to us. He led with purposeful attention to detail and a sense of compassion. John and I would develop a strong friendship over the next several years. He admitted me into his inner circle of friends, his carefully guarded homosexuality and his marriage to his partner, Maxwell, a lifestyle that also included large amounts of alcohol consumption.

Managing a flight attendant workforce brought me in contact with a diverse group of men and women, with equally diverse issues, problems and human stories. The 1980s in New York City was a decade of terror in the gay community, with the explosion of AIDS—primarily among men between the ages of 18 and 40. It is no secret that most men working as flight attendants were gay. That I was heterosexual was the anomaly.

Soon after being promoted to senior flight attendant, I was assigned to a special flight that was to depart Kennedy Airport flying direct to Panama City with a layover of thirty-five hours and then a return to New York. It was not a regularly scheduled flight, so the crew was pulled together based on availability. I was to be the senior flight attendant aboard a Lockheed L-1011 with a full crew complement of ten flight attendants. When I arrived at Kennedy and checked in, I saw on the crew manifest that all but one of the flight attendants were male. I wondered what poor female flight attendant would be with all these guys. I also had a spark of terror wondering what motley bunch of men I would be with for the next two days. As it turned out, all of the other men were gay, some of them bordering on flamboyant. The female flight attendant was an innocent young woman from North Carolina who appeared to be shell-shocked for the entire trip. She was treated like a little princess by all the queens. I, on the other hand, was treated as the target of sexual innuendos and advances. Throughout my life, I had grown accustomed to being hit on by men and women, some of their advances innocent and casual, but others direct and aggressive. It was not uncommon while flying as a flight attendant to be touched, pinched and propositioned.

When we got to Panama City we were transported to our layover hotel where the crew made plans. Several got together to go into town and find trouble. Others disappeared into the lobby and off to their own worlds. I chose to separate myself from the crew. It was late afternoon, and as I did on most layovers, I found my way to the bar for drinks. I always went for the alcohol, the buzz. Alcohol took away the harsh rigidity of having to be fully functional.

I easily found the bar. As I drank, I started to talk with others at the bar. Jim was from Great Britain. He was doing consulting work in Panama for an American energy company. After a while, our conversation turned to drugs. He moved a bit closer to me and asked if I was interested in getting some high-quality cocaine?

I said, "Of course."

We left the bar and made our way to a taxi outside the lobby. Jim told the driver, in Spanish, to take us to a destination in what appeared to be a run-down part of Panama City. We paid the driver and asked him to stick around for the next fifteen minutes to take us back to our hotel. The driver answered, "Si, senor." In the apartment building we came to a directory that showed the apartment numbers and names. Jim rang 4C and a man asked who it was. Jim replied and slowly the door opened. An unshaven, dark-haired man greeted Jim and looked me over carefully. We entered the small apartment. The dealer beckoned us to have a seat at his kitchen table. He went into another room and returned carrying a clear heavy plastic bag filled with the better part of a kilo of cocaine in crystal rock form. He asked how much Jim wanted.

Jim looked at me and asked how much I wanted. I asked him how much. He stated for a hundred US dollars we could get two ounces. I had $150 with me, so I told him that I would put in $100.

Jim said we would take four ounces. The dealer measured the rock carefully, inserted it in a small container, accepted our $200 and escorted us to the door. Our taxi driver was waiting for us. He returned us to the hotel with enough cocaine to feed a party of ten for an entire evening. There was no sleep for me during this layover. It was impossible given the amount and quality of cocaine that I snorted. The trip home was challenging.

Many times over the next five years, I found myself crossing into the borderlands of deep, dark, uncontrolled behavior in an alcohol and drug-induced state of madness. During the three years of working in management at Eastern, my alcohol use increased to a daily intoxication. I awoke each morning with the primary thought of when and how I would get my next drink. After each day's work, I sought out my true love, not Helen, but alcohol! My most intimate thoughts and actions came as a result of my relationship with alcohol or the ménage a trois with alcohol and cocaine— or even crack at times.[18]

After Lynn's Bar was sold off, I had no problem finding another watering hole. I took my drinking to another bar closer to my home so that if I was driving, I could more easily make it back. The Tavern, on Kissena Boulevard, just off the Long Island Expressway, three blocks from my apartment, became the spot. Patrons of this bar were locals, off-duty police officers, sanitation workers, fire fighters, postal employees and lowlifes of all backgrounds. This was also a place where drugs were readily available. I could support my love for cocaine easily from this hangout. The Colombian connection was a part of this bar. Carlos, who worked in the deli three shops down, lived in Jackson Heights and was a part of the Colombian drug cartel operating in metro New York. If I had 90 dollars, he had high-quality rock that would keep me buzzing for an extended evening. One of the problems with cocaine, as with other addictive drugs like meth, heroin and crack, was that there was never enough. For me, the combination of a rapid-fire stimulant and large quantities of alcohol would render me electrically wired, irrational and physically charged for days at a time. Holding a job, let alone having a relationship with Helen, became ever more challenging.

I would carefully schedule my binges to coincide with my own time off and with Helen's flight schedule to allow enough time to be high. Only in hindsight could I see the tremendous amount of duress and energy attached to pulling off this frequent scam.

I knew at some level that I was in trouble. In 1987, John Scully was forced to resign from Eastern based on a vicious false story circulating among more senior management. I was moved to Kennedy airport to work under another manager who, unbeknownst to me, was scrutinizing my work to look for any indication of an alcohol and drug issue.

On the twelve-mile ride from work back to Flushing every day, in heavy traffic on the Van Wyck Expressway, I got off on the service road to stop at a bodega. I bought three, sometimes four 16 ounce cans of cold Budweiser, individually wrapped, to drink on the way home. I thought if I had a drink in a paper bag and used a straw, no one would know I was drinking beer. I stuffed the empties under the driver's seat. At home I had six to ten more beers. Rationally I understood that this behavior probably wasn't normal, but I decided to avoid and deny the destructive daily pattern. Spiritually, I was so buried in sickness that I was blind to the truth, unwilling to have the eyes to see where I was. This pattern continued pulling me deeper into the darkness, moving me further along the path to death. How long could this pattern continue without having some major ramifications?

Spiral Downhill

Helen had been purposely leaving more often to do her own thing and had recently left without providing any message as to where she was or who she was with. A year earlier, I saw a copy of *Playboy* in the apartment. Since I hadn't purchased the magazine, I asked Helen where it came from. She said matter-of-factly that she had subscribed, that she enjoyed the articles. I thought that strange. But she had stopped wearing makeup and started wearing more masculine clothes. When I saw her with other women, I realized she was a lesbian and had been living falsely with me.

I knew that my relationship with Helen had deteriorated largely due to my absence, both physically and emotionally, but her coming out was devastating. I was heartbroken. The foundation of my world was crumbling.

Over the next several weeks of hard drinking, I managed to find my own apartment on 147th Street, a prewar fourth floor walkup, with on-the-street alternate side parking. It served the purpose and, to my great joy, the Triangle Lounge was three short blocks down the street. The bar became my home away from home for the next year.

And the next year was hell. The tumultuous breakup of my eight-year relationship with Helen created a void that my drinking and drug use could not fill. Between January and March 1988, every free moment was filled with alcohol and drug consumption.

At JFK, I worked beside several other in-flight supervisors, one of whom became a close friend. Skip Sanford was one of the warmest, best-looking, friendliest people I had ever met. His ability to connect with people was magical. He was originally from El Paso, Texas, born to a Mexican-American mother whose husband abandoned her and the three children early on. Skip had a sensitive and compassionate heart.

He also had a liking for cocaine, so the connection between us became more than a professional one; we shared an occasional cocaine and alcohol binge. Over time, he came to me to ask if I could get him some cocaine. I had the connections to easily fulfill his requests. He and I would team up and hit the streets for an extended binge that would take us into dangerous areas of Jackson Heights to procure more drugs. Skip spoke fluent Spanish and was intimidating at six foot two.

Following my breakup with Helen, about a month into living on my own, Skip and I got together for a night of partying with heavy drinking and drugging. We stopped at several bars in the area around Flushing. One of them was a seedy place along the Long Island Expressway, probably the fifth one that night, now early morning. I was sitting on a barstool, in the middle of a conversation with Skip. The next thing I knew, a concerned-looking Skip was picking me up off the floor. He asked me if I was alright. I had passed out and had fallen with a huge thud. Skip had turned his head to look in a different direction and in the middle of a sentence, I was gone. This type of experience would happen more often over the next months.

On many nights, particularly Friday nights leading into weekends, I would make my way down the street to the Triangle Lounge not to return to my small apartment until later Sunday afternoon, days into an alcohol and drug-induced state of terror. The Lounge was my new watering hole, and I came to know the bartenders and clientele fairly quickly. Even during these dark times, I could still connect with people; I still had a compassionate heart and a friendly spirit.

The quantity of drugs that flowed through that bar was unthinkable. Patrons routinely snorted cocaine in the bathrooms, and drug deals occurred inside and outside the establishment. Most of the clientele were users to some degree and the owners looked the other way most of the time. I befriended the major dealers, and sometimes accompanied them into dangerous and uncertain situations. I often had no memory of my actions because of the amount of alcohol I consumed. The cocaine acted as a counterbalance to the alcohol. The more cocaine I snorted, the more I was able to drink. I often blacked out.

St. Patty's Day Debacle

The five boroughs of New York City comprise of neighborhoods, each with its own distinctive culture tracing back generations, to the days of immigrants coming through Ellis Island and settling into areas with familiar language and culture. Flushing was no different, with families who had passed along homes, friends and traditions. Bars were collection spots for the working class people who lived in the area. The Triangle Lounge, like the Tavern before it, had a clientele of firefighters and sanitation workers, with a smattering of police officers who partied heavily.

St. Patrick's Day in New York City was a big deal. The parade in Manhattan brought together firefighters and police officers from across the five boroughs in a day of celebration that provided an excuse for excessive drinking, rabblerousing and inappropriate behavior en masse.

Several of my drinking associates were firefighters and they invited many of us to join them in Manhattan to party after the parade. I had requested the day off in order to join in this celebration. And party I did, so much so that the last memory I have was sometime in late afternoon at an Irish bar on Third Avenue in the Murray Hill section of Manhattan, snorting cocaine with other partygoers. What I remember next is lying on my couch hearing the phone ringing at 2:35 pm on March 18, a Friday, the day after St. Patrick's Day.

I was supposed to be working on that Friday, not waking up from a blackout, still drunk and in a stupor. The phone ringing was my immediate manager looking for me, trying to find out if I was alright. Monday morning, I knew I was in serious trouble.

As I entered my office, I was greeted by my supervisor and his boss, who took me immediately into a closed-door office and fired me from my management position. When they asked what happened and where I was, I responded that I had become drunk and completely lost track of time. The damage was done. Rather than end my career with Eastern Airlines after nine years of service, they gave me the opportunity to continue working, but demoted me back to the position of flight attendant. I accepted the offer. I was resigned to the embarrassment of my behavior and the humiliation of stepping back into the flight attendant ranks.

I had managed over a hundred flight attendants. I had been an advocate for the company in several high profile firings and subsequent arbitration hearings. And I had been challenged by our local union representative, who openly accused me of being a company man not sympathetic to the rank and file. It was a tough time for me. But not as challenging as the next year would be. To this day, St. Patrick's Day, 1988, is a day of grave remembrance, a celebration that comes and goes without my participating.

I wasn't sure I had the strength to go back to being a flight attendant; I would be flying with people I had just supervised and rumors were everywhere as to why I might be returning. There were moments when, in the quiet of my small apartment, I sat in darkness trying to make sense of my life and where it had deteriorated to. I knew that my life was out of control, but I was not ready to make the changes I needed to make; in fact, I did everything I could to avoid going down that rabbit hole. It was too much for me to consider. I had to make it through what was in front of me. After three years in management, I had enough seniority to get a schedule to work three days on and three days off. During trips I would drink as heavily as I could and still be sober during the daytime. On days off I would again drink heavily and snort as much cocaine as I could find. I would attempt to limit the heavy use to the front end of my days off to afford me enough time to recover.

During the entire time I worked for Eastern Airlines, I continued to run, both literally and figuratively. As early as 1981, while living in Manhattan and in preparation for running the New York Marathon, I established a training regimen of between sixty and seventy miles a week, running every day, including at layover locations throughout the country and Mexico. As my alcoholism and heavy drug use worsened over the years, I continued running, to try to reverse the ill effects of pervasive abuse and as penitence for destroying my vessel. I would wake, knowing I had to be at work in a matter of hours, clumsily find my running shorts, a T-shirt and running shoes, and hit the streets for a five or six-mile run. That would jar my insides so brutally that I was forced to sober up. The pounding and sweating expunged the toxins that blurred my eyes, thinking and spirit. When I managed my time well enough before flying to afford this punishment, it was a salvation that brought me back to some semblance of normality, a minimum of clarity from which I could work. It was a good thing, as there were rough times ahead.

Over the next months, I continued the pattern of acute self-destruction. I intentionally chose flight schedules that had ample hours on layovers during which I could drink and get sober enough to work the following day. I selected aircraft that afforded me my own first class galleys so I could pull the curtain and surreptitiously make my own vodka tonics along with the drinks for the first class travelers. There were times that when either going to a layover hotel or ending the day, I drank as many as six vodkas, believing I was masking the smell with peppermint Breath Savers.

I learned sometime after leaving the airline that some fellow workers knew I was imbibing, but no one knew the extent to which my energy was engaged in this pattern of behavior. And the days off continued to escalate in their damage and duress.

It was during this period that I teamed up with a new friend, Jerry, a bartender at the Triangle Lounge. He was a jovial soul who was deeply engulfed in cocaine and alcohol, the perfect person to align with. Our collaborative escapades took us to the seediest of places. Smoking crack became a new standard. Crack cocaine was everything it was made out to be and more. Smoking crack instantly opened the door to a breakdown in any semblance of rational thought, dissolving the ability to decide between right and wrong; any voice of conscience was quieted. And the pervasive aspect of crack was that you needed and wanted more.

One evening, a Friday night when I had the next five days off from work, I showed up at the lounge around five. Jerry and several other of my drug connoisseurs were at the bar, drinking and laughing. I soon found myself in the bathroom snorting cocaine. Jerry and others had large amounts of cocaine, and as their friend I was invited to participate in their consumption. I gladly acquiesced. The last thing I remember was a bar packed with regulars at eleven o'clock. After countless trips to the bathroom, Jerry, Ernie, and Jessica decided that they wanted to push the high further by finding some crack to smoke. They invited me and I joined. I recall jumping in the back seat of Jerry's car. I knew that we were on route to Jackson Heights, but what I did not know was where we went after our trip to Little Columbia.

The next thing I remember is opening my eyes in the back seat of a Chevy with three other people, Jerry and Ernie in the front and Jessica seated beside me. It was daylight, but not the morning light of the next day, rather the afternoon sunlight of the day after that, Sunday. The vehicle I was sitting in was on I-95 North, twenty-five miles to the north of Richmond, Virginia. I had been in a blackout for well over twenty-four hours, still awake, just not conscious. When the shock set in as to where I was, I asked why we were in Virginia. With a puzzled look, they responded that we had just done a drug run and had several kilos of cocaine in our trunk. I had apparently been an active participant in the drug run. I did not know if I was coming or going, so I decided to remain quiet. On the nine-hour trip back to New York, we continued to pump cocaine into our bodies. I got back to Flushing around ten, found my way back to my walk-up apartment and collapsed. The dark side of my world was enveloping me.[19]

Who's Riding Shotgun

Another evening of drinking and drugging in 1988 led to an irrational decision to drive to Jackson Heights in search of more crack cocaine. I was driving with two women who had joined me in the evening's activities. We wanted more. I thought I had balanced the cocaine against the alcohol well enough that I could function okay. It was after three in the morning and the streets of Queens were quiet except for trucks making their early morning deliveries.

I was going through a series of lights on a crossroad above the Van Wyck Expressway. Traveling at the speed limit, I drove through one green light, another ahead and then another, but this green light had turned red. I looked at the woman next to me and did not see the red light until I turned back to the front of my car. Both women screamed, "Look out!"

A semi was coming from my left, not slowing down, not seeing that I was cruising through the intersection. Panic instantly engulfed me as I readied to being hit by the truck. My whole body prepared; and in the next instant, I felt a whoosh of air pass through me. I opened my eyes to get a glimpse of the truck that had just passed through our vehicle. As my eyes followed the semi off to the right, sitting in the passenger seat was someone completely different from the woman who occupied the seat moments before. Sitting next to me, looking deeply into my eyes during the elongated seconds that followed, was an angel. I could see through her body although it was as an opaque image, yet demonstrably present and loving. There were no words spoken, just a look of utter compassion and love at the miracle that had just occurred. It was shocking to have lived through what certainly would have meant serious injury, if not death, for me and the others traveling beside me. But as powerful as that realization was, the fact that a divine messenger had been there to protect us as well as to have shown me such divine intervention was remarkable on one hand and curious on the other. Me, why me, and what did it all mean? I had just been in the direct path of a semi, yet the only impact was a whoosh of air and an angel sitting next to me. We pulled over and decided to return to Flushing and ended the evening. My angel departed as quickly as she had appeared, but her image remains with me today.

Machinists Strike, 1989

In March 1989, the International Association of Machinists, one of three unions at Eastern Airlines, went on strike over the company's refusal to honor concessions desired by the union. In quick order, the other two unions, the Air Lines Pilot Association and the Transport Workers Union, which represented the flight attendants, followed suit and brought the sixty-two-year-old company and its 50,000 employees to a halt. The airline would never regain its capacity and ultimately would collapse in 1991. This was a turbulent time for the employees and for me. The company was attempting to keep a small contingent of their more profitable routes open using scabs, who crossed a vicious picket line. The Eastern Shuttle out of LaGuardia was one of the most lucrative business units of Eastern Airlines. I had been in management for three years and was therefore considered an enemy of the worker. Some of those in the unions were not interested in facts, but rather in drawing their own conclusions based on beliefs alone.

I had been flying as a flight attendant for the better part of a year when the strike occurred, a paying member of the TWU, but I started receiving phone calls from anonymous callers threatening me with violence, accusing me of being a scab. That I never crossed the picket line did not matter much to the thugs that were accusing me.

One night, a Wednesday in late March, I was walking out of the Triangle Lounge to make my way back up the street to my apartment. Three men jumped out from behind a parked car along 147th street. It was after midnight and I was inebriated as usual. The attack occurred quickly, with all three men coming from my left side in a blur, punching me and eventually kicking me when I had fallen to the ground. I was too slow to protect myself, so there were several blows that made direct and painful contact. As it happened, another person was on the other side of the street; he began yelling for help when he saw the attack. His booming voice was enough to scare off the attackers, forcing them to hightail it on foot. I did not know who these men were, but it was obvious to me that I was on someone's list as a scab. From that day forward, I carried a six-inch hunting knife, concealed and ready to use, should I be attacked again.

It was a brutal time for many of the good people I had come to know at Eastern Airlines. I continued to get threatening calls despite my reporting them to airline officials and the police. I was in a bit of a sensitive place owing to my drug use and connections, so dealing with the authorities was a last resort.

The Last Year

After Eastern Airlines shut its doors following the machinists' strike in 1989, I lasted a little more than two months before my money ran out, forcing me to leave New York City and relocate back with my mother and brother in Scotia.

After my father's death in 1982, my mother, who had been renting a house in Rotterdam, decided to purchase a home in Scotia, not far from my cousin, Rosie. The three-bedroom colonial on Washington Road was built in 1913. The street, lined with beautiful old trees, was a quiet, mixed-generation community including retirees and younger families.

Scotia, New York is small town located across the Mohawk River from Schenectady, home of General Electric, the principal employer that was the barometer for growth and prosperity in the 1950s and 1960s as well as the architect of depression that set in from the 1970s until now. Generations of workers passed through the doors of GE. My parents' generation all worked there. After the end of the Second World War, the GIs returned to find good work for good wages. Many of them bought small homes in Rotterdam, the next town over, and settled down to raise their families. This was a middle-class community with a generational history defined by hard work, nice kids and the American dream.

When I was eight, after we had returned from the Philippines, we visited family in Schenectady. Wallace Street in Scotia was the home of the Robin family, cousins on my maternal great grandmother's side in the 1800s, when James Michael O'Hearn came to the United States from Wales. He settled in Schenectady when it was still rural farmland.

Ruth and Ted Robin were two of the most loving people I have in my memory. Although I would only see them intermittently, with my family traveling as we did, each visit was memorable and sustaining. They had two children, Little Rosie, as we called her, and Franny, short for Francis.

Franny was a child with Down syndrome who was never treated any differently than any other child in the Robin household. Today, this is not particularly remarkable. But fifty years ago, children born with Down syndrome were placed in institutions where they would live out their short lives in controlled and despicable conditions. Not Franny. Ruth and Ted had made it their priority to raise Franny just as any other child would be raised.

Scotia residents all knew Franny. He would peddle his bike around the neighborhood and everyone would keep a close and loving eye on him. Franny's nature was loving and friendly. The ingredient that made Franny's inclusion into mainstream life during a time where children with disabilities were not recognized or supported, was his parents' unconditional love.

Ruth was a music teacher in the public schools. When we visited she played the piano, sang and laughed, usually with a drink in hand. Every visit to the Robin family was a party, filled with joy and laughter. It was not hard to love them. Ted was a printer; his business was a printing press located in their garage. I do not know if Ted decided to have this business at his home in order to be present and supportive in raising Rosie and Franny, but my intuition always led me in that direction. Our visits always included music, food, drinking and, in the summer, a cookout. We would set up the croquet game in the back yard and have fun smacking the hard ball with the mallet.

After Ruth and Ted died some years later, Rosie, who never married, took ownership of the house on Wallace. She, too, was a schoolteacher, working with developmentally handicapped special needs kids in the

Saratoga School district. Rosie played a large role in supporting me with mom in my early years of recovery.

On my father's side of the family, there were two sisters, Aunt Thelma, in Camillus, New York, just outside of Syracuse, and Aunt Marleen, the youngest sister by four years. Marleen and her husband, Frank Jackson, also my godfather, lived in Pattersonville, New York, in a small cape with a finished upstairs and a basement rec room that had a ping-pong table.

Of my father's family, I was closest to the Jacksons, mostly because of my cousin, Sally, who was less than one year younger than I was. Sally and I had a strong connection from day one. There were two other siblings, David and Betty, both old enough that our paths rarely crossed. All the kids were attractive. Aunt Marleen was a beautiful woman, tall, with striking features like the other Splann kin, but more so with Marleen. She was a gem and her children were blessed to have their mother's beauty.

I especially looked up to David, who was eight years my senior. My earliest recollection was on our return from overseas and seeing him a sixteen-year-old playing basketball with his friends. It was hard not to look up to him. He was good looking, athletic and friendly; and, he exuded a warm heart.

Several years later, David and a buddy of his took a road trip to our home in Pennsylvania in his 1966 Corvette Stingray. How much cooler could this guy be? He graduated from Colgate and went on to law school in Virginia where he met his wife, Lauren. After several attempts at passing the bar exam and failing, David moved on. Alcoholism and heavy tobacco use ravaged this beautiful man later in his life, eventually killing him well before his time. I loved David.

Alcoholism not only infused my immediate family, but destroyed others in my extended family. My uncle Frank died before his time from drinking and poor health. My other uncle, Eugene Short, Thelma's husband, also died from complications attributed to long-term alcohol abuse.

Then there were the children. I was not the only one to hop on the alcohol bus. Sally's older sister, Betty, eventually made her way to sobriety through AA, straightening out her life after a rough start. Aunt Thelma's family story was one of tragedy after tragedy. Eugene and Thelma had five children, four girls and one boy. Their son was taken too soon as he walked home from church, hit and killed by a drunk driver. The oldest daughter, Pamela, was killed one rainy evening trying to negotiate the turn from East Genesee onto Hunt Drive, where the family lived. Eugene, also a veteran of the Second World War, drank heavily and died an early death. Carissa, Tara and Mary Catherine, the remaining daughters, all had their escapades with drinking, drugging and abusive relationships.

The Short girls were spirited and attractive young ladies. The Splann DNA provided strong and attractive offspring and the three daughters were all knockouts. When the entire Splann side would get together, which was only a few times in my recollection, trouble times three would occur.

One get-together, brought about by marriage, ended with the three fathers going on a bender that they tried to live down for years to come. My mother frequently avoided family reunions owing to the certain disaster that would occur. I often wondered, even as a young boy, whether the thread that bound the destructive behavior of our fathers was somehow linked to their war service. I have come to realize not only the sacrifice of our father's generation, but the sheer horror of the war. Those who made it back were never the same. At least this was my experience in the Splann family.

Moving from Flushing to Scotia meant having a permanency with my mother and my brother, Danny. It served a purpose in keeping me alive and sustaining me, but it inhibited the independent lifestyle I had known for many years apart from my family. That I was broke, unemployed and in a state of disarray in body, mind and spirit made the transition necessary.

My initial thoughts were to rebuild and return to living as an adult male should, away from his mommy.

The next year would be my darkest yet. I felt like a failure on many levels, but I wasn't willing to acknowledge my addiction, nor was I ready to stop drinking. I was so entrenched in alcohol consumption that all else paled in importance.

After a lifetime of smoking and drinking, my mother's health was starting to deteriorate. She, too, became a drinking buddy. Most afternoons into the early evenings, before we would attempt to eat a dinner that I prepared, we began our ritual of drinks.

A Longing

My culinary skills were honed after living in New York for the past decade where eating great food and drinking wine had become an obsession. For many years, Helen and I turned our attention to a particular type of wine, exhausting the various vineyards, comparing and contrasting our way to intoxication. We went from cabernet to French burgundy, from bordeaux to chardonnay then back to pinot noirs. We spent countless months tasting California zinfandels and delighted in learning the delicate exuberance of champagnes. What she and I did not experiment with, my friend John Scully and his partner Maxwell filled in the gaps. John and I became well acquainted with Portuguese ports, usually the final digestive after having had several other bottles between us. In all my drinking escapades, none were more enjoyable than those attached to wine. In fact, after being fired from my management position at Eastern Airlines, I would join John and Maxwell as the three amigos, working as professional wine pourers for Tewksbury Winery during summer festivals, as well as other formal wine tastings sponsored by the vineyard.

Over the years with Eastern Airlines, my professional and leisure travel also provided me with opportunities to dine at many great restaurants across the country as well as in the countries visited. I came to know certain cities by specific restaurants and more precisely by favorite dishes that select restaurants would serve. New Orleans was one of my favorite dining cities, as was San Francisco. I visited New Orleans many times and found amazing cuisine from raw oysters to po-boy catfish sandwiches and must-have beignets from Café Du Monde. The very best crabmeat omelet was served at Brennan's in the French Quarter, and the most spectacular oyster bisque was served at Galatoire's on Bourbon Street. But, as will always be the case, New York City is by far the greatest city on the planet for food, bar none.[20]

Ben

Shortly after relocating to Scotia, I fulfilled a desire that I had for some time by finding a dog to call my own. I had always wanted a Newfoundland, but there were none to be found within a two-hundred-mile radius. Instead what I found was a litter of St. Bernard puppies, through an acquaintance of my mother's.

After my father's death in September 1982, my mother, with my coaxing, decided that she would take up golf. She had learned the game while living in the Philippines and always rued the fact that she hadn't continued playing. The Whispering Pines Golf Club, in Rotterdam, New York, was an executive course, shorter than a standard course, and close to our home. When I worked for Eastern I would fly up from New York City to visit and we would play golf together. The club was owned by three brothers and my mother became acquainted with them.

When I was looking for a Newfoundland, one brother mentioned a breeder he knew that bred champion line St. Bernards. As luck would have it, they had just had a litter a little over a month before. I called and there were still a few puppies available. I drove to the farm outside of Albany. At the front door I was greeted by a friendly couple who took me to the barn where the puppies were. I had never seen more adorable animals in my entire life. There were five eight-week-old pups, all balls of fur and big paws pushing each other aside trying to make their way to my open arms. Two were taken leaving three puppies, two females and one male. The owner apologized that the male would not be able to be shown because he was too white. She told me that because of this she would sell him for $500 as opposed to the others, which were $750.

After holding the whiter puppy in my arms only to have him lick my face with unabashed love, I told her that I did not have any interest in showing the dog; I was looking for a best friend. I said, "I'll take him."

Ben came with me and was my companion for nine-plus years, until he was too ill to go on. I loved Ben, slobber and all.

I trained him not to go in the street and never fed him anything, but veterinarian-approved dog food, except for a piece of apple once in a while. Ben loved apples. Just the sight would instantly bring about rivers of uncontrollable doggie saliva. When Ben was a full-grown adult St. Bernard, he weighed two hundred pounds and was six feet long when he laid down. He was so large that he could walk up to a table and place his huge head right on the table setting or walk up sideways to a couch and simply roll into a lying position. I trained him not to impose on our eating or couch sitting though. I wondered what Ben would have been like if, like most people, I fed him human food and allowed him full run of the house. At his slim, fit weight, it was hard to imagine what *overweight* would mean to this dog.

Humble Pie

Aunt Marleen had a friend who was a supervisor at SUNY Albany. He came through with a temporary job for me, seven dollars an hour to put in fence posts around the campus for an upcoming end-of-school-year concert. It was springtime 1989 and the job market was abysmal. I took the job gladly with the hope that I might eventually get full time status. Because it was a state job and it was full time, even as a temporary employee, I was entitled to the great benefits given to state workers.

Pounding fence posts for eight hours a day was grueling, and while it built muscle to adorn my thin athletic body, it was hard for me to rationalize doing menial labor after being a university graduate from the Maxwell School, and accomplishing everything I had to that point, despite the poor judgment associated with my drinking and drugging. I fell prey to feelings of victimhood in those first days, slamming fence posts into the dirt.

I worked with two other men. We completed the fencing and readied the area for the upcoming concert, which was to be a series of bands culminating with The Cars as the headliner group. I knew the music from The Cars, so when I was asked to work the concert, I eagerly accepted. My assignment was to work the stage area, assisting the roadies and ensuring that all electrical and lighting elements worked properly.

The concert came and went. I was still assigned to the grounds department. My next job was to work with a team of men to remove, gather and return all the posts to the storage garage on the perimeter of the campus. I moved around to various shops based on need. I worked most of my time between the carpentry and electrical shops.

SUNY Albany was designed for an arid, desert-like environment rather than the harsh conditions of upstate New York, where cold, wind, ice and snow were a certain reality. The exterior grounds consisted of concrete squares edged with acrylic caulking to keep moisture out of the subflooring. My assignment was to identify critically damaged areas of the campus flooring, and to remove, repair and replace with new caulking. I spent months by myself working on those concrete slabs. Each morning I would gather cases of acrylic caulking, two stainless steel industrial strength caulking guns, styrofoam cylindrical inserts to place in the open cracks between the concrete slabs, and water to quench my thirst. I would load up my electrical golf cart and off I would go to do my thing. The solitude of this work played very well to the many mornings where I was still hung over, still feeling the effects of heavy drinking from the night before. The sun beating down on me during the day helped sweat the alcohol out of my system. Most days it worked well.

After work at SUNY each day, I drove back to Scotia and went immediately to my new favorite watering hole, The Scotia Tavern, a few blocks away from my new home on Washington Road. It was close enough that I could negotiate my way back safely when I was drunk.

I became a regular, taking up a bar stool most afternoons and drinking enough that I was inebriated upon returning to my mother, who by that time had downed a couple gin and tonics herself. After greeting my mom, I would grab a beer from the refrigerator, light a cigarette and chat with my drinking buddy before moving to the kitchen to fumble around while making some dinner. This was my pattern for months. Weekends started on Friday nights after work. I would go to the Tavern, get blind drunk, return home and pass out. On Saturdays, I tried to delay my first beer to at least mid-afternoon, but the start times kept moving up as the weeks went by. I still managed to be a runner, particularly on the weekends, after awaking with a heavy head, blurry eyes and a saturated brain. This was the best way for me to come back to Earth and regain a semblance of reality. I was blacking out at least two nights each week. Stopping drinking was difficult once I began. Just as with cocaine, there was never enough alcohol to satisfy the desire or to numb the pain.

Late in the summer I attended a get-together at my cousin Sally's house in Rotterdam. Friends gathered for a barbeque, drinks and fun. Sally had been married since 1979 to Samuel Clausen and had children of her own. At the gathering were many of Sally's friends, some of whom I knew. Blanch, one of her best friends from high school, had been a girlfriend of mine for a short time. She was there with her husband and kids as well her cousin, Cherie Conners. As at most get-togethers, drinking heavily was part of the expectation. We lived up to and surpassed this goal, partying well into the next day. Cherie and I hit it off and made plans to connect at a later time. She was a divorcee with two young girls living in Berne, New York, a rural hilltop community outside of Albany in the Helderberg Mountains, not far from one of my family's summer destinations, Warner Lake. Cherie lived in a mobile home off Route 441 and waitressed during the daytime. She had recently divorced a man who abused her routinely. They were still in court proceedings, with a lot of hostility between them, a perfect mess for me to insert myself given my track record up to that point. Why would I have chosen to connect with anyone healthy? That would have been impossible, since I had deteriorated to being a sponge soaked in alcohol.

For the next seven months, I would spend a day during the week and weekends in a trailer drinking myself to unconsciousness, attached to a hard, young, chain-smoking woman who provided a safe haven for my drunken state.

In early 1990, it became clear that even for Cherie, a woman of modest means and lower than low expectations in life, putting up with a man who was perpetually drunk was not sufficient for her. We ended the relationship and I was left trying to sort through yet another part of me that was dissolving away.

I was rapidly approaching the ultimate decision, whether to live or die. The bottom was in sight. I was blacking out five out of seven days a week and driving blind drunk. I had lost any semblance of my true self. I didn't know it at the time, but my body was so toxic with alcohol that a small blood transfusion to any healthy person would have rendered them immediately unconscious from the alcohol content of my blood.

The internal fires needed to be quelled, but how would I find my way?

CHAPTER 5 REFLECTIONS

[15] *Many years later after much therapy and extensive study, it became clear to me that, astrologically as a Taurus, I was imbued with a strong desire for material security, wealth and pleasure, none of which were going to be realized as a starving waiter.*

[16] *The Divine, with an accompaniment of masters and angels, has always been with me, despite my inability to see, feel and know this truth. In early 1979, I did not have the eyes to see; but intuitively, in the quiet of my infrequent stillness, I knew that something was there. I could, in moments of emotional reflection, sense a voice from within, crying at the choices I was making.*

[17] *My ten-plus years working for Eastern Airlines fostered my running away, staying disconnected and living a life that was perpetually transient. It also became a pattern of living that allowed me to go deeper into self-destructive behavior, as would be my path over the decade of the 1980s.*

[18] *How did I arrive at such a dark place? It happened quietly, stealthily, poisonously over time. Drinking was normal in my family when I was young. It was natural for me to take it up myself. But I had moved beyond any form of normality as my capacity for alcohol and drugs increased from 1985 forward. I was not cognizant of the negative effects of my alcohol and drug use. The physical aftereffects of cocaine binges lasted for days and left me deeply depressed physically, emotionally and spiritually. I tried to keep the professional façade together, but I was living a Dr. Jekyll and Mr. Hyde counter-life of a raging alcoholic and drug user. And my relationship with Helen suffered as a result. She became more alienated from me in response to my pattern of use and abuse that prevented any real and genuine*

connection. I understood this at some level, but was desperate to keep the relation-ship going, more as a life buoy than in the loving spirit of union and flow. I did not know it consciously, but I was hanging on by a shoelace and trying to kill myself.

[19] *Throughout my life and up until the darkness in 1988, I heard a voice from within, quiet and subtle, yet present in moments of despair and uneasy solitude. Even as a child I felt a nudging, a faint pulse from within that I somehow knew was there, despite having no assurance other than intuition. I had an inner per-ception that I somehow did not fit into this world in its construct, that I was never quite aligned to the ebb and flow of others. Perhaps it was due to my being an ad-opted child, given up by my birth mother, yet there was more to it than this. Deep within, there was something else present. What it was I had no idea. There were times in my life when I would pray, not the typical prayer of the obedient Catholic, but rather humbly seeking truth, asking for grace and understanding. Like so many others who came and went before me in their suffering, my prayers during this time were pleadings of deep and dire need, of desperation. After one evening of heavy drinking, while I was lying down, I heard a voice that I understood to be God's and observed his face looking down at me lovingly, shaking his head as a disappointed father would, saying, "My son, I love you."*

[20] *I learned many years later into sobriety, with a view through past life regres-sion, that I was in fact a man of the Renaissance, a lover of the finer things, sensual and exquisite parts of being human that our souls long for. I was born to strive for an abundance of beauty, texture, delight and sensual pleasure. Even during the dark times, I would find great pleasure in delicious food, the endless bounty of Mother Earth's offerings in the succulent bouquet and artistry of flow-ers, fresh rain, the salt air of the sea shore, the intoxicating scent of a woman and the majesty of a symphonic orchestra as well as the miracle of each act of kindness that I witnessed. I knew these things and they touched my heart deeply. Even then I had the eyes to see, blurry and red, but present nonetheless.*

INSIGHTS AND TOOLS

Be a Peace-builder - in order to build peace, it is essential to find peace from within. The fires that burn within each of us manifest in a myriad of ways as we interact in our world. Oftentimes, our internal firestorms are hidden from our conscious behaviors, embedded in subtle innuendos, sarcastic refrains or by our unintentional actions. Take time to observe yourself as you interact with others. Are there individuals that unwittingly garner negative thoughts and actions? Are there certain people that simply stir your anger or contempt? Pay attention to situations that pull you into judgment and self-righteousness. These are signals that may require you to look at your own inner firestorms, those parts of your psychic reality that you are projecting onto others. After all, we create our realities by the choices we make. Choose to build peace by being peaceful within.

6

BE PRESENT

Learning to Live Differently

We are connected in more ways than we can imagine. As energetic entities, human beings are electromagnetic superconductive miracles that exchange energy between themselves and others. Is your output positive or negative energy? Pay attention to those you interact with and you will see quite clearly how your energy is received. Being present requires tuning in on the frequency that touches others from a point of love, compassion and understanding. This frequency is of a higher order, resonating from the heart.

The present is a canvas upon which we can paint infinite possibilities. Living outside of the present in sickness, denial and darkness limits our view, creating a myopic, caged existence, as was the case with me in March 1990. How does a soul arrive at the point where there is only one choice to be made, life or death? There were no what-ifs or middle-ground complexities to consider for me in that dark period of 1990. It had come down to whether I chose to live or die. I was perfectly capable of making this choice. Death presented the sole question of *how?* But that was never a challenge in my thinking. Any number of means could work. Living, on the other hand, would require monumental change and pain; I would have to confront massive amounts of fear, anger and loss. Yet I had come to a juncture in my life, at age thirty-five, when something had to be done, one way or the other. I simply could not endure any longer. How had my life spiraled to this point?

The picture was grim in March 1990. My entire life was spinning out of control. I was incapable of thinking straight and acutely sick on all fronts.

A Recurring Nightmare

I had a recurring dream over the months before I hit bottom. In the dream, suicide was an option. I lay in eerie darkness, in hues of brown, rust and deep blood red. I was outside my body and could see it still and rigid. A black veil moved slowly from my feet toward my head, wafting inches above my body. As the veil reached my waist, then my abdomen, moving upward toward my chest, I saw that death was imminent. I would awake, heart racing, head pounding.

I was sick mentally, emotionally and physically. I had lost all hope. I had blackouts five days every week. I could barely put sentences together. My eyes had gone dim with yellow and perpetual red where white once was. I was dying and the recurrent dream foretold my future.

To Live or Die

March 29, 1990, was a typical day at SUNY Albany where I was working with Steve changing ballasts in lighting fixtures around the campus. Steve noticed that today I was particularly low, not at all conversational and deeply depressed. I told him that I needed to use the restroom and I slipped away from the job. I needed to be alone to collect my distorted thoughts. I felt as though I was coming apart at the seams. What to do? *I could kill myself* was my first thought. It would have been much easier than the other choice, which flooded my soaked brain. Without thinking and almost as though being controlled by someone else, I decided to call my doctor's office, a general practitioner I had seen a couple times for colds and a sinus infection. When the receptionist asked me if it was an emergency, I said, "yes."

She asked what the situation was.

I said, "I am suffering and need help."

She told me to come right in.

I returned to Steve and told him that I wasn't feeling well and needed to leave to see my doctor. Steve told me he was happy that I was doing so. It was around 11:30 am and the drive from Albany to Rotterdam took about 20 minutes. During the ride, my mind was consumed with whether I should steer the car in a different direction, get a gun from my brother's dresser, and end it all. The alternative of meeting with the doctor meant telling him that I was depressed and needed help. *Was I ready for this?* Even in my state, I knew that if I chose to seek help it would radically change my life. What I knew, but did not acknowledge was that I was alcoholic, sick and damaged. To make this choice would not be easy. *Did I have the courage?* I do not remember having any dialogue with God for a long time, but this morning, I asked God to help me, pleading with him to show me the way. Tears formed in my eyes as I continued to drive to the appointment. [21]

I told my doctor I was deeply depressed and needed help. He reacted quickly. Later that day, at Ellis Hospital in Schenectady, I met with Dr. Habib, a staff psychiatrist, who within sixty seconds asked me, "How much do you drink?"

It was the first time in my life that I was honest in sharing that information. I told him the truth, that most days I would consume between twelve and twenty cans of beer, with occasional shots of liquor. I told him that most nights I would not fall asleep but rather pass out. I told him that I had no recollection of my actions most evenings, that I had been drinking heavily for the last ten years and less in the previous ten. I told him I could not remember a day in the last five years where I had not drunk alcohol. I told him that when I lived in New York City, I combined cocaine in large amounts with drinking nonstop for days at a time.

Dr. Habib said I needed to stop drinking. When I mentioned that I was considering suicide as a viable option, he wanted to admit me to the hospital immediately. After I convinced him that I would not be taking my life that evening, he reluctantly let me leave, but he said that if I did not contact him at nine the following morning, he would be sending police and an ambulance to pick me up. March 29, 1990 was the day I stopped putting alcohol into my body. But, life did not get easier.

Year One of Sobriety

I now faced the question, what *next?*

To stay out of a forced hospital inpatient program, I agreed to attend an outpatient rehab program affiliated with Ellis Hospital. Life Start was an alcohol and drug rehabilitation center on Union Street in Schenectady. The six-week program consisted of two-hour sessions three days a week, mostly with a group of others trying to find a glimmer hope for living without substance abuse. During this program, I learned in great detail about the progression of alcoholism, the stages of deterioration and the symptomatic phases that a human being goes through as the disease progresses. I learned that I was in the later stages of the disease and, according to the researched data, death was not far off for me.

This surprised me because all along I had maintained the justification that somehow I was not as sick as one might think, that I had some control. The program showed me that I was gravely mistaken. Consciously, I was not cognizant of the fact that I was attempting to kill myself; yet, I was and in a savage manner. The catalyst for this self-imposed brutality remained a mystery; even if I had been told straight-on, I would not have had the capacity to understand. I was very sick.

As toxic as I was on that 1990 day, I understood the duress and work attached to my decision to live. The recovery process was torturous. It required a level of strength and faith of monumental proportions, particularly during the first year.

My cells and body systems had normalized to the ingestion of alcohol in large quantities for such a long period of time that removing it blew circuit breakers, shutting down systems and leaving me reeling in horrendous sickness. I had trouble sleeping for months. Digestion, from intake through processing to excretion, was in shambles. Diarrhea was normal for me during the first two years. The whites in my hazel eyes did not return for multiple seasons.

My intellect and vocabulary were decimated. I struggled to string a cogent sentence together for well over a year before words started to come naturally.

When I started drinking alcoholically, which was close to twenty-years prior, my normal emotional growth stopped. It took me years to uncover some of the rudimentary emotions that others feel naturally, such as anger, love, self-worth, security, joy and gratitude. There was demolition to be done before reconstruction could occur.

Dr. Habib recommended Alcoholics Anonymous as an organization that would help me. One thing was certain: I needed help. For the first time in my life, I openly acknowledged that I, left to my own devices, could not do it. The hiding, the falseness, the massive amount of energy required to live alcoholically and maintain a pretense of normality, the uncertainty that I might kill someone while driving drunk or be arrested and thrown in jail—all these daily segments of my self-contained and totally self-consumed life had been exposed. I needed help. The dark, deep clinical depression set in just days after removing the alcohol. [22]

Dr. Habib had prescribed a new magic drug, Prozac, as a counterbalance to the depression and anxiety that surely occurred. I made it through one week taking Prozac and then threw it away. I returned immediately to my job at SUNY Albany, working on ladders with machinery and tools. The drug caused not only dry mouth but dizziness. No Prozac for me. But I was willing to try anything to get from hour-to-hour, minute-to-minute with the possibility of feeling better.

Toward the end of my outpatient rehab, my counselor strongly reinforced my attending AA. The AA schedules showed many types of meetings— open ones, closed ones, step meetings, gay meetings and those for drug addicts as well. I reviewed the schedule and found a Saturday morning meeting in Schenectady at a place called the Clubhouse. *How friendly that sounded*, I thought.

Saturday came and I left my Scotia home at 9:20 to find the Clubhouse, which was in the old Italian neighborhood of Mt. Pleasant. My inner voice chattered anxiously about attending an AA meeting.

I knew that my father had attended AA during one of his more challenging periods with his own alcoholism, but never stuck to the practice. I was open, but scared. There was a stigma in my belief system of AA having down-and-out drunks and seedy souls who were the dregs of the earth. Now I was marching into a place of uncertainty. All I knew is that I was told this would help.

I rounded the corner onto a street of older homes. Ahead on the left was a building with a sign saying Clubhouse, with lots of men and women strolling inside, some of whom looked pretty normal to me. Finding a place to park on the street a few blocks away, I parked, took a deep breath and walked toward the Clubhouse. *What could happen? I will just go in and keep an open mind.* The door opened to a hall that emptied into a large room with tables and about a hundred chairs. I went to the coffee station at the back of the room where two people poured coffee for the participants.

One of the people working the table was a middle-aged black man who I thought looked very poor, and yet his smile was beaming. I thanked him for the coffee and found a seat at the perimeter of the room in what I thought would be a safe area.

The leader, sitting at a table in the front, quieted everyone and welcomed the crowd to the Saturday morning Clubhouse meeting. He then read the twelve steps of the program and a section from a hardcover book about AA. All I remember is his referencing the Big Book and saying that this organization is anonymous. He then told his story of alcoholism. As I looked across the room, I saw people of modest means, some in torn ragged clothes. There were men and women of color, some shaking with what were the effects of drinking, some looking quite healthy. I felt uncomfortable, like I was in a foreign land of people who were much sicker than me. But I resisted the urge to leave and sat quietly in my seat as the meeting progressed. My visual observations temporarily overpowered my listening, but I was brought back to reality when I heard the speaker say, "Are there any topics that you'd like to discuss?"

A man sitting to my right had raised his hand, "I would like to talk about gratitude."

Gratitude! What possibly could this group of misfits have to discuss about gratitude? The moderator nodded. "Anyone have another topic to discuss?"

A woman in the middle of the room with auburn hair falling below her shoulders and piercing eyes said, "I'd like to hear about surrender."

Now that was a topic that resonated with me. *Where was this going?*

People shared their experiences of surrendering to the power of alcohol and of their gratitude to be alive today. People openly shared heartfelt emotions about the harsh reality of their lives, the sadness, terror and loneliness of the alcoholic path. Tears filled the eyes of some who listened to the sharing, including me. I could relate to the pain and desperation people were expressing. This was the first time I ever heard another human being capture the loneliness and self-absorption, the darkness of being consumed by alcohol. I was amazed that others actually knew what that felt like. It was a remarkable moment for me. In that instant, I knew that if I was going to make it, AA would play an integral part. And it did.

Over the next several years I became active in AA, working the steps, going to prison to conduct meetings with inmates, sponsoring alcoholics and living true to the principles and mantras. I formed a circle of associations and friendships with other alcoholics, going for coffee at Stewart's after meetings, traveling to other AA meetings with them and reaching out when I was in particular pain or struggle. I strongly believe that without AA, especially early on in my recovery, I would not have made it. It was one thing to suffer, but another to do it with the support and understanding of others on a similar journey. Knowing this made the trek that much more possible to accomplish.

A couple months into my recovery, I quit my job at SUNY. Without the stress and responsibility of having to go to work each day, my job became getting better. The process was painfully slow, one step forward and four steps back.

Contending with the physical damage and the effects of abuse demanded patience and courage, as did the emotional rollercoaster attached to learning how to live again. And that was exactly what was necessary. [23]

The twelve steps of the AA program started with admitting that I was alcoholic, that my life was out of control. This was not a stumbling block for me since I was very clear about my alcoholism, not to mention the many areas of my life that had become dysfunctional.

Steps two and three brought into play a "higher power," which for many drunks was a monumental obstacle that would prevent their finding sobriety. I was at such a low point, where I felt as though I was being dismantled one piece at a time, the concept of a higher power (God) was a blanket I could easily wear to find comfort. It was no stretch for me to bring God into the picture since my outlook was so dark. Despite my Catholic upbringing, with its dogmatic interpretation of God's wrath, I was able to find solace in a loving God, one that I had held close as a child. And loving was the operable word and feeling that I needed from the Divine.

I had regrets and painful memories associated with the nightmare of active alcoholism. Early in rehab it occurred to me that one area of my life that had fallen from grace was my integrity, my word, the promises that I would make and break routinely.

Learning to live sober took discipline and change; one change was to eliminate "if I only could" and "I wish I" from my thinking. These phrases were pathways to the pain of the past, reminders of broken promises and lost integrity that permeated my experience during the past decade or more of my life. Most egregious were the promises I made to myself, those pleas for sanity and peace, for a glimmer of light that never would come. I could not make it if I did not turn off the incessant thoughts of my past mistakes; there were countless times that, if I gave them attention, would come to infuse me with such sorrow and sadness that it would be overwhelming. To not have my word, my integrity, would negate any constructive reason for living differently. I also started to learn that life was to be lived in the present, not in the past or an uncertain future. This was a new idea for me, but it made perfect sense.

The woman who suggested the topic of surrender at my first AA meeting was an extraordinary human being. Joanne K. was thirty-two years old, single, with three children, all from different men. She was a recovering heroin addict and alcoholic whose life was replete with challenges most people could only find in a nightmare. She lived on her own from age thirteen, on the streets, living among uneducated and vicious men who took complete control and advantage of her. She was one of the most interesting people I had ever met. Her life was a saga, yet she managed each day to stay clean and sober despite the many challenges she faced.

When I met her, she was living in a third floor walkup in an old house in the inner city section of Schenectady called the Hill, near I-890 on Crane Street. Before the Second World War, Crane Street was the Italian section of Schenectady, a neighborhood that Irish and Polish families would sharply advise their young girls to stay away from. *You know those Italians—they are trouble.* My mother, having grown up on the Hill in the Irish neighborhood, always had sharp criticism and barbs of disdain for those nasty wops. The Hill, where Joanne and her three children lived, suffered from years of deterioration after GE pared back its headquarter manufacturing operation from the high point of 50,000 employees after WWII to a tenth of that in 1990. Schenectady was in serious decline. The Hill was notoriously one of the worst sections in the Capital District and the entire state of New York. Drugs, prostitution and crime plagued the area where Joanne lived so modest a life.

A strong recommendation in early sobriety was to avoid, at all costs, romantic attachment of any sort. The first year it was strictly forbidden to have a relationship. Early recovery was a confusing time emotionally, where any sense of clarity in matters of the heart was muddied by misfiring of synapses and the inability to rationally put one foot in front of the other.

Divine Messenger

One Tuesday in September, after a noon AA meeting, I pulled into a parking space in front of a Stewart's convenience store for a cup of decaf. When I came back out, I saw that my driver side rear tire had gone flat. *What else?* I thought.

Placing my hot coffee in the cup holder of the console and preparing to change the tire, I closed the driver door when suddenly a man of around twenty-five with blond hair and bright blue eyes, dressed in jeans and a flannel shirt walked up to me. Without skipping a beat, he said, "Wow, that's too bad about the tire; let me give you a hand. I have exactly what we need."

I smiled and said, "Thank you."

He said it was no problem and that he was very happy to help me. In an instant a hydraulic jack materialized and he had changed my tire. When he was done and he approached me from the back of my truck, time slowed, and I saw a glow around my helper. He stood in front of me, gazing into my eyes.

The glow around him permeated my spirit and was cellular, as he then spoke these words: "I am here to tell you that you are infinitely loved. Your prayers are heard and the Divine wanted me to tell you that you are never alone. Remember this Michael, son of the Blessed." He smiled at me with a love and warmth that I feel even now. He turned and disappeared as I watched him take several steps. I stood stunned as time and reality returned in the living moment.

Discovering Real Love

Relationships are hard enough, but given the infant reemergence of lost feelings, they can be dangerous in recovery. I made it to the holidays of 1990 before Joanne and I acknowledged having strong feelings for each other. It was a mismatch of huge proportion, no doubt, but there was a unique and strong connection between us. We were from very different backgrounds, yet Joanne's unique blend of intelligence, experience and compassion attracted me on many levels. I had never met a person who had been through such profound and prolific hardships, nor had I ever met a woman whose natural beauty was as elegant and complex as hers.

For the next two and half years we were together. I know that my presence with her provided a catalyst for her to move up and out of poverty, to gain a stronger sense of her own strength, and capacity to love and to see the divine part of her essence that was deeply buried beneath pain, suffering and loss. When I met her, her strong six-year recovery charted a course of commitment that helped me greatly. We attended several meetings each week and supported each other in physical and emotional ways that were healing and restorative. She helped me immensely in finding the part of me that could love, be passionate and drop my guard enough to find an authentic piece of myself: the heart of my soul that, up until this time, was held captive to fear and silence. It was the first time in my life that I felt genuine love. For this and her, I hold tremendous gratitude and admiration.

The time had come in early 1991 for me to seek employment again. Having been a mid-level management professional at Eastern Airlines prior to being fired, I had strong skills. I thought perhaps I would be able to again secure this level of employment. The Reagan years had brought about a tight job market in upstate New York; jobs were hard to come by, let alone high-paying management positions. After negative responses to a myriad of applications, I knew I would need to set my sights much lower.

I saw an advertisement in the Albany *Times Union* for relay operators at AT&T. Wow, this sounded like an interesting way to get a foot in the door at a major communications company. I responded and received a letter directing me to come to their corporate office in Clifton Park the following Monday morning at 9:30.

The morning was cool and overcast. The prelude to winter could be seen in the silhouettes of the barren trees. Pulling into the parking lot, I proceeded into the office complex to join a large crowd of applicants. More than fifty people filled the large reception area. I quelled my anxiety as best I could. At 10:00 a woman greeted us and said we would be taken to a testing center down the hall for the first in a series of tests for the relay operator position. I entered a large classroom, took the next available seat and awaited further instructions.

The same woman told us we would be taking a series of three timed tests that would evaluate our ability to quickly and effectively answer a variety of verbal comprehension, math and spatial relationship questions, all relevant to being successful as a relay operator. She went on to describe briefly that the AT&T Relay Center was specifically for people with impaired hearing in the state of New York to have equal access to communications via the telephone with others who were not disabled. The relay operator was the communication expert who facilitated this equal access by being the voice and hands of the communication. I was interested. Each of the three tests was approximately twenty minutes, with the goal being to correctly answer as many questions as possible. It was a heads-down, all-out brain dump.

Afterward, all the applicants were taken back to the reception area to await the results, which would take thirty minutes. Those who passed would be asked to move on to the next round. The wait was nerve-racking. The same woman emerged through the doorway with a paper in her hand, and said, "If your name is called, you will be moving onto the next round of testing. For those of you not called, thank you for your time and interest in AT&T."

Seven, eight, ten names and no Michael, but then I heard her say, "Michael Splann." Relief and excitement replaced anxiety. More than half the applicants had been cut in the first round.

On to the typing test. I had a flashback to the start of my senior year in high school. I had taken all the required courses necessary for college admission and now had elective opportunities. My mother insisted I take typing as a half-year course. I can hear her telling me, "You'll need that skill at some point." And she was right. We had ten minutes to type as much of a document as we could. Speed and accuracy were the goals. There was no correction key, so what we typed was what we typed. Each of us was given a two-page document folded in half to conceal the contents. We were instructed to position the paper in a copyholder. The signal was given, and we opened the paper to see that there were two solid pages of writing, more than we could possibly type in ten minutes. I concentrated on accuracy. My fingers beat a musical rhythm as I plowed through the test.

Of the twenty remaining applicants, I was one of the five selected for employment at AT&T. The pay was $278 per week, with a varied schedule. My professional life moved from the airline industry to communications.

More Challenges

During my first year of recovery, late in November 1990, my mother's health deteriorated; she had a fever and was unable to eat. She never was much of an eater. At this point she was about five foot two and 110 pounds on a good day. Her diminutive size had to do with the fact that she was a heavy smoker for decades and loved her gin. A duodenal ulcer had plagued her for years. Now the blockage between her stomach and her intestines had become serious. Her doctor sent her to the emergency room at Ellis Hospital, where she was to be readied for surgery.

The ER staff quickly took my mother into one of the exam rooms, where they attempted to put feeding tubes through her nostrils. She may have been frail, but she was not going to let that happen without a fight.

She screamed, "Stop! Michael! Michael, help!"

I rushed into the room and yelled, "Stop this now! There must be a more humane way to do this."

The lights went out in my mother's eyes. Sometime later I read that, particularly with the elderly, illness, injury and trauma can cause neurological damage. The damage began that evening at Ellis Hospital. From then on the mother I knew would slowly slip away. No one else saw this but me. I knew my mother energetically and spiritually; I understood the damage that was done and it was devastating.

After a three-and-a-half-hour operation, my mother remained in the hospital for the better part of a month. What distressed me most was her memory loss and inability to grasp the here and now. She was severely disorientated for the first couple of weeks; she was agitated and unaware of the time, the date and where she was.

The doctors attributed her condition to the trauma of the operation and the severity of the blockage. I, on the other hand, had seen her cross over the line in the ER. Where she would end up was questionable during that hospital stay.

My brother, Danny, still living at home, refused to visit our mother. He said, "It's too hard for me to see her like that."

I was not buying that, but I let it go nonetheless. I was still in early recovery and trying desperately to remain diligent to my meeting schedule and the routines that I had built to stay sober one day at a time. Anger at my brother's inability to be present for our mother was a luxury I could not afford, so letting it go was the healthy choice. The truth was that the anger lay buried along with the festering cauldron of rage that I had carried with me since childhood. This was not the time to deal with it. Shortly following my mother's surgery, Danny decided, after years of being cared for by our mother, that he would make a break. He packed up his pickup truck and moved to Wilmington, Ohio, to be close to his childhood friend, Bobby Keene.

My mother regained enough strength to return home following an arduous recovery process. She was sufficiently connected with reality to know her name, the date and the answers to other small, but purposeful questions that the neurologists would ask to determine the nature and severity of her mental failing. Yet, I knew that she was not all together. There were extended periods of clarity when she exhibited the unique characteristics that defined Kathleen, and then other times when bizarre behaviors would emerge. My whole life she drank her coffee black. Now she wanted cream and sugar. It was a small shift in her usual behavior, but it struck me as remarkable. And after a half century of smoking Camels, she just stopped smoking and never mentioned cigarettes again. My mother's psychic world had shifted into a downward spiral that manifested in more troubling ways over the course of the next year.

The slow progression of the disease was deceiving during the first several months of the downslide. Following the surgery, my mother's affect seemed perfectly normal most of the time, with her more cogent, truer self in evidence during the morning. In the afternoon and evening, I noticed disorientation that only I was sensitive to.

As time went on, life in our home started to unravel. My mother developed Sundown Syndrome; nighttime brought on confusion and disorientation. Kathleen became increasingly agitated and required my reassurance and loving consolation. Sometimes she forgot who I was and called me Larry or even Jim, her brother who had passed away years previous. After a night of repeated interruptions, she would awake without any knowledge of what had occurred or any sign of the confusion from the past evening. I, on the other hand, had become the caretaker of an aging woman suffering from the early stages of dementia. The challenges had just begun.

Usually, it's a daughter who becomes the parental caretaker, according to healthcare providers that I would meet over the next year. It was unusual for a son to take on this role, especially caring for the parent at home.

I was thirty-five years old, in the process of trying to regain my life, starting over in every possible way and now the primary caretaker to my ailing mother. This was not the story I would have written for myself or the path that I envisioned when I thought of being a grown-up. Each day was a new chapter of duress—emotional, physical and spiritual.

My Aunt Bernadine, ten years older than my mom, and her husband, Curtis Herskind, lived in Niskayuna, an older, more affluent community consisting largely of GE executives and more recently the next generation of professionals. The school district was one of the better ones in the Capital District.

Bernadine and Curtis would make it a point to look in on my mother several times a week. Their involvement was intermittent and generally earlier in the day, when my mother would be lucid, for the most part, and conversational.

When I approached my aunt and her husband to let them know what was happening with my mother at night, they would say that she seemed fine to them.

Several months into this deterioration, they paid a visit to our home and asked my mother whether she was feeling alright. I was in the kitchen and overheard my mother say in a fearful whisper, "He's stealing from me and wants to do me harm!"

I said this was not the case, that I was caring for my mother. But nothing dissuaded my mother's accusations. It was an extremely difficult time.

Curtis, Bernadine's husband, pulled me aside and said that I should stop taking advantage of my mother, that he had contacted my brother, Danny, who also told him that I was stealing from her.

I told him to get out of my house.

Bernadine and Curtis were the only family that I could possibly have received help from. Losing their confidence was devastating and hard for me to comprehend. It looked like I was going to have to go it alone. Luckily, cousin Rosie, who lived a few blocks away, came over and eventually saw that my mother was deteriorating. And although Rosie was helpful during this challenging time, she did nothing to shed light on the situation with my godmother and her husband. Rosie's observation of my mother's condition did, however, provide me with a sliver of recognition that I wasn't losing my mind.

In November 1991, on a rainy Saturday that was cooler than typical for that time of year in upstate New York, I scheduled my errands in the morning to ensure that I was home later in the day. I had just finished running my usual four-mile run and come back into the house when I saw my mother in the family room, sitting watching television. I checked on her and told her that I was going upstairs to take a hot shower. When I came back down the stairs, I went into the kitchen to look for my mother. She wasn't there. I called out to her. No answer. Outside, the rain continued to fall. A feeling of fear came over me as I started to realize that she was not in the house. I checked the closet. Her raincoat was still there. I put on my rain slicker, exiting the house and started walking rapidly, shouting, "Mom, Mom!" I went down Washington Road to the right, then I turned back, running to the left toward the main busy Saratoga Road, Route 50. As I approached the corner and looked to the right, north, there was my mother, walking in her bare feet along the sidewalk without a coat and in a fog. My heart ached with both deep compassion and relief at the sight of her aimlessly wandering. I caught up to her in a flash and covered her with my raincoat. I guided her back to the house, where I dried her off and pondered what to do. It was a dark time in so many ways.

I could no longer care for my mother; that was certain. *But what could I do?* I needed to investigate options. What followed was months of investigation and a series of meetings with my attorney to understand what was legally necessary to manage the house and what little my mother had.

Early on, before my mother became ill, she had my name added to her bank accounts, just in case something happened. That I was on her accounts allowed me to get a small home equity loan to cover the expenses of getting her into assisted living.

I was able to get her into an adult assisted care home at the end of Wallace Road, blocks away, despite her vocal objections. Getting her to physically go to live there was one of the most challenging hurdles that I was to overcome, since she had enough mental capacity to have a strong opinion regarding her moving into this controlled environment.

Her condition continued to erode rapidly over the next nine months, meaning she required the next level of care. Getting her into a nursing facility was not an easy process.

After her surgery, we discussed the fact that if something happened to her, the house would be taken as an asset. I knew that much of the law. Before she declined mentally, she decided it was in our best interest to add my name to the ownership of the home. This decision ultimately meant the difference between losing the house to Social Services for full-time nursing home care and continuing to live in the home.

Transitions

When I relocated from Flushing to Scotia in 1989, and after working at AT&T for several months, I received a phone call from a recruiter for NYNEX, formerly New York Telephone, saying that they were in the process of hiring employees for several of their companies. I applied. After I completed their battery of tests successfully, I was slated as a potential candidate for employment. Shortly thereafter, I was called and offered a position with the publishing side of the enterprise working in Troy, NY.

My job at AT&T, while a solid and secure position, afforded me a schedule that was inconsistent from week to week, making it very challenging to care for my mother. The position with NYNEX would mean a steady Monday-through-Friday work schedule that made it that much easier for me to care for her. I made the move and began working in the national Yellow Pages unit on the third floor of an impressive building in Rensselaer Technology Park. While the pay was similar to what my

AT&T job paid, the physical environment and hours were much better. I had a more structured schedule, which worked much better for care of my mother, for AA meetings and for my personal relationship with Joanne.

The building housed close to four hundred employees, many of whom had multiple decades of service to the phone company. The entire work force was unionized, with a benefits package that was completely paid for in addition to a non-contributory pension program. Nepotism ruled in this work environment, with three generations within my line of sight each day. Grandmothers, mothers and children were commonplace, in addition to cousins, in-laws and other associated relationships.

I was alarmed by the pervasive attitude of entitlement that emanated from this unsophisticated, uneducated and arrogant group of workers. What made it even more perplexing was the fact that the benefits included full tuition reimbursement for higher education, an amazing gift that went unused by the work force, many of whom were younger individuals without the family duties that prevented so many others from taking advantage of the benefit. And for the few of us with college degrees, we were looked down upon by blue-collar union members living a life of false entitlement.

The next decade would be telling, for many would eventually lose their jobs and the accompanying contract benefits in the throes of a changing competitive marketplace. For me, working at NYNEX Information Resources served a purpose in more ways than one.

During my tenure there, a woman several years younger than me, whose mother had recently retired from the phone company after thirty plus years, took a liking to me. Marie Jane had been an employee for twelve years at that time. She would arrange to run into me routinely, always smiling and making friendly conversation. She was an unusual woman. Sometimes she dressed as though her work was a fashion show. She would show up looking like a highly paid secretary, wearing short, color-coordinated skirts and high-heeled pumps, her long, bleached blond hair adorned with clips and combs. She was unique, for sure; and she was on a mission to acquire my interest.

At the time my relationship with Joanne was strained by problems with her three children. The oldest had become pregnant by an abusive man, the middle child had severe behavioral issues in school and the youngest was an out-of-control trouble maker; all of these problems resulted from the total dysfunction occurring in the family. To make matters worse, Joanne had tried to quit smoking for the better part of a year but just could not make it happen. By this time, I had been a nonsmoker for well over a year, and that put an enormous strain on our relationship. Taken together, despite the strong feelings that we shared, these differences started to make our relationship challenging.

I was deeply torn, for I loved Joanne as I had not known love before. Yet, I knew that we needed to separate.

Despair Sets In

I was thirty-eight years old, never married, without support, living with my mother, whose health was rapidly failing, and holding on by a shoe-string financially. And to add insult to injury, I was in relationship with a woman I cared deeply for, who was strapped with endless issues attached to her children, all this while trying to live my life sober.

One night, I walked into the quiet house in Scotia, now occupied by only me and my Saint Bernard. Overwhelmed by uncertainty and realizing that the dreams of that twenty-two-year-old Syracuse graduate in 1977 had been dashed into oblivion by a life out of control, I wept. It seemed to come out of nowhere. The well had broken and up came the incredible loss and sadness associated with a life shattered and abused. I leaned against the door jamb separating the small kitchen from the den in the back of the house. Tears poured out uncontrollably. The years of duress, the unrewarding work and grieving for an ailing parent combined with the loneliness of my journey, all coalesced into hours of weeping. I slid down the door jamb into a sitting position in the kitchen, I hung my head and crossed my arms on my knees to hold up my falling head and continued to sob. I managed to lift my head and open my eyes at one point to find the massive head and large black nose of my best four-legged friend, Big Ben, sitting immediately in front of me, inches away from my face, just looking at me, concerned and supportive, as though he felt every pang of raw emotion. It was a remarkable moment, knowing that my dog was not only sensing my despair, but attempting to show his love and unconditional caring. He was an extraordinary animal and my dearest friend. I loved Ben and he loved me.

From Love to Insanity

Marie Jane represented a polar opposite of Joanne.

In the summer of 1993, after I got my mother into the assisted living center, Marie Jane wore me down to the point where I made the choice to end my relationship with Joanne. It took months for me to find my way to this decision. In spite of the great complexities in Joanne's life, she was an important part of my world, a person with whom I shared intimacy and tremendous growth. I had learned the rudiments of loving. To end this relationship was heartbreaking to both of us, yet the truth was clear that our differences became too much to manage. I knew that I wanted some semblance of normalcy, a chance to live according to what I thought was the American dream of family, home and love.

Little did I know that what was ahead would be anything but love; it was, rather, a lurking nightmare that would define the rest of my life.

My inner voice was urging me to tread carefully. I was not capable at this point in my life of knowing that the divine was nudging me, whispering in my soul to trust my intuition. In the infancy of my spiritual life, I failed to see the freight train barreling toward me in the human form of Marie Jane Fratoria.

After several dates, I realized she was not much on depthful conversation. Our discussions were always superficial. I thought maybe she just needed more time to open up her real self to me.

My mother's condition worsened to the point where she needed to be moved to a skilled nursing facility with around-the-clock care and attention. She had become ill with a serious respiratory infection which landed her in the hospital. The doctors treating her quickly ascertained that she was suffering with more advanced stages of dementia and would require nursing care. *But where would I move her?* My investigation took me from private homes to state and county nursing facilities, all of which had a waiting list that could take weeks to open up. I started to look in bordering states of Vermont, Pennsylvania and New Jersey as a last resort.

Marie Jane was aware of my situation and told me that her grandmother, with whom she had a very close relationship, had been in the Albany County facility until she passed away a couple years earlier. She said that she would check with her mother to see if she knew anyone at the county home.

As it turned out, Marie Jane's mother had a close relationship with the director of the nursing facility and made a phone call that resulted in being able to find a spot for my mother. I was grateful beyond words to have such assistance, the likes of which my own family never provided.

Marie Jane's mother, a large woman who had worked with the phone company for many years, seemed like a generous soul. She had a friendly demeanor and a dialect that pinned her as a resident of Troy—a vocal quality that identified her as one of the falsely entitled blue-collar workers. She was to reveal her true self in years to come as a vicious, crude and evil person walking around in sheep's clothing.

After my breakup with Joanne, I had reservations about a relationship with Marie Jane.

I caught wind in the internal NYNEX job postings of hiring within our cellular arm, NYNEX Mobile. There were customer service specialist positions at the Metro New York headquarters in Orangeburg, an affluent community in Rockland County, on the west side of the Hudson River, adjacent to Westchester County and a stone's throw from New York City. This might be my ticket out. *But what would I do with my house, my dog, and the visits with my mother?*

I applied through the company to the internal posting and received word ten days later that I had been accepted to the position. I informed Marie Jane of my decision, and without much emotional reaction she said, "I'll just come and visit you." I thought this would be my way to escape the hard press being waged by Marie Jane.

Traveling to the Orangeburg area to explore places to live, I found rentals to be very expensive. I expanded my search into New Jersey, which abuts Rockland County. Eventually I found a listing in a private home in Ringwood, New Jersey. The apartment was a one-bedroom basement apartment that opened up to the lower deck of a split-level home right on Ringwood Lake.

The lake community was picturesque; residents were professionals working in the City for the most part. The landlord I rented from lived upstairs with her son, a teenager who I would rarely see or hear.

I was able to negotiate having Ben join me, which made living there all the more acceptable. The hard part was transporting the two-hundred-pound doggie. Ben was no traveler; in fact, riding in a vehicle terrorized him. Getting him into my SUV was no easy matter. Even if he had enjoyed riding, which he clearly did not, finding a way to get this monstrosity of an animal into the back of my truck was challenging. I had to force him to the back of the vehicle, then lift his long front legs and paws into the flap of the truck. From there, I would have to pick up the remaining three feet of dog to get his back legs into the truck. Ben would hug the floor of the vehicle for dear life, paws locked into place, face between his paws, motionless for the entire trip, however long it would be. Ben was so large and long that it was difficult for him to climb stairs, which kept me from living in a location with more than three steps. Ben's length between front paws and back made climbing traditional stairs impossible for him. In all the time I lived in Scotia, Ben never made his way upstairs to the second floor. It was a trek that he would not even contemplate. The Ringwood apartment worked well since there was a level walk-in from the backyard. Ben was a happy dog.

We did not have a television hookup in the basement. During the week, Ben and I would listen to music from my cassette player and listen to the radio, mostly NPR.

I came to appreciate the solitude those months provided to turn my attention toward writing, reflection and getting to know myself much better. I had been through a lot of change in recent years, all of it a blur of putting one foot ahead of the other.

I gave serious consideration to how my life should proceed. I considered marrying and having a family, attending the Culinary Institute of America in New Hyde Park to become a chef, and exiting altogether to live a bohemian life in Tuscany, a place that spoke to my soul. Both the CIA and Tuscany came with the certainty of wine, for what would a chef be without the sacred ingredient of deep rich Burgundy or Chardonnay? And how could I possibly live in Tuscany without the sweet nectar of beautiful Italian Frascati? What remained was the part of me that felt alone, purposeless and inappropriate to my age, station in life and full potential. Perhaps marriage was the answer; after all, I was in my late thirties and a bachelor. I knew I was not gay, so living absent from a female life partner seemed to be living falsely.

It was also a time where Marie Jane's persistence and assertiveness played into my strong feelings of loneliness and separation. She was relentless. She called me incessantly and made several weekend trips to the Ringwood apartment. She wore me down, even though I knew how shallow and absent she was of any real substance. I decided that I would take a chance, a long shot no doubt, but the time had come to move forward.

On Halloween 1994, I proposed to her, giving her a beautiful ring. She was elated. I thought that perhaps her parents, with whom she still lived, might feel the same. As I would find out later, in spite of their hatred and loathing of me, they were happy to pay for what was to be a grand marriage ceremony, Cinderella carriage and all.

The next year was filled with frenetic planning. In late 1994, I realized that working in Rockland County, a three-hour ride from the Capital District, was not conducive to planning a wedding. Luckily, I was able to transfer to a job at the NYNEX Mobile retail store on Central Avenue in Albany. Shortly after returning, I used the remaining funds from the home equity loan to complete the home improvements and repairs necessary to sell the Washington Road home. I was in full gear now, trying to live up to the American Dream. What was missing was having a fresh start, a new home. Marie Jane and I started looking for homes, both resale and new.

In a matter of months, the house sold. I now had the proceeds from the sale of the Scotia home plus my savings to purchase the new home. Our search took us into the country in Raymertown, a quiet rural area ten miles east of Troy, where there was a small new community of colonial homes being built by a local builder. We worked with the builder's daughter, an architect for the firm, and designed a gorgeous two-thousand-square-foot custom home on a cul-de-sac with more than two acres of land. The lot abutted beautiful mature oak trees to the south. It was a dream come true, Italian marble tile in the open foyer, nine-foot ceilings on the first floor, antique pieces used for bathroom fixtures, gorgeous cherry cabinets, wide-plank maple flooring in the kitchen and dining area. The entire back of the house was open and sunlit. In September 1995, two months before our wedding, we moved into the Raymertown home.

November 4, 1995, a gray Saturday in Albany, at Holy Names Catholic Church, we were married by Father Franklin, Marie Jane's longtime favorite priest. He also presided over the school that she had attended as a child. Her mother had also attended that school and her future grandson would be walking the same halls in years to come.

The entire wedding and reception was a Marie Jane and mother extravaganza, showing off the storybook princess who married the prince turned frog. Of the 250-plus guests who made their way to the hall in Saratoga that afternoon, you could count on two hands the number of invitees that came from my side of the union. It was a spectacle of grand proportion and I was the trophy husband that poor Marie Jane had bagged. The Hall of Springs reception, one of the premier venues in the tri-state area, included a live band, sit-down dinner, and to top it off, at the end of the reception, a horse drawn carriage picking us up to take us through the quaint town of Saratoga Springs to end up at the Victorian turn-of-the-century Adelphi Hotel, right in the heart of the historic town. When we settled into the honeymoon suite, the first thing that was on my mind was to get something to eat. In all the activities, I had not eaten since early morning. We made our way across Main Street to Lillian's for a hamburger.

The most memorable part of my honeymoon night was that delicious hamburger—not quite how I imagined it would be. Little did I know, but that hamburger would usher in five of the hardest years of my life. So many times I would go inside myself questioning how I had made such a colossal mistake. In my heart I knew what I was getting into with Marie Jane: the incessant chatterbox speaking at me, as opposed to having a civil conversation, one of sharing and listening. It didn't matter what I said, did or thought to do, it would be challenged, usually with a level of screaming insanity that would shake me to my core. Many times during her fits of rage she would pick up the phone and call her mother to bring her into the malaise, chiding, accusing, and spewing of incredibly toxic barbs.

And she was compulsive, perpetually writing religious passages on sticky notes, in writing so small that she would fill up the small space with repetitive phrases, much like a student would do when caught by the teacher doing something wrong and having to write on the blackboard over and over again their crimes. There would be hundreds and hundreds of sticky notes saved in drawers, boxes and any other receptacle she could find. On top of this, Marie Jane was a hoarder, saving every receipt, box, bag, tag, and piece of clothing ever purchased. Our newly built Raymertown home had a full dry basement that was impassable because of the collectibles she had amassed. It's a good thing I liked to cook because, aside from boiling water or placing a premade dinner in the microwave, nothing would have been made.

Six months after James Mitchell was born and after so many failed attempts to get him into his own crib, or into his own nursery that I had devoted hours of time and energy adorning, I realized that Marie Jane was completely unable and unwilling to get him out of our bed. I loved my son, but I also wanted to have some normalcy of having him sleep in his own bed and develop a secure sense of himself. I was unable to sleep with a baby continually lying next to me, fearful that I might roll over in my sleep and somehow suffocate him. Demoralized, I moved into the spare bedroom, where I remained for the rest of our marriage.

We separated in the spring of 2000. *So much for the fairy-tale marriage and my yearning for living the American dream*, I thought. Yet, I knew that I wanted a companion, a lover and someone to journey with in this lifetime. The dye was cast in my first marriage, now with a small son, embroiled in contentious litigation, trying to be a good father to a son I always wanted and heartsick at yet another failure added to my long list.

So when I again opened myself up to the possibility of romance, I did so consciously seeking a partner of stability, intelligence and grace. This time I would get it right!

Another Debacle

Rodney and Beth had joined us for dinner early in my courtship of my second wife, the psychologist, at a quaint bistro in the old section of Albany. It was late summer 2001, before 9/11. Rodney, a co-worker at the bank, had many years of experience. He was a fun-loving drinker and smoker, but he had a good heart and spirit. Beth, his stay-at-home wife, met Rodney in Ohio, where she worked for him when he was a branch manager.

The dinner was stilted right from the get-go, with the doctor boasting by telling them that she was a world-renowned psychologist and had achieved her educational success at the early age of twenty-five.

"Oh, how nice," Rodney replied. Rodney and Beth were not pretentious, so title meant very little to them. The evening started out cold and went downhill from there. The next day, Rodney, in as caring way as he could find, made it clear I should not invite them to dinner again. He described my fiancée as arrogant, stuffy, haughty, snooty and superior.

Rodney and Beth, as well as another friend, Max, and his wife, Laura, attended our wedding on March 9, 2002 in New Hampshire.

While I enjoyed speaking with and getting to know several of my wife's friends, I always felt like a second-class citizen in my own home or, more accurately, her home. At a dinner party at our home early in the fall, I was sitting at the beautifully dressed dining room table with two other couples. In the middle of a lively conversation, one of the guests turned to ask me what specifically I did in my professional world. As I was preparing to answer the question, my wife condescendingly interceded: "He's just a trainer." I was aghast. She changed the topic quickly.

At Christmastime 2002, my wife, who loved to entertain her gaggle of professional friends, had smartly decorated the beautiful Union Street home with a perfect blend of holiday ornaments, garlands, and festive adornment. Martha Stewart would be pleased.

She often complained that she had all the friends and I had very few, or at least few she considered worthy of her acquaintance. This time, however, I had invited several of my co-workers.

Max, Laura, Rodney and Beth arrived to join the Christmas party. Considering the way they had been treated earlier in the relationship, it was a stretch for them to attend the Christmas party. My wife welcomed them cordially. But after that, she stayed well clear of my friends. It was humiliating and infuriating to be treated this way, especially to my friends. Days later, I asked Rodney and Max if they enjoyed the party. They both said, "No, not really." They had felt out of place and as if they were being treated like foreigners.

I appreciated their honesty. But once again, I was torn emotionally. I had gone from an incredibly destructive first marriage right into another debacle. I questioned my own actions. I thought, *Did I not see this? Was I blind to think this was the relationship I always dreamt of? Did I intentionally create this toxic malice?*

One lesson learned from my second marriage was the importance of respect in a relationship, whether friendship or, as in this case, marriage. She held no respect for me, as was apparent to anyone who observed the tenor of her demeaning and emasculating style.

The Christmas party was only the second time Max encountered my wife, but it made a lasting impression on him. He refused to have anything else to do with her; he always had an excuse. I began to wonder why he would always have some other appointment or event that precluded him from accepting an invitation. I found out one day at Yankee Stadium.

Several of the regional managers decided, as a team building activity, that we would charter a bus to take our leaders to an afternoon Yankee baseball game in the early summer of 2003. We were all diehard Yankee fans. This was not your typical charter bus trip, though. Max, Rodney, Steve, Nicole, and several of the branch managers in the Capital District converged on our Broadway office early that Wednesday morning, coolers filled with beer, wine, soda and water. Box lunches and ample snacks accompanied us on the ride south. Leaving Albany around nine with half the bus filled, we set out to pick up our Hudson Valley contingent in Newburgh, New York, approximately an hour south on the Thruway. The drinking did not officially start until we picked up Theresa, another of our regional manager friends, and her many managers. The game would start at 1:45 pm, so we had plenty of time to make our way to the Bronx, to the House that Ruth Built.

My godfather, the same man who gave me my first baseball glove, took me to Yankee Stadium for the first time when I was six. I took my son, James, to his first game when he was six as well. Mickey Mantle, Roger Maris, Yogi Berra and Tony Kubek were among the players little Michael aspired to emulate as I grew to love the game. But today, it was Derrick Jeter, A-Rod and the boys slugging it out against Cleveland. I was always up for a trip to Yankee Stadium. Onward to the Bronx we went on that sunny day in June.

It did not take long for Max, Rodney and Steve to pop their first beer. Others joined in, and the party began. By the time we arrived in the Bronx, half the bus, twenty-five or so bank employees, had a buzz working, and it was only noontime. The drinking continued once we arrived in the stadium, several groups going in their own direction. Max, Theresa and several others joined me as we found our way into the upper right field bleacher seats, on what would be a sunny and warm June afternoon. By the start of the game, Steve and a couple of the branch managers were showing signs of drunkenness; one of the managers, feeling the effects of the heat, got sick in the stands—embarrassing, but indicative of the out-of-control behavior that turns level-headed adults into errant teenagers.

As a recovering alcoholic, watching how alcohol strips away people's inhibitions reconfirmed the intelligence of my decision to stop drinking.

Max was always up for fun and this day was no different. He decided that our seats were not good enough, that we should go down after the fourth inning and try to find open seats behind home plate. Arguing with him when he was drinking was never a good idea, so I acquiesced. The four of us left the nosebleed section and headed toward home plate. Max was also very lucky and had a way of manifesting what he wanted. Voilà! He saw a group of four seats several rows back from the netting behind the plate. We watched for fifteen minutes to see whether or not people would return and to scout out if ushers were checking tickets. Then we made our break. No problem! Now we were close enough to see the curves and breaks in the pitches.

At the top of the sixth inning, I excused myself to use the restroom. Max, still drinking beer, also needed to relieve himself, so he joined me. He was intoxicated but cogent enough, while standing next to me at the urinal, to suddenly speak from his heart about his feelings toward my wife and the angst he was holding onto.

"Michael, I love you and can't tolerate the way she treats you. You deserve better than that. She's mean-spirited and a bitch," he said. His eyes welled with emotion. "I didn't want to hurt you by continuing to make excuses not to join you, but I'm afraid I will not be able to control myself and I'll tell her to fuck off."

Hearing Max come clean on his feelings was a relief, on one hand, to know why he wouldn't accept any of my invitations. On the other hand, his comments rang true, and I knew he was right.

I again had made another grave mistake in choosing a partner, a wife that saw me as a target for throwing daggers at my soul.

Albany Pro Musica

The guest list for the Christmas party in 2002 included Dr. Mike Waldman and his wife, Stella, whose son, Aaron, dated my wife's oldest daughter, Maggie. Mike was good-hearted and outgoing. He was about my age. I learned that evening that he sang with a well-regarded choral group called Albany Pro Musica. I had heard of this group's performances in the past and thought about singing as something that might relieve the duress that seemed to have no end. I overheard Mike and Stella talking about their upcoming concert.

I said, "Tell me about your group."

Mike said, "Albany Pro Musica had about fifty core members. The group performed a cappella with a wide repertoire. The group also performed what he called masterworks performances, usually with the Albany Symphony or other large orchestras."

"Are you interested?" Mike inquired.

"Definitely," I replied.

Mike said there were auditions being held for an upcoming masterworks performance of Beethoven's Ninth Symphony. The fourth movement was the chorale, "Ode to Joy," which would require well over a hundred voices. The venue for this performance would be the Roman Catholic cathedral in downtown Albany, a magnificent and austere setting for such an incredibly emotive symphony. I was up for it.

Albany Pro Musica was directed by David Griggs-Janower, chair of the music department at SUNY Albany. David had a PhD from Indiana

University and was nationally respected as a great choral director. He had built a small empire at SUNY Albany, with an exceptional quantity of vocal sheet music, catalogued and ready for use by his true love, Albany Pro Musica. His professorship at the university provided him the resources and the venue to rehearse every Tuesday evening from 7 to 9:30 pm. I auditioned and was brought in as a baritone to sing with the larger masterworks group. This would be my interview for acceptance into the core group. I was excited at the prospect of singing once again, with trained vocalists and musicians and a world-class director.

The pace and quality of the rehearsals were rejuvenating. I immediately felt at home. My spirit soared with the opportunity to sing beautiful music with talented singers, trained working musicians, composers, teachers of music or professionals, like me, who had the gift of voice and music accompanied by the desire to sing. And sing we did. My first performance at the cathedral with the Albany Symphony, Beethoven's Ninth Symphony, under the masterful direction of David Alan Miller, was spellbinding. I had never had the opportunity to experience a ninety-two-piece symphonic orchestra from just behind the brass section. This was by far my most thrilling experience to date.

Miller explained to the chorus during the dress rehearsal that he was stepping outside the normal tempo other maestros acquiesced to. He had researched the Ninth Symphony and ascertained that, in his view, Beethoven wanted the tempo of the symphony to be much faster than other renditions of this piece. The soloists, all nationally renowned artists, found the pace to be brutal, especially the tenor, whose solos were most affected. But Miller was determined to advance the tempo.

We entered the stage following the third movement. Once the 120-member chorus was settled, Miller tapped his baton on the music stand; the orchestra and the singers, donned in tuxedos and gowns, standing on four tiers of stage risers behind the musicians, gave him their attention. The fourth movement began.

Just prior to the chorale, Beethoven guides the music into a blend of jagged and beautifully ensnarled cascades of horns competing against a flurry of strings and then gently, with anticipation, leads the music into the first soloist's deep bass outpouring. In the middle of the chorale, the tempest of majestic staccato rises to a climactic infusion of biting strings. Miller's cadence felt like a rocket ship taking off, the bows of the violins beating rhythmically, biting each thirty-second note in unison. I thought I was going to lift out of my shoes. It was sensational and magical. I was lifted to a place I had not ventured previously. It was an experience I would never forget and a performance that to this day remains my favorite performance of this timeless masterpiece.

David Griggs-Janower invited me to join the core group following this performance. I gladly accepted. And there were other amazing moments while performing with Albany Pro Musica, performances that changed my life, moving me so deeply that I felt the presence of the divine. David had studied Johann Sebastian Bach for his doctoral thesis so he had an intimate and profound love and understanding for the intricacies of Bach's musical genius. David had dreamt of performing one of the most complex and beautiful compositions ever created: Bach's Mass in B Minor. For him, this was the pinnacle of performance, something he wanted to direct and perform his entire life. It was time, for he knew that he had the very best ensemble of voices he had ever brought together over the twenty-five years he had directed Albany Pro Musica.

This was the most difficult and detailed music I had ever come across. One of the blessings afforded to me while singing with this group was the opportunity to study and get inside the spirit of great composers. One cannot sing such intricate and exquisite compositions without hours of study and without getting inside the soul of the composer. J.S. Bach was masterful beyond my imagination, for this piece was not only the entire Mass, but was composed entirely from the hand of God.

Over several months, David would start each rehearsal by sharing his knowledge of Bach's intentions as expressed in musical passages within the Mass. I will never forget the eight bars of penetrating music symbolizing the hammering of nails into Christ's hands during his crucifixion. David's passion and knowledge of this masterpiece brought illumination and brilliance to our performance.

Two hours, a hundred and ten voices, accompanied by a fifty-two-piece orchestra, performed to a sold out Troy Music Hall audience of 1,200, we brought David Griggs-Janower's dream to fruition. There have been moments, divine moments where I could feel firsthand the imprint and whisper of the Divine moving within. This concert was one of those indescribable and life-altering experiences. Standing on the upper riser, in the middle of the performance, fifteen seconds before again bringing the basses and baritones into the Mass, I took a moment to look to my right and then to my left, acknowledging the hundred plus singers, all there sharing this magnificent experience together, and I was infused with the breath of God. It is one thing to experience majestic presence alone and apart from others, but an entirely different one when sharing something as intimate and full-bodied as performing music clearly ordained and created as a gift to humanity. I felt the collective spirits and souls of all those singing together, combined with the incredible beauty and expression of the musicians. But what was visceral and so deeply heartwarming was to watch David, standing on his podium, utterly consumed by the experience. I still see him, his eyes and spirit dancing to the cadence of sheer bliss. It was one of the most profound experiences in my life.

The other masterpiece we performed, two years later, in April 2008, at Troy Music Hall, was the Brahms Requiem. Again, the lush textured music of Brahms brought together another dazzling performance, one that lives indelibly and emotionally riveting.

These and other performances created picture-frame moments that remain powerful slices of my life in the first decade of the twenty-first century. In 2004, a group of twenty-six singers were invited to tour in France, performing nine concerts at some of the most spectacular cathedrals in the world, Notre Dame, the Cathedral of Rouen, Mt. Ste. Michelle, and various small-town chapels along the way.

As part of our tour in France, we were invited to sing at the sixtieth anniversary and commemoration of D-Day at Omaha Beach in Normandy. World leaders, dignitaries from across the planet and some of the remaining allied forces soldiers, mostly in their late 80s and 90s, attended this austere commemoration. Choking down our tears, we stood shoulder to shoulder and performed several hymns in honor of the fallen. We were deeply moved as we opened our mouths to sing. Later, I went down to the beach, walked along the shoreline, and imagined the horror and violence suffered in that infamous battle.

We were invited to tour in Spain two years later, in early spring 2006. I had met the love of my life, Janeen, in Lenox, Massachusetts, in May of 2005 and invited her to accompany me on that tour. She jumped through many challenges to make herself available to do so—finding childcare and support for her two sons, who lived in Port Jefferson, New York, ensuring that she had the time off from teaching, and all the many preparations necessary for a nine-day excursion.

Seville, Granada, Montilla and Malaga were among the locations we visited and performed. Having Janeen next to me, sharing in the marvelous travels, new cities, culture, food and the unique beauty of the Spanish people with their rich heritage was a delight beyond words.

I had heard many years prior that if one could travel easily with a partner, it was a good sign of compatibility. This was certainly the case with

Janeen. Our relationship since has encompassed traveling, moving and discovering new experiences together. Ours is a modern day love story, replete with drama, familial warfare, beating the odds and surviving endless change and challenge. I know firsthand that there are angels among us in human form. Janeen is an angel brought to me by a force much greater than me.

Moving to Troy

In November, 2009, Janeen and I sold our Niskayuna home, taking a $90,000 loss, and found a brownstone rental on Second Street in Troy directly across the street from the world class venue, Troy Music Hall, where I had performed with Albany Pro Musica. It was the most beautiful street in the town. Our top-floor bedroom window provided a view of turn of century rooftops that gave the feel of living in Europe.

Painful Admission

Uncovering what lies in our unconscious is hard, so coming to the realization that all my actions, all the painful turmoil attached to trying to be a good loving father to my growing son was for naught, pulled heavily on my heartstrings. By 2010, it had become evident to me that my relationship with James Mitchell was vaporous and at best, a struggle, both for him, for Janeen and me. He was well into adolescence, with stronger ties to his mother and her parents, not to mention his being subject to their perpetual vilification of Janeen and me. It did not matter what I did: his spirit was not aligned to me, and I was waking up to the reality that it wasn't in the divine plan for our relationship to improve.

James would ask to remain with his mother more and more during times when he was scheduled to be with us. The most loving action to take was to be present to the reality of the heartfelt loss.

CHAPTER 6 REFLECTIONS

[21] *This was the crucible moment of my life up to age 35. No other time had held such urgency and terror for me, for I knew that this would be a turning point, one way or the other. What was left of my intact sanity was tethered by a shoestring, teetering on the brink of making a decision to commit suicide. One thing after another seemed to be slipping through my fingertips. People, possessions, jobs and most indelible, my sense of self. My humanity was being challenged in a life and death psychic roll of the dice.*

[22] *Conscious leadership demands presence of body, mind and spirit. One of the greatest tools we possess as human beings is choice. Our thoughts create our intentions, which lead to our choices. Choices then determine our reality.*

What reality do you choose? Being present to choice gives you the opportunity to choose differently. Most of us operate on autopilot, living our daily existence in a pattern that becomes second nature, just the way we do things. Honest self-appraisal may lead us to the position that, the way things are, might not be the most optimal way to live our life, both personally and professionally. When we become present to our choices, we step into an elevated state of awareness. And when we are aware of our state of awareness, we step into consciousness.

I have learned by my own example the power of consciousness in making choices to lift others up, spending the extra ten seconds actually connecting with the human being in front of me. That human being—your employee, your spouse, your child, the neighbor, the person you meet on the street—they all feel a different connection when you tune into being present.

This higher degree of connectivity is in opposition to lower, duller frequencies associated with the many tentacles of fear. Put aside the fearful lower frequencies and choose love, caring and compassion for others. While you may think of this as a simple task, I assure you that it requires practice and a commitment to your own transformative power.

[23] *Not only did my addiction wreak tremendous havoc and damage psychologically, but physically I was much sicker than I knew. In fact, when I stopped drinking I had pickled my brain so much that stringing a complete and understandable sentence together was challenging. The whites in my eyes took nearly one year to heal and I suffered from deep depression for the first several months. All my organs and the various systems, including my digestive, were attuned to a daily dose of alcohol. Sleeping became a nightly adventure into nightmares, dark sequences of unrelated and entangled vignettes of disjointed people, places and events. It was a time of harsh chiseling and dismembering of old, non-working pieces of myself.*

INSIGHTS AND TOOLS

Be Present - Aside from what we may perceive, there is only this moment, nothing more and nothing less. Yet most of us live our lives attuned to re-living the past or fearful of an uncertain future, both of which pull us away from living fully engaged where life happens—now! When you turn off the autopilot governing your behaviors, you become aware of being aware and you step into the presence of living consciously. From this vantage point, you have opportunities to make life-filling choices, for yourself and for those you lead and love. Start each day acknowledging the breaths you take, the place you stand in and the environment in which you live. Make a commitment to being present to those you interact with, whether at work or in your home. Spend the extra seconds to actually be interested in the person in front of you. When you ask, "how's it going?" mean it. When you smile, do so from the presence of love. Where there is disappointment, discouragement or failure, experience the feelings fully, letting them pass through you. Don't hold onto that which pulls you downward. Let it go!

7

BE A SERVANT LEADER

From Self-Centered to Selfless Caring

There is no room in our human adventure for closed-mindedness, ignorance, prejudice, or any agenda that supports separation and distance from others who are different. Limiting beliefs about color, ethnicity, religious affiliation, sexual orientation, politics and many other topics separate us rather than unite us as a human family. We share the same emotions. Parents' love for their children is not limited to one nationality or part of the world. We all mourn the loss of a loved one and share in the joys of intimate connection. Love is not a geographical or cultural phenomenon. It is a universal reality.

Two thousand ten would be a turning point for Janeen and me. We were living in our third and fourth floor brownstone apartment in downtown Troy and great change was afoot. Our oldest son, Martin Dufner, still living with us, was attempting to take on higher education at Hudson Valley Community College, after securing additional support needed to accommodate his writing disability. Our son Matthew, however, had been accepted into Hobart William and Smith Colleges, on the banks of Lake Geneva in the Finger Lakes region of Central New York. Matt was in his spring semester of freshman year when Janeen and I were entertaining the possibility of relocating and changing my employment from the bank.

It did not take long for Martin to decide that further education was not his ambition. Hooking up with what appeared to be rather dark and lower vibrational friends, he became agitated more and more at having to abide by parental dictates. And quite honestly, his affect and behaviors were counter to where his mother and I were heading. The signs were clear that it was time for him to make his break from us. He was ready and so were we.

Martin broke my heart sometimes. His aptitude and verbal abilities were stunning and sharp, while his ability to live under the construct and rigors of a broken educational system rendered him a special needs student. His early years were marked by pervasive issues, and he seemed to have an internal bent toward anger, resentment and a caustic, less-than-acceptable level of respect and acceptance of his mother's many efforts to support and guide him. She had become the receptacle of his ire, vilified and targeted by his verbal aggression. He was a tough kid, not in the sense of violence and brutality, although his stature and physical frame were intimidating and intrusive. He was tough in the way he operated in his world, carrying a dark energy that others felt.

When I met Martin, he was at the age where his growth seemed to be out of alignment with his ability, giving him the appearance of being uncoordinated. He needed to grow into his immense size.

Janeen, Martin and Matthew moved from Port Jefferson, Long Island to Niskayuna in June of 2006. The boys were to enter their sophomore year. As much as Janeen and I tried to make the transition as painless as possible, there were factors outside our control that would make their entrance quite challenging.

There were many trials and tribulations raising him during his high school years. With his athletic prowess and his enormous size—he was six foot two and 220 pounds with shoulders the size of small buildings—it was logical to attempt to get him into the sports programs at Niskayuna High School. Mom and I made calls, set appointments and tried every avenue possible to open the right doors for him.

Martin met with the coaches and was invited to join the football team. Practice was to begin in August. Weeks before school officially started, however, Martin hooked up with a young lady who, unbeknownst to us, was the school troll, a dark urchin who had made quite a name for herself. She and Martin became a thing just prior to starting the school year, leaving his brother Matt in a most precarious position. Martin was eleven months older than Matt, but they had established a pattern from when they were small where Martin would ruin Matthew's good works, either by destroying any project he was working on or by creating such discord with friends that both boys would be picked up and not invited to parties, playtime and other normal activities. Now entering a new high school, Martin had already ruined any hope of Matt having a chance at a fresh positive experience. While they were separate people, the truth was that they came into school as brothers and everyone would quickly attach Martin and his troll girlfriend to Matthew.

In 2007, the boys began their junior year. Matt was particularly sensitive to the way others saw him, largely because of the loss of any real fatherly connection from his birth father. Neither of the boys had a strong positive male role model.

Janeen's ex-husband was a couch potato, a lazy and uninterested man who was unable to hold down a job, was in and out of mental health facilities, and suffered from bipolar disorder.

Both boys were negatively affected. Matt felt hurt and was psychically damaged by his father's lack of interest, casual disregard and complete inability to connect on any meaningful level. The combination of this loss and Martin's continued caustic behaviors led to Matt checking out, choosing to not attend school and to lie in his bed for days at a time. Janeen and I did not know exactly what we might find at the day's end with Matthew. We were very concerned about possible suicide. Something needed to be done.

Matt needed an alternative situation to mainstream high school. We started exploring options. On a cold early December morning, while driving to one of my branch locations, I picked up my cell phone and dialed private boarding schools throughout the tristate area, in the hope of finding a good place for Matt. I had jotted down several schools, including Darrow School, located in rural New Lebanon, New York, in the Berkshires near the Massachusetts border.

A friendly voice answered the phone. "Hello, this is Jamie. How can I help you?" After a fifteen-minute conversation in which I explained the duress our family was experiencing, Jamie indicated that Darrow was not your usual private boarding school. Darrow was an alternate living and learning environment with support and alternative learning programs for kids who don't fit the mainstream educational system. *Wow, it sounds great,* I thought after the call. I called Janeen. We were relieved to find an alternative that might make sense in a troubling and urgent situation. Matt was interested, so we made plans to visit the school during the upcoming winter break. On a particularly cold morning one week later, we traveled to the hillside boarding school, originally a Quaker village. Meeting with Jamie and touring the school, Matt and I found the environment inviting. And Matt immediately took a liking to the idea of getting away from his entangled situation, not the least of which was an opportunity to get away from Martin and their father. We decided to have him attend Darrow, which saved his life. Matthew thrived there and in June of 2009 graduated a new young man, confident, athletic and with a renewed spirit that would propel him further into his academic pursuits.

Unbearable Heartache

I worked hard at being a good father to James, keeping my schedule with him and providing whatever support I could, given the toxic conditions created by the incredible ignorance and hatred of the three-headed monster of mother and grandparents.

I broke from Marie Jane in 2000. While I was at work on a Friday, she packed her bags and took James to her parents' house and advised me that I would not have access to see my son. He was four years old and I was not accepting any ultimatum precluding me from seeing him. Infuriated, I drove to my in-laws' house demanding to see my son. Marie Jane's father, George, came out into the carport to engage with me, since I was not leaving. In a feeble attempt to threaten me, he advised that he had more than enough money to legally take me on. I decided it probably would not be a good idea to slam him into the ground, so I took a deep breath and said, "Excuse me! But I think you forget that I work for a bank. I have access to more money than your worthless idle threats!" He then thought it appropriate to tell me that his wife, Bertha, would like nothing more than to slice me up with a butcher knife and then vomit on my insides. I had always wondered just how deeply both parents hated me. I couldn't have gotten any clearer picture than that.

And the battle began, one that would carry on for years.

Proud Son

Summer break 2010, Matthew was home after his freshman year at Hobart. He had been academically successful, but his first year was consumed with rowing. At six foot four and as lean and strong as he was, he didn't stand a chance walking onto campus. Crew at Hobart, was a big deal, with Ivy League competitors vying for highly sought after trophies. Matt remembered me telling him the story of my first week at Syracuse University and being drawn to the crew team. For me, it was not a positive outcome; I was not tall or heavy enough for crew. I always carried this as a disappointment and Matt had absorbed my story about it.

He, on the other hand, was aggressively recruited. And it was grueling, requiring hours of daily practice, torn hands and early mornings in the cold of upstate New York. Janeen and I traveled to support him at regattas across the Northeast, with the biggest event being the New York State finals outside of Binghamton. All the competitions were exciting, but this one took the cake. Matt rowed as the fourth man in the eight-man shell and they went into the final competition with West Point the team to beat in the two-kilometer race. The gun went off and the ten teams exploded into their cadence. Janeen and I watched excitedly as the race was making its way toward the final push. Tension built as the announcer focused on the two teams vying for position, West Point and Hobart. We watched from the sideline as the noses of the two shells traded first place, not once but twice, then over and over again with alternating strokes. It was going to come down to a photo finish. It was everything one might ever hope for in a collegiate competition.

After twenty minutes the loudspeaker clicked on and the announcer said, "the photo finish showed that Hobart won!" Janeen and I jumped and screamed as Matt came up from behind, embracing us jubilantly. The tradition in this competition was for the losing team to give their shirts to the winners. We watched as the West Point team met their competitors with high fives, hugs and the eventual trade of shirts. Matthew relished the win, as did we, his glowing parents. Matt had turned into quite the athlete and had come so far from the pudgy, insecure young teen I first met in 2005. It was clear to me that all he needed was the guidance and eager support of a father willing and able to teach him how to excel in sports. Both Matthew and Martin learned to be competitors with my instruction and coaching. They were big boys. I immediately saw their talent and inserted myself in their lives. Matt was a state champion! This was as much a success for Janeen and me as it was for Matt that day.

Time to Move

By mid 2010 my relationship with James was deteriorating rapidly, especially as he grew in his adolescence. For many years, I had put aside promotions and advancements in favor of my strong allegiance and dedication to James. In my present marriage, had Janeen not moved from her successful teaching career and uprooted her two sons, our relationship would not have been fully realized.

Countless senseless conflicts ensued with James's mother and grandparents, so many attempts at providing him with great vacations, teaching him how to play baseball, basketball and even golf, yet nothing remained strong enough to embolden the father–son relationship. My best efforts were for naught.

Things change. People evolve. Dreams disappear. And hearts break. This was the case with me. I put up with years of abuse and a complete lack of appreciation for either my generosity or my strong commitment to be a role model for my son. I had to fight my way all along the path, only to be led to a dead-end street from nowhere. I learned a great deal about myself, which in the long run provided me with a much deeper appreciation for love, compassion and humility, but still I was left heartbroken.

I chose a different path, one that now supported me, my wife and my son Matthew. James may have been born of my genetics, but Matthew truly became my son, the one who showed up, the one who loved me for who I am, the one who let me love him fully, the one I adopted as mine and the one who at age seventeen went to his birth father and gained his agreement and signature to change his name from Dufner to Bianco-Splann. Our shared destiny was now in place.

With this growing separation from James, I started my job search, looking to leave the company that had now become oppressive and unproductive. And for the first time in many years, I now was willing and able to relocate. But where and how were the questions. My search took me all over the country, from one financial institution to another. Boston, Houston, Washington, D.C., Philadelphia, Ithaca, and Chicago were among the cities I visited for interviews. My success at the bank where I worked was impressive and opened the door to several opportunities, but no takers. I was talented but expensive.

I managed to travel for interviews without taking time off from my job. I did not raise red flags or prompt attention. But the months of my job search without landing the perfect offer led to some dark times. We persevered by staying united. Janeen was my savior during this time, always supportive and uplifting.

Then I received a call from a major bank in Arizona. A district manager position was available in Tucson, leading the retail branch locations in a large market. Janeen and I looked at each other and just shook our heads. Arizona? Neither of us had thought of relocating to Arizona. Being of a progressive and liberal disposition, the thought of relocating to this state made us ponder the possibility. But we remained open to the idea.

Several phone calls later, I was invited to Phoenix for the final step of the interview process. It was midsummer. The desert heat when I walked out of the terminal at Sky Harbor Airport in Phoenix felt as though I had opened the oven door at a pizzeria. It was only 112 degrees, milder than it had been earlier in the week, I was told. And the desert brown landscape was certainly not New York. It looked moonlike. But, it was an adventure, and I was always up for a new experience.

After a night at the downtown Sheraton, I had a morning meeting scheduled with Russ Bowen, the senior vice president of retail banking. I walked to the corporate building and went to the fifteenth floor, where I was greeted by Cora and Marnie. The first interview was with Mr. Bowen and the director of human resources, and the second, an hour later, was with two district managers, who would be my peers. Since this franchise in Arizona was primarily in-store banking locations, I told my interviewers about my many successes building and leading an in-store franchise in New York State. They were impressed by the level of creative leadership and methodologies that I had employed previously as well as the high performance awards garnered over the past several years. The interviews went very well.

Back in Troy, New York, my cell phone rang around six in the evening, as I was walking to meet Janeen after her yoga session. Not only did the bank in Arizona want me for the position, but they offered a relocation package of $25,000. When I discussed the offer with Janeen, we agreed that I should accept.

This was going to be a huge change, not only for us, but for Matthew as well. It was a dramatic decision for Janeen, in that it would mean giving up, for the third time, a tenured teaching position and ushering in a new phase in her life.

Matthew was getting ready for his sophomore year at Hobart. Our decision to move to Arizona caught him by surprise.

Summertime in Troy, New York, brought with it a terrific farmers' market by the Hudson River. The three of us had a ritual of shopping there on Saturdays, bringing home fresh arugula, mixed greens, tomatoes, farm-fed poultry and occasionally grass-fed bison. We also discovered a friendly Lebanese restaurant within walking distance. The proprietor and his son welcomed us graciously, and it became a favorite alternative to summertime cooking, especially in the oppressively warm summer of 2010. Janeen and I decided that sharing the news with Matt would be best communicated over delicious Middle Eastern cuisine. Food--quality food--was something we valued in our household, and Mediterranean was on our list.

As we ate the delicious salad, we announced to Matt that we had accepted an offer and would be moving to Tucson, Arizona. Matt reacted with a palpable fear that caught me by surprise. Janeen and I had discussed whether he would want to remain at Hobart, thinking that would be his choice.

Several seconds passed before words found their way to his mouth. "Tucson!" he exclaimed. "What about me?" No possible way to have misinterpreted his response. It was very clear that Matthew wasn't ready to have us leave him on the east coast. He was coming west with us.

We did not understand the challenges associated with moving across country. There were a monumental number of moving parts attached to uprooting ourselves and moving to the Sonoran Desert. And desert it was. As much as there was huge change to occur, we did not anticipate how physically, emotionally and spiritually draining this move would be.

Not only was I starting a new position with a new company, but my beautiful wife would be resigning her tenured position at Bethlehem High School; and now our son was to switch schools too. But which school? And more importantly, how would we make the transition at such a late juncture, for it was August and transfer application deadline had long passed. Our collective energies were aligned positively, so we simply accepted the many challenges we would face together. This was the genesis of what would become a core triad family unit, Janeen, Matthew and me, truly combining our lives in unison with each other. This pattern set the stage for many years to follow and provided a strong catalyst for growth, expansion and primacy of our unity.

The start date for my new position was set at August 16, 2010. We had a short window available to make the move. The good news was that we had downsized less than a year earlier when we sold our home in Niskayuna.

The challenging news was that we lived in an eighteenth-century walk-up brownstone with almost impossible steps and curved hallways, making an already daunting move that much more difficult. The move from Niskayuna to Troy almost disabled us completely. This time we would hire professional movers to lug boxes, furniture and goods down the four flights of stairs. It did not, however, mitigate the extensive packing that Janeen primarily performed. As for me, having little time available prior to starting in my new position, it made sense to go ahead and scope out the territory to find temporary housing, get a lay of the land and better understand the logistics of Tucson. There was still the question of Matt.

Quickly and efficiently we identified both Arizona State University in Tempe and the University of Arizona in Tucson as possible schools for his transfer. But the time for transfers had come and gone, so there was a sense of urgency associated with getting Matt settled in a new place of learning. Matt would come with me ahead of Janeen.

I kissed Janeen goodbye at the Albany International Airport, and Matt and I boarded our flight west. Our goal was to visit Arizona State the first day and then travel to Tucson, 112 miles south on I-10, to visit the University of Arizona. We stayed in Tempe the night of our arrival. Matt and I arose early and headed to the campus at ASU. It was summertime in the Valley of the Sun and the heat never relented. We met with a couple university representatives to gain access and to learn about the university. Matt was unsure of what he hoped to pursue for his undergraduate degree. We visited the school of architecture and design, which was something Matt was leaning toward. Because it was summer, very few of the 50,000 undergraduate students were on campus. This made it easy to get around the expansive campus, but we did not have the visceral excitement of 50,000 undergraduate students filling the space.

Matt was overwhelmed, yet enthusiastic as we moved around during our short visit. We grabbed a bite to eat at the student union building. I told him how different the campus was from Syracuse, where apart from the short seasons of spring, summer and fall, most of my memories were of blistering cold, feet of snow and a student body dressed like little Michelin men and women, bundled from head to toe, just trying to make it from point A to point B. The few scantily dressed female students we passed sparked Matt's interest. This wasn't Geneva, New York. He liked what he saw.

That afternoon we drove to Tucson, the city that would become my home for the next two plus years. Driving down I-10, we passed large hills that protruded from the brown hard-packed desert surface and looked like dinosaurs. There could not have been a place on the planet more different from where we had just come. The color green seemed to be in very short supply and the ruggedness of the terrain indicated something hostile, yet beautiful in its own way.

As we became more acclimated to the environment, we would learn that these hill formations would change colors depending on the angle of the sun, the season and the elements. Sunsets would be some of the most luminous events we ever experienced. The flora and fauna of this region was breathtaking, but it was a constant reminder of the danger of exposure. We came to respect the unforgiving ecosystem around us. Cacti dotted the landscape. Saguaros, some of them thirty-plus feet high, stood as sentinels, arms reaching upward, spines extended as a protective armor. Spring flowers painted the desert with yellow, aqua blues, vivid magentas, pinks and deep coral. Matt and I noticed the beauty and fierce hostility of the land we would come to call home-- including the varied animal life supported by this raw environment.

There were rattlesnakes, king snakes, lizards of many varieties, tarantulas, scorpions, poisonous spiders, wild javelin, bobcats, vultures and mountain lions that were always around, hidden for the most part, but that would show up when we least expected them.

Through a temporary housing company, I found my way to a condominium complex on the northwest side of the Catalina mountains, which form the picturesque backdrop for Tucson and its suburbs. Oro Valley sprang in the early 2000s. Higher-end subdivisions dotted the wilderness, with bigger, more spacious spreads on higher ground. The area included Dove Mountain, one of the most beautiful desert golf courses on the planet. The PGA held its annual Accenture Tournament at the magnificent Ritz Carlton course, where I was fortunate enough to play on several occasions.

A week before starting my new assignment, I decided to play a round of golf at one of the local courses in Oro Valley. It was the hottest time of the year, so getting a tee time was no issue. On my cart, moving from the first green to the tee box of the second hole, I stopped adjacent to the tee area. The good news is that I looked to my left several feet ahead of where I had parked, for there, coiled in a spiral of spotted grey, brown and black was a rattlesnake, now letting me know of his discontent by rattling his tail. I snapped a picture with my smartphone, but I thought twice about whether it was a good idea to send it to Janeen. I decided against it.

Janeen and I rented a two-bedroom unit in the Boulder Canyon complex during the first couple months in Tucson. This condo community allowed for a small percentage of units to be rented. Rental companies handled the arrangements, since Tucson was a destination for snowbirds, most of whom came from either the upper Midwest or Canada. With our relocation package in place, we chose to reside there to give us enough time to learn more about our new habitat. Some units were being completely refurbished and sold. We decided several months into our stay that buying one would be advantageous, for our intentions were to make this our home.

Janeen had left her teaching career, but her established SAT coaching business followed her to Arizona. As a high school teacher in Port

Jefferson, New York, she had used her teaching position as a catalyst for parents to send their teens to her for SAT verbal coaching. Her ability to meaningfully connect with sixteen- and seventeen-year-old students was remarkable.

Janeen is a great teacher. It's one thing to be intelligent and resourceful, but with Janeen, it is her heart that separates her from her peers. Her students felt her passionate calling and responded to her energy. And with the students feeling as strongly as they did about her teaching ability, the parents followed suit.

During the first year in Tucson, Janeen was able to continue her SAT coaching, since she met with students over the phone. But when she left teaching, the feeder system dried up, rendering her business devoid of students. This was a loss for her. I felt her despair and disappointment in losing this part of her professional practice. It would take time to heal. To assuage my own discomfort in knowing that each day I was leaving her alone, I thought of getting a dog. But we had had some terrible experiences with dogs so we decided to go slowly.

This time, Janeen and I didn't have a teenager begging us for a dog. This time it was our decision to make. We still bore the scars of our previous Armageddon of dog ownership, but nonetheless we agreed to explore the possibility. We went to the Humane Society of Tucson. We found an unusual environment where the animals were not only treated well, but were kept quiet by piping classical music into the kennels. It was brilliant. Many breeds were represented, from chihuahuas to bloodhounds to boxers to pit bulls. The volunteers at this humane society were gentle, loving people who cared deeply for the animals. There was one older volunteer named Mason who Janeen and I took an immediate liking to. His gracious affect helped defuse our anxiety. We told him about our past experiences with dogs in New York.

Mason assured us that we would find what we were looking for. He said he would be at the center tomorrow. "Let me take a look at our dogs. Based on what you are looking for, I think we'll come up with a solution."

"We'll come back tomorrow," we said to each other. Saturday morning came and we jumped in our car and proceeded across town to the humane society.

We arrived at the center around eleven and met Mason, who had been expecting us. The look on his face gave away his enthusiasm. "I have the perfect doggie for you," he said.

He took us through the kennel to a crated area with three medium-sized dogs, all sleeping to the sound of Vivaldi. "There. That one." He pointed. "His name is Jake, and he's a special dog."

In front of us was a ginger-colored dog of about fifty pounds with obvious Labrador marking and a wrinkled face that Mason claimed was of the Shar-Pei lineage. He guided us to the petting area outside the main kennels and said he would get Jake and bring him out to us. The first meeting was rather uneventful. Jake was obviously traumatized. But there was something about him that both Janeen and I were drawn to. After discussing whether Jake would be the right dog, we decided to take him home with us. Poor Jake didn't know what to do. We had gotten him some chew toys hoping that he would entertain himself, but he did not even know how to play. What form of cruelty had he been through? The name Jake did not fit our new family addition. But what should we call our new friend? After spending time with him, I grabbed his cute jowls and told Janeen that he was a moosh-doggie. Moosh led to Moshe, Hebrew for Moses, who was in some sense a savior. It seemed appropriate for him and for us. But the question was always, who saved whom?

Shortly after Moshe joined us, we noticed that he was struggling to keep food down. Janeen tried to find the right food for him. She combined cooked chicken with rice so that he might gain strength. This was a short-lived experiment; his digestion was clearly a problem. We took him to the veterinarian at the Human Society and were told that there was no visible medical issue. The vet felt strongly that something was not right about his condition though. She recommended exploratory surgery to ascertain whether there were internal issues with Moshe. We explained that we did not have the funds for surgery and the doctor graciously agreed to perform the surgery gratis. Janeen has always been extraordinary in her ability to not only ask for what she wants but to get it. In this case, without getting the humane society to pick up the costs of the surgery, we would not have been able to keep our four-legged friend.

Nothing seemed abnormal in his internal organs and the veterinarian concurred that it might be allergies or a food sensitivity. After the surgery Moshe was wrapped in a medical body sock, protecting the incision. He was quite unsteady, having been anesthetized for the surgery. We now lived in a three-bedroom condo on the second floor of the north side of the complex. So I picked him up ever so gently and carried him up the stairs. We are convinced that this emboldened my loving relationship with Moshe.

Another veterinarian at the animal hospital across town prescribed a hypoallergenic dog food that seemed to do the trick. Moshe was on his way to a healthy life with Janeen and me. What we had only dreamt of previously had actually come true.

It took time and love to bring Moshe out of his past abuse. Slowly he loosened up and began to get close to Janeen and me. One of the greatest gifts we have ever received has been Moshe.

In Tucson we came to believe that rattlesnakes lurk around every corner, and rattlesnake bites to dogs was a huge concern. We investigated rattlesnake dog training and reluctantly decided to get Moshe trained to protect him and us from attacks. Because the training is done with live rattlesnakes, Janeen let me take Moshe to his scheduled appointment. We drove down Tangerine Road, well into the desert, to the training facility.

The instructor, a man in his late thirties, said there would be three parts to the training that involved smell, sound and sight. First was the sound of the rattle. The man guided us away from the kennels onto a hard-pan desert driveway. He placed an electric shock training collar on Moshe and told us to stay where we were, and he went several yards away to some small covered cages, each about three feet square. He took off a cover and I could see that there was a medium-sized rattlesnake in the cage. He brought the cage to about twenty feet from where we were standing and told me to walk slowly toward the cage with Moshe. As soon as Moshe noticed the sound of the rattle, in an instant he went from standing on all four legs to being airborne, jumping vertically higher than my six foot one height. The trainer had pushed the button on the control in his hands to deliver a shock to Moshe's neck. The dog was terrified.

"Wow, was that necessary?" I asked.

The trainer said that perhaps he had set the controls too high.

On to the next exercise.

This time the trainer went to another cage and brought a solo snake out of the cage, holding it in his hand. Placing the snake on the ground outside its cage, he backed away, instructing me to move Moshe toward the snake, whose rattle had been removed. As I walked Moshe within ten feet of the snake, he turned to the snake, clearly smelling it. Zap again! This time Moshe only leapt a couple feet in the air. Sound and smell learning was complete.

There was only sight left to train for. The man grabbed the loose rattler and put it back into its cage. Then he called to us to come further into the desert area where there was another cage sitting by a large saguaro cactus. Inside this cage were several rattlesnakes. As we moved closer, the man waited to observe when Moshe first brought the snakes into focus. A turn of Moshe's head and the recognition of the snakes prompted the last jolt of electricity. This time it was apparent by Moshe's terror that he was done. And so was I. I paid the man for his training and packed Moshe back into my car, petting him to calm him down and we proceeded to go home. It was challenging for Moshe, but equally challenging for me to see him shocked by the electrical nodes around his neck. But rattlesnakes were to be taken seriously, I reassured myself, mostly out of guilt for having put him through the torturous training.

One early evening, with the sun setting as darkness rolled across the desert, Janeen called to me in the kitchen that she was taking Moshe out for his evening walk. The door shut and within five seconds opened again. Janeen came in and closed the door behind her. She excitedly told me that as she was walking down the twelve steps leading outside, she spied what appeared to be a snake slithering to the right along the ground.

I asked, "Are you sure?"

She was sure she had seen a snake.

We couldn't live afraid to leave our second floor home. "I will take Moshe out for his walk," I said. Janeen said she would join me. Darkness in the desert comes on quickly, so by the time we exited our condo, flashlight in hand, it was nearly dark. Slowly we proceeded down the stairs. Knowing that Moshe had been trained gave us a bit of comfort, but we were still consumed by the fear of running into a rattlesnake in the dark.

Path lighting along the walks next to the buildings provided cone-shaped illumination, but there were also trees and other plantings that could easily hide a venomous reptile. We made our way to the bottom of the stairs, holding Moshe closely to us. We shone the flashlight from side to side. No snake. I thought, *Did Janeen actually see a snake?* We proceeded left along the sidewalk. Hearts raced as we walked ever so slowly. About fifteen feet from the entrance to our stairway, I shone the flashlight to the right and up. On the tree trunk right in front of where we stood was a six-to-eight-foot rattlesnake clinging to the five-inch diameter trunk, right at eye level.

Janeen and I both screamed as I pulled her and Moshe away from the tree, moving as quickly as we could in our panic. From that day forward, we were uneasy and constantly vigilant in that environment, always on the lookout for a creepy crawler. It would not be the last time we encountered rattlesnakes.

Danger had been a casual acquaintance of mine throughout my life, in one form or another.

Earlier Danger

It was a six-hour drive from Syracuse to New York City on a good day. Barring snow, wind, or traffic jams, I would make the trip several times during the spring semester of my senior year at Syracuse University. It was March 1977, a gray, rainy Friday around 5pm, when I crossed the Tappan Zee bridge from Nyack into Westchester county on route to visit Sandy, the sister of my housemate, who was attending Columbia University.

Sandy had visited her brother, Sam, my roommate, earlier in the spring, and wouldn't you just know that we hit it off big time. Almost immediately we bonded and ended up moving rapidly to becoming sexual playmates. Both Sam and Sandy came from money, big money from a Midwestern family deeply connected to corporate wealth. And Sandy, an attractive, freckled redhead with deep blue eyes, was brilliant and charismatic and she touched the part of me that was attracted to uniqueness in feminine form.

Sandy lived on the fringes of the university neighborhood in a two-bedroom apartment on West 117th Street in Harlem. Harlem in the 1970s was no place for a middle-class white guy. Gentrification would come twenty years later. At this time, it was a haven for the oppressed, beleaguered and poor. The area was rife with violence, prostitution and drugs, but visiting Sandy outweighed the potential danger.

Finding a parking spot for my beat up 1972 Plymouth Fury was challenging, for the car resembled more of a boat than a vehicle. I finally found a space two blocks away. I made my way to her fourth floor walkup, anticipating a warm welcome and two days of bliss. The best laid plans of mice, men and college students were for naught this time. But, unbeknownst to me, Sandy had pulled away. My trip this time was a surprise visit that ended very poorly.

Cell phones did not exist at this time, nor did much of the technology of modern day living. Sandy was unprepared for my arrival on that Friday evening. I knocked at the door once, twice and a third time. I then heard noise coming from inside the apartment. A man cracked open the door, with the chain lock in place on the other side. "Yes, how can I help you?" he said in a deep voice.

"Is Sandy home?"

"Who are you?" he asked.

"I'm her boyfriend," I said.

The door closed quickly and for thirty seconds I heard muffled voices from behind the door. A dark energy swept through me. I sensed trouble. The door opened. Sandy was standing there disheveled, with a just-got-out-of-bed look.

"Hi Sandy, what's going on?"

Joe, the unknown guy in question, was her sleeping mate and new boyfriend. "I didn't get a chance to talk to you about him," she said.

"No, shit!" I said. "Fuck you, Sandy."

I retraced my steps back down the flights of stairs, through the front door of the apartment building and on to West 117th Street. I was hurt and furious at the same time.

It was 8:30 pm as I walked the two blocks back to my beat-up Fury. Rounding the corner, I spied my light blue boat. Someone behind me said, "Hey motha-fucka!"

I turned around and saw a disheveled thin male, about thirty years old, coming toward me with a knife in his hand.

I was annoyed more than anything else; my stronger emotions were focused on my anger and disappointment with Sandy. Out of some corner of my mind, rapid fire reflex kicked into gear. When the drug addict was about four feet from where I stood on the sidewalk, I caught his direct glance and then feigning surprise, looked over his left shoulder and said, "Hey John!"

The would-be attacker, caught off guard, turned to see who I was talking to. I clocked the left side of his face with a strong right just as he turned back to me, upon realizing that there was no John behind him. Right, left, right, right, left to the head. He folded forward and I caught him with my right knee directly to his nose, causing him to collapse head first into the concrete sidewalk. I wasn't done yet. I kicked him in the head with my Frye boots repeatedly. He was now unconscious.

There, laid out half on the sidewalk and half on the street, lay my knife attacker, unconscious and bleeding profusely. He hadn't picked a good time to attempt to rob me. I pulled away, collected myself and turned to see if anyone had witnessed my retaliatory attack. I opened the door to my Fury, started the monster, put it in drive and headed out of Harlem for another six-hour trip upstate. *Ah, the trials and tribulations of dating*, I thought. What we go through for young infatuation.

Ten years later, the center of my affection would be not the curved, sensual shape of a beautiful woman, but rather alcohol and cocaine, with occasional heroin and meth. Either way, my desires would lead me into perilous adventures. That I lived through many of these dangerous episodes can only be attributed to the support of angels, masters and forces beyond understanding.

Life-Changing Events

Some events shake us to the core and create indelible incisions in our psyche. My life has had its share of lasting impressions, markers delineating chapters of growth and development along the path.

I was eight years old on November 22, 1963, a day that, for our generation, changed the political landscape, rendering the American experience as dangerous and uncertain. President John Kennedy's assassination taught a nation--and a world--that permanency, security and civil order were on shaky ground. As kids we didn't truly understand the significance of this death, but we knew enough to feel the collective heartbreak, the mass outpouring of sadness, loss and disorientation.

My family had recently moved back to the United States from the Philippines. My father was stationed at Olmsted Air Force Base--now Harrisburg International Airport--along the Susquehanna River. We lived in New Cumberland, where my parents had enrolled my brother and me in third grade at the Saint Theresa parochial school. At around eleven in the morning, the speaker above the teacher's desk squawked on with its usual clicking and clacking. Mother Superior's voice crackled with a visceral feeling that something was terribly wrong, "We have just learned that President Kennedy has been shot. All classrooms are to immediately proceed to the church." Our teacher, herself a nun, ordered the twenty-five students, now caught in the confusion of hearing words that would linger in our memories for our lifetimes, to stand up, form a line and march through the halls to the church. We knew the drill. Within minutes the entire student body, along with the teachers and administrators, were seated. The priest, visibly shaken, commenced the service. Tears, weeping and confusion ripped through the students. As children, all we knew was that our president had been shot. It wasn't long after this that we learned he had died. We were sent home after the Mass and the next several days captivated an entire nation's emotions.

These types of events crystallize moments in time that define where we were and who we were with. They affect us collectively, transcending our uniqueness and individuality.

Other collective moments were less dire, but equally affecting. The man who most memorably channeled America's sadness and grief during the days after the president's death was the veteran newscaster Walter Cronkite.

The sixties were turbulent years, with massive changes occurring in every aspect of the social, economic and cultural foundations within our country. The space age was upon us and the race between the US and the Soviet Union to land humans on the moon formed a backdrop for it all.

Kennedy had set a goal for the United States to land a man on the moon within a decade of his inauguration. And it was again Walter Cronkite who best expressed the excitement at NASA's technological triumph on July 20, 1969, when that goal was achieved. The evening was a warm one in our Middletown residence. We were captivated by the prospect of landing on the moon's surface for the first time. I had grown up in the era of astronauts. From John Glenn to Neil Armstrong, these men were our childhood heroes. My father, who was active Air Force during the early part of my life, reinforced the importance of the space program.

Popular culture was in a major transition too. Four kids from Liverpool, England, made their American debut on the *Ed Sullivan Show* in 1964. The Beatles changed everything. These charming and talented musicians stepped onto the stage at CBS Studio 50--now the Ed Sullivan Theater--in New York City and brought a nation into the era of British rock. More importantly, the power of television to connect with a national audience by bringing live broadcast into the living rooms of millions of Americans created a new world order. As nine-year-old Michael, I knew that music was to play a vital role in my life from that day forward.

9/11

On September 11, 2001, I had just tuned in to public radio on my ten-minute trip from my Academy Road residence in Albany to the Broadway office where I was preparing for a sales leadership training program. "Breaking news. We are just now learning that a plane has flown into the World Trade Center. Details are just coming in," the announcer said. How odd, I thought to myself, pulling into the parking lot. It was a spectacularly gorgeous September morning, sky clear blue with the chill of early fall in the air. Entering the building I could see that several of my colleagues had gathered in the executive conference room, where the TV was tuned into what was happening 150 miles to the south. I felt a chill in my bones as we watched the second aircraft hit the other tower, exploding into a ball of fire and debris. The reporter's gasping reaction captured our collective response, for we now understood in a second that this was not an accident. At the same time, reports were surfacing that another commercial aircraft had been detected off course and heading toward Washington, D.C., while additional reports were coming in that another aircraft was being monitored as off course and unresponsive over Pennsylvania. My first reaction was to think, *where else will see attacks?* Was this an orchestrated series of attacks against federal government installations? Were we in danger ourselves due to the close proximity of the federal building, three blocks from our headquarters? What was happening? Were we under a greater attack in the homeland?

My thoughts swirled around how it was only a matter of time before we in the United States experienced what other parts of the global community had been living with for generations. Terror, in its most insidious fashion, creates internal angst, pulling us from a sense of security and peace. The internal firestorm associated with terror takes away any sense of calm, adding gasoline to an already burning ember of fear, exploding into a massive searing fire within. That became the collective experience of so many around me following the attack. I felt the massed tension that everyone was experiencing. And being familiar with New York City, I especially felt the pain and realization of tremendous loss, not just for those who died, but for loss of peace, familiarity and the exuberant spirit of New York City. No surprise in how New Yorkers responded during this tragedy. When confronted with collective malaise, New Yorkers are resilient, loving and able to put aside differences to join together to support each other in bold ways.

But Wait, There's More

Other events, too, have come to define my life. Saturday morning, January 8, 2011, began with a bright, clear blue sky similar to that of 9/11. Janeen and I had intentions of enjoying a weekend together in the desert. The coffee was brewing and we donned our robes, prepared to settle in for a quiet and enjoyable morning, perched on our comfortable couch viewing Mount Lemon in the distance. I was half finished with my first cup of black coffee when my BlackBerry rang. I had a separate phone for personal use to guard against any possible conflict of interest. The BlackBerry was strictly for my job.

On the other end was the operations manager, Roberta, who said she had just gotten a call from Nick, the assistant branch manager at one of my branch offices, in the Safeway grocery store on Oracle and Ina. Nick said there were gunshots fired and confusion in the store. Roberta did not have any further information, but told me she wanted to let me know. I said I would handle the situation and hung up.

I told Janeen what I knew and said, "I should go to find out what happened, just to make sure the team is okay."

Gunshots in the Tucson area are not unusual. It was common to see people with guns in waist holsters. At gas stations, in supermarkets, at malls, and even at Rotary meetings, carrying guns was the norm. The Second Amendment in Arizona takes on a whole new meaning. So when I heard that there were gunshots fired, as troubling as it sounds, it was not unusual.

Today, however, would be a different experience altogether. I jumped into a pair of jeans, a collared sport shirt and a blazer. I took a last sip of coffee, kissed Janeen and told her, "This won't take long. I will be back shortly." That turned out not to be true. Within ten minutes of receiving the call from Roberta, I was on my way to the supermarket, three miles away.

Approximately a quarter mile from the intersection traffic was starting to back up. I decided to pull off Oracle into a strip mall about 150 yards from the intersection. I started walking toward the cross street, Ina. Off to my left, I could hear what sounded like helicopters. As I approached, the noise grew louder and I now could see three rescue helicopters on the pavement, rotors still turning, while another two were flying in tandem jockeying to land at the Ina entrance to the shopping plaza. Something was terribly wrong. This wasn't just some random gangbanger shooting. As I made my way on the north side of Ina along a dirt pathway, I saw police stationed at the intersection, completely shutting down Ina. Ambulances were arriving as I continued to move along the path to the side entrance. Things were happening fast. I saw a stretcher being rolled from the entrance of the Safeway to one of the medevac helicopters. I later realized that I was watching Congresswoman Gabrielle Giffords being taken from the scene after being shot in the head by a deranged young man.

I reached for my cell phone to call Janeen. I said, "Baby, whatever happened here was huge! This looks like a war zone." As I was speaking with my wife, I could see that local reporters were starting to arrive at the scene, trying desperately to cross Ina and get closer to the action. Local police were screaming to anyone trying to cross the road, "Get back! Get back!" No one was being permitted to come into the plaza area. Clearly it was being secured as a crime scene. But I had employees inside the store and I remained unsure of what had occurred. Janeen, still on the phone, was anxious and concerned. "I need to get inside," I said.

She said, "Be careful."

I said, "I'm going in."

I hit the end button on my phone and placed it in my belt holster. I took a deep breath, looked right, then left. I saw many police officers on the south side of Ina, directly across from where I was standing. They had secured the perimeter around the shopping plaza. Police dogs were in plain view. Stepping out onto the road, I walked with a deliberate gait to the other side of the street without a single notice from any of the many police officers, FBI personnel and dogs in front of me. I had chosen to be confident and purposeful in my action, but what I had not anticipated was being completely invisible to everyone around me. It was as though I had stepped into an alternate reality. I continued moving toward the front of the Safeway store. The front of the building looked like a MASH unit, with gunshot victims being attended to on the ground. Several others were taken out on stretchers, with the most serious being placed in the remaining two rescue choppers and the others placed in waiting ambulances.

The scene was something out of a horror film, but I calmly and stealthily moved ever closer to the secondary entrance to the store, farther into the shopping area. I passed police German shepherds, who didn't flinch or have any reaction whatsoever to my advance.

I banged on the glass doors of the entrance closest to my branch office. I spotted the Safeway assistant store manager on the other side of the door and caught her attention. She realized who I was and came over to pry back the sliding doors to let me into the store. Grateful that I had actually gotten into the store, I proceeded immediately to my branch office, where Nick and Leeann were visibly shaken and instantly relieved to see me. I hugged both of them and then asked what happened, since it was all a blur to me at that point. Leeann was particularly anxious and visibly traumatized. As I backed away from the hug, she caught her breath, still with tears in her eyes. I sat her down at one of the customer stations and held her hand. "Tell me what happened."

"It was about 9:45am, and I was in the process of setting up a marketing table outside the main entrance to the store. It's a beautiful morning, so I wanted to be able to greet shoppers and invite them to bank with us," she explained. "I took our folding table outside to find the best place to set up. I saw that Congresswoman Giffords and her team were also setting up on the north side of the entrance. I decided to have our table adjacent to where she had set up on the other side of the doors. After unfolding the table, I returned to the branch to get other supplies. Nick was preparing for the opening at 10am as I gathered supplies. It was about 9:50am when I made my way back to the entrance and out to the table. I set up the display with our bank flyers and realized that I still needed several other items. I came back to the branch and gathered what I needed and turned to go back outside when a regular customer of ours, who had come in the door closest to the office, called over to me as I was walking. She and I had formed a great relationship, so I turned around to walk toward her."

Leeann's breathing seemed tight and her eyes continued to well up as she relived what had just occurred minutes earlier.

"Just as I did, I heard a commotion and what sounded like gunshots, pop, pop, pop, in rapid fire. There was instant confusion. People were running, screaming, and several of the store employees were moving toward something happening just outside. Then I saw a couple people fall to the ground right at the entrance. It was surreal. I ran back to the branch office, opened the door and screamed to Nick that someone is shooting at us. We both hid under a desk as the scene was unfolding."

Leeann, now weeping, attempted to regain her composure. I held her hand and reached out to put my other hand on her shoulder to provide some degree of comfort. In between her shortened breaths and sobbing, she told of how close she was to being in the middle of the onslaught. "If Diane had not called out to me when she did, I would have walked right into the gunfire as it was happening. I could have been shot and killed," she said. And as much as I wanted to comfort her, she was absolutely right. It was only by the grace of another person calling to her that she was prevented from walking in front of a bullet.

A few minutes later the phone rang. "This is CNN calling. Do you have any information that you can provide us regarding the incident now being reported at your location?"

I did not have any solid information and knew that it would not have been appropriate for me as a bank executive to provide any information to the media. At 10:30am, less than an hour into a major event, the media was on top of it. I shook my head in wonderment as I continued to assess the situation. Calling my direct report manager, I advised what had happened to the best of my ability, telling him that I would stay with Nick and Leeann until we had the situation under control. He stated that he would ensure that all relevant bank personnel were informed.

Within one hour I received a call from the bank CEO's staff, checking on our wellbeing. "I will be calling you every thirty minutes to check up on how you are doing," the representative said.

Seven hours later, we were released by the FBI. The grocery store had turned into a crime scene, like one you might see on *CSI*. Blood was visible in several locations, including the branch office, where two victims were initially treated. Yellow crime scene tape crossed a large section of the main store entrance, where the bulk of the shooting had occurred. The store employees, visibly in shock, wandered around the Safeway zombie-like, some experiencing uncontrollable tears and others appearing to be caught in a nightmare with vacant and lost looks on their faces.

Both branch employees calmed down over the hours of waiting. My spirit was engaged in supporting everyone within my grasp, minimally by sending them love and compassion, but also in remaining open to listening with great empathy. It was simply impossible for those around me to find any justifiable reason or rationality for what had materialized on that sunny bright Saturday morning. And as much as I held my own feelings in check, the impact was visceral and profound. It would take days to fully realize the extent of this event and the trauma associated with experiencing such a heinous act of terror. And I had not forgotten about my miraculous trek from the sidewalk to the interior of the store. *How was this even possible*, I thought.

In my position with the bank I led eighteen branch offices primarily located in the greater Tucson area, but inclusive of outlier offices to the north and south of the city. I had planned a manager meeting for Monday, two days after the shooting. Given the enormous psychological impact on the community following this event, I thought it necessary to hold the meeting as scheduled. A pall of sadness and loss had infiltrated the community of Tucson after the shooting.

Monday morning, I arrived at my office early to prepare for the manager meeting. As the managers arrived, I greeted each one of them warmly with hugs. The managers came into the building already feeling the collective response of disbelief, all aware that the killing had occurred within twenty-five feet of our branch office, that our two associates were in the heat of this tragedy. Without saying a word, everyone knew how dangerous the situation was for Nick and Leeann. All the material that I had planned on delivering to the manager team was eliminated from the agenda. The only topic this day was to share our grief and our sadness to support each other in trying to find some way to deal with the event. We gathered around the conference table and began the meeting with a moment of silence.

I said, "I don't know what to say, team. Having been there, witnessing the horror of such cruelty and insanity, I am heartbroken." Uncontrollable emotions surfaced and I was overcome with such deep loss and sadness, all I could do was weep.

In an instant, I was surrounded by several managers weeping along with me, holding each other and just standing together in complete wholeness, literally holding each other up. It was a moment of vulnerability and humanness I will never forget. In that instant, everyone put aside their worries, their beliefs, their insecurities and came together in a unison of shared emotions.

The incident became an international event, with media from around the globe converging on Tucson. I saw Brian Williams broadcasting from a hillside location directly across from the side entrance to the shopping plaza I had used. Satellite broadcast mobile vans littered the west side of Oracle for well over a week. Within days, President and Mrs. Obama came to Tucson in an act of national reverence and tribute for the grave losses that had occurred.

That I had been there haunted my psyche as the days unfolded. I became quite emotional with Janeen the following Sunday as I relived the ordeal, trying to find the right words to express my utter sadness and the experience of being in the middle of the event, as I was. It was as though I had no control over the emotions that were surfacing. As much as I pride myself on remaining composed and under control, not this time. Surely, I was suffering from the shock of the event. That the entire Tucson community was collectively imbued with the totality of what had occurred added a palpable darkness to my already frayed emotions.

After all, we were just humans having a spiritual experience together, one that would continue to reside deep within my memory.

Divine Light

I have often wondered why unexpected divine interactions occur in my life. From my earliest recollection, I have heard the voice within, soft yet visceral, deep within my spirit, whispering to me, nudging and calling me to notice something being missed or supporting me from an alternative reality. And these divine intersections, while sporadic and unannounced, have occurred out of the blue, unsolicited and surprising.

It was early springtime in upstate New York, 2001. My doctor fiancée and I were now living together in our expansive home, lying on our bed discussing upcoming events as the cool rain blanketed the Saturday afternoon. There were small windows of warmth and lovely sharing between us that always pulled me closer to my wife to be. Unfortunately, these memories are fleeting and overpowered by the incredibly harsh and vicious entanglements between us as we moved forward in our relationship. This day, however, was one of those magical times where we felt close to each other and eagerly shared our vision of a bright future. As I lay there, draped sideways across the bed, gazing into her eyes, we chatted about plans for our upcoming marriage in February 2002. It was a rare occasion that we found ourselves intimately engaged in sharing an optimistic event ahead, one for which I recall feeling such appreciation and gratitude. As she was talking to me, I listened intently.

Then, in the middle of a sentence, all of a sudden her eyes opened wider. She looked awestruck and shocked. Her affect changed as she sat up and continued to look at me as though something dramatic was happening. "What is it?" I asked. Her eyes were the size of silver dollars. "Oh my God," she said. "Your face! It's illuminated with bright light." Now standing in the middle of the bedroom, she continued. "All of a sudden your eyes lit up, your face became filled with sparkle, and there was an aura surrounding you."

I was completely caught off guard and did not know what to say.

"What are you feeling?" she asked.

"I was just filled with such love and compassion while you were sharing your thoughts with me," I said.

By now the light had faded and we were both together again as we had started. It was a moment when divine love filtered through me, not just within but as though I was the conduit, the channel for its magnificent expression. It was another reminder that I was not alone, but rather connected to a spiritual reality beyond the limitations of our 3-D construct. Despite this ten-second visitation of divine energy, the relationship continued to follow a destructive path. Yet it was, for me, another divine occurrence and message of union with a greater power and love.

Trying to Understand

Days after I met with my managers following the shooting spree in Tucson, the bank provided both Nick and Leeann counseling services to address their trauma from the incident. I was also offered counseling, but I declined, stating that I was fine. As I would continue to be reminded by sudden infusions of uncontrollable emotion, though, I was anything but fine. The effects of the event were psychically embedded in me, causing intermittent breakdowns. I was perplexed by my inability to manage my emotions and particularly curious as to exactly how I was able to make my way into the store that Saturday morning, despite the police, FBI and dogs that secured the area around the crime scene. *How could I have made it through the secured area without anyone even noticing me*, I thought over and over again.

After several days of experiencing these emotional outbreaks, I decided to try and find support. Janeen and I reached out to our naturopathic doctor to find the right counselor. As it so happens, there was a spiritually centered alternative practitioner working within the health center where our doctor practiced. We were referred to her and set an appointment that next Friday afternoon.

Jennifer was a middle-aged woman with a beautiful smile and grace that exuded from her eyes, as though she was walking with an internal light. It became clear to Janeen and me that Jennifer was gifted. I provided her with the grisly details of my trek into the crime scene, along with the fact that I was clearly invisible to the authorities as I made my way across the street, parking lot and MASH unit set up in front of the store entrance, to eventually get inside the store.

"How could this have happened?" I asked.

Jennifer smiled and said, "let's see if we can find out why you were able to do this."

Jennifer was trained in eye movement desensitization and reprocessing, otherwise known as EMDR, a technique not unlike hypnosis. She explained that in order to expose the trauma held in the unconscious state this procedure supports bringing the trauma forward and replacing it with positive emotions. We listened intently and agreed that it was certainly worth a try.

Jennifer repositioned her seat to be directly in front of me, only a couple feet away. Gazing directly into my eyes, she reached for a blue pen sitting on the desk. "I want you to focus only on my pen," she said. Holding the pen a foot in front of my nose, she began to move the pen from left to right and back in a slow cadence as she spoke. "Take me back to standing on the curb across the street as the situation was unfolding in front of you. What are you experiencing?" Concentrating on the pen moving back and forth, I started to recollect and share what was happening. Taking Jennifer through the ordeal, I gave specific details, sharing what was going through my thoughts as I walked into the police line, the FBI, the dogs and the many first responders who were attending to those wounded. But nothing was coming as to how I had been able to magically wind my way unnoticed and into the store.

Frustrated by failing to gain any understanding, I remarked to Jennifer, "but I still don't know how this happened."

"Let's try it again. Once more I started at the same place and again traced my path into the store. And again, nothing to answer the question. Repositioning herself slightly, she said, "one more time, Michael. This time concentrate on where you were in your psychic state as you were talking to Janeen on the cell phone. Step outside your physical body to elevate yourself as an observer." She began to move the pen back and forth as I once more went inside to relive the experience.

Jennifer must have known that there was something happening beyond my ability to see directly into what was occurring. This time I started by remembering the conversation with Janeen, sharing with her the incredibly horrendous scene that was unfolding in front of me. I was able to separate myself, almost as a third party observer watching me from a distance. "I'm going in," was the last piece of communication with Janeen. Energetically there was a convergence of purposeful intent which, from a distance, provided what appeared to be a sudden burst of power. In an instant, I was able to clearly see what I had missed in the previous attempts at understanding how I was able to achieve access while remaining unnoticed. From the vantage point of the observer, there appeared a friend that I had met once before while under hypnosis in past life regression. And this friend was an angel. Yes, wings and all. When I ended the call after speaking with Janeen, he appeared, sweeping in at that very moment. Standing beside me as I looked across the street analyzing my route and making the decision to go for it, my very tall, shoulder-length-blond-haired angel opened his left wing and covered me as if with a cloak. Stepping off the curb and moving with assuredness, he completely shrouded me with his wing as we both glided across the crime scene. As startling as this was, it made perfect sense, as I was invisible to everyone that morning. Once I arrived at the side entrance, in an instant, he was gone.

I have had these extraordinary events throughout my life, all of which occurred suddenly, without provocation or intent. The divine support and periodic reminders of the unfiltered and unconditional love have clearly shown how deeply connected we are to a much grander construct, one of infinite possibilities. As a conscious leader, I realize that leadership comes with profound responsibility as well as the imperative of serving those I lead. [24]

Optimal Sunlines

In seven years, Janeen and I have moved seven times across four states covering three corners of the United States. Significant change became a constant in our lives, requiring huge amounts of faith, hope and action. Our moves were prompted by my work in banking, but prior to our making any decisions, we consulted several astrologers, including Robert Hand, renowned and deeply respected in his field. We had learned that, based on our birth charts and the associated planetary alignments, there were locations on the planet which provided us with optimal potentialities. Our investigation showed that for Janeen, her best locations were along a sunline from just west of Indianapolis southward through the Yucatan peninsula of Mexico to the west coast of Costa Rica and Nicaragua. For me, the Olympic range in the Pacific Northwest, the south of France and the southeast of Great Britain were places where I would find the greatest potential. Sound crazy? Perhaps, but nonetheless we had become believers based on the work undertaken over the past decade.

After Matt was accepted at USC in the three-year graduate program in architecture, Janeen and I decided that rather than make the move from Atlanta to the Seattle area, we would look to transfer to the Los

Angeles area as a means of supporting Matt in his new academic endeavor. It just so happened that a similar position with the bank had opened up in Los Angeles. I applied, interviewed and was able to transfer with Bank of America into this market position.

Driving in LA

Having traveled domestically and internationally, I have experienced the dangers of driving in cities like Mexico City, Boston, New York, Rome, and Hong Kong, but nothing compares with the density and duress of greater Los Angeles traffic. Add texting, legal cannabis and the ubiquitous nature of people identifying themselves by the type of car they drive, you have an environment of impending danger every time you step into your automobile. Accidents, dented rear ends and deaths seem to be the every-day occurrence.

In November 2014, while driving to my office in Torrance, CA, I was coming to one of the many lights on Hawthorne Boulevard. Foot on the brake and slowing as I approached a red light ahead, there was a sudden jolt from the rear passenger side of the vehicle. The loud crunch of a young woman's late model Oldsmobile smashing into my Honda Civic thrust me forward violently, turning the small auto around in the middle of the three-lane busy road. A sharp pain was felt in my lower back, later deter-mined to be two budging discs. I continued to work for several months as the pain continued to exacerbate requiring that I seek medical attention. Cat scans and an MRI determined that in addition to the back injury, I had broken two ribs. The ultimate recommendation was to have surgery. Both Janeen and I, over the years together, have relegated western medi-cine only as a last resort, but in this case, met with an orthopedic surgeon and pain management doctor. The diagnosis and medical opinion was to stay out of work, especially based on the amount of driving my position demanded.

So for the next five months, I went on short term disability, following the course of medical treatment including chiropractic adjustments and acupuncture three times weekly as well as a series of epidurals to help manage the pain. Cutting into my back was not an option we were willing to entertain. But during this time, my position as Consumer Market Manager for the South Bay Coast market was filled. When it was determined that I was able to return to work, I was given sixty days to find a comparable position. The only opening was in south Orange County, a one-way trip of more than two hours. So I expanded my search.

Pacific Northwest

While Matt's graduate program continued for another year and a half, we were able to have supported him in getting off to a great start in the 3-year program. He was in the groove, making our decision to leave Los Angeles that much easier. Yet, for Janeen, moving from Los Angeles to Tacoma, Washington, was challenging on many fronts. No more sun everyday. Gray skies, unrelenting rain and a less than desirable rental situation dampened spirits.

In retrospect, during our time in Los Angeles, especially being on short term disability, where I was greatly limited in performing normal daily activities, I felt like a caged animal. Unable to drive, exercise, and operate with normality seemed to intensify uneasiness and a depleted feeling of usefulness and purpose. And, I had developed an acute distaste for the pervasive entitled collective personality of Los Angeles. Perhaps living where we were in the Grove area, adjacent to Beverly Hills and West Hollywood, deepened my sense of disdain for the privileged who flaunted their wealth driving Porsches, Lamborghinis and other high-end performance cars on 3rd Avenue. And as much as I tried to relinquish this aversion, the disparity I witnessed between the haves and have-nots, particularly the Spanish speaking working class that tended to the lawns, constructed the multi-million dollar homes and waited tables at trendy restaurants, tugged at my heart strings. So when the chance became available to leave this paradise, I was first in line.

We moved to the Pacific Northwest for a new position at the bank, charged with managing operations, including risk and other related areas in an expanded territory. This job would demand a he-man level of energy, time and learning. Perhaps naïvely, we believed our vision would come to fruition. Our own company, Illuminate Ambitions, Inc., with expertise in bringing consciousness to leadership, working with organizations to install, train and leverage our consulting services, along with an expanded coaching client list, all were part of our business model and more importantly, where our passions resided. Certainly after publishing the first book, hiring a publicist and investing significant time and money in our new website, we felt strongly that our lives would have taken a turn toward bringing our dream to fruition. And Los Angeles gave us the progressive environment to succeed, so we thought.[25]

Origin of this book

After the release of *Conscious Leadership: 7 Principles That WILL Change Your Business and Change Your Life*, published in the summer of 2015, many individuals reading the book inquired as to how I had arrived at the principles elucidated in my writing. It was a great question. Janeen frequently remarks that I came into this life knowing certain truths, being aware of spiritual realities that others seem oblivious to, tenets of deeper, more illuminating connection that are life-filling and resonating to a higher calling. I do possess the ability to see with different eyes and hear with a different internal knowing. Where this acute understanding comes from remains a mystery, but embedded in my soul are beliefs that not only elevate Janeen and me, but when embraced by others, create a powerful dynamic that ultimately can change the world we live in. It's not complex, yet it is dramatically different from what our 3-D construct teaches, reinforces and controls in our collective society. At the heart of my knowing is the infinite power of love, compassion and understanding, attributes in short supply, particularly among leaders from across the gamut of human enterprise. When we boil down all the superfluous, self-centered belief systems, the greed-sponsored capitalist model and the false rigidity associated with organized religion, we come to a place of human connection. And this lost connection is also witnessed in our complete disregard for Mother Earth and the incredible beauty of the animal kingdom as well as our firm reliance on war, violence, female subjugation and hatred of everyone different from us. This reality is my truth, for we are only here for such a short time. What we do with our lives matters, not just to us but to those we touch. I knew there was much more to accomplish, a greater vision to uphold.

For many years, I have worked with an incredibly talented life coach and spiritual mentor, Dr. Jan Seward. Her valuable insights and creative approaches to life have enriched me greatly as I have taken on my own calling. "There's an unfinished, frenetic energy infusing my soul," I told her. "I know that my book has the potential to significantly improve how leaders engage others, bringing about much greater employee satisfaction and accelerated revenue, both of which are goals for most companies," I said. "What are my next steps?" I asked.

"Everything in its time," she reminded me. Yet, time was ticking away and we were trying desperately not to feel impatient or discouraged. That I was still working at the bank with its drain of energy and passion made the months ending 2015 more challenging.

An epiphany started to take shape in early 2016, as Janeen and I continued to move through our lives, trusting and maintaining our own integrity while exploring all possibilities. In 2012, while still residing in Tucson, I started writing an autobiographical account of my journey in this lifetime. My mission was to uncover what kept me down, those indelible pain points and transitions in my life that led me to where I am. This project was set aside for the time being.

Then in 2014, I decided to write about my experiences as a leader within the corporate structure after three decades. My leadership work at the bank provided me with ample fodder to experiment with the principles espoused in my first book. That was the starting point. But there was additional work to accomplish. Those who had read my first book wanted to know more. Why not use what I had started in 2012 as a springboard to telling the story of my life and how I had arrived at the principles in *Conscious Leadership*? But when and how to accomplish this project?

Since writing for me demands continuity of time and energy, spending an hour here and an hour there would not work to complete the second book, I went back to the model I used to write my first book. The concept and outline for *Conscious Leadership* emerged mid 2014. How would we bring it to life became the question? We had enjoyed cruising in the past and decided to take an eleven-day cruise from San Francisco to Alaska. In September 2014, we did just that. Every day at sea, seven days to be exact, were spent writing. Janeen and I found a quiet place in the very back of the sailing city. Parking ourselves at the back window in the dance lounge on the seventeenth deck, I plugged into baroque music and entered the alternative reality of writing. The manuscript was completed during the cruise. This same approach would be necessary to produce the second book. To cruise or not to cruise?

This time we decided to take a different approach, staying landlocked at a beautiful full-service bed and breakfast in the Olympic range of Washington State. We knew that in order to bring this project to life, it would be necessary to sequester ourselves away from distractions while minimizing the amount of labor associated with normal daily living. No cooking, cleaning, bed making, or other menial duties for this project.

Packing up our Chrysler 300 with all the necessities, including our incredible dog, Moshe, we set out to Sequim, Washington. The inn owner was fully aware of our mission to write and provided us with a wonderfully secluded suite in a separate building, away from the main lodge. All the essentials were provided, in addition to a writing desk and chair set up in front of a springtime bloom of gorgeous trees, flowering bushes and a duck pond.

Janeen and I settled into our temporary home for the next ten days. Moshe, a constant companion, also settled in as he found his way under the desk by my feet. Opening my MacBook, cleaning my glasses, a cup of black coffee to the right of my computer and a quick glance at my beautiful wife, quietly rapt in her own work, and I was ready to start. Shifting my thoughts to the work ahead, I looked up to find a hummingbird floating at eye level just outside the window in front of my desk. Coincidence? No, I think not.

"Thank you little bird. I love you too.

CHAPTER 7 REFLECTIONS

[24] *The vulnerability I showed in meeting with my managers following the shooting event of January 8, 2011, allowed me to connect from a human point of view. Every time I step into my humanness with those I lead, I become a servant leader, one who possesses the ability to lift others up. To connect as a servant leader forges relationships on a human scale. After all, are we human beings having a spiritual experience or spirits having a human experience? Take your pick. Either way, recognizing our capacity to serve those we lead brings about deeper connection and a shared purpose, calling on everyone to bring their best forward.*

[25] *Over the years, I have become confident enough to express openly my own vulnerabilities, those internal issues usually kept under cover and shielded from view. I know today that while there is risk associated with opening up and sharing my psychic shortcomings, to run away from authenticity negates all that I hold so deeply. Beyond the abandonment issues attached to being given up at birth, other insidious fears surface around security, money and comfort. The thought of not having a gainful source of income continually ignited the burning embers of my internal fears. For many years, particularly in starting our own company and writing my first book, our hopes and dreams centered on leaving corporate America and bringing our message to life in others. This dream still sizzles and enflames my passion. So, how will we advance our lives to fulfill what has been a manifest destiny?*

INSIGHTS AND TOOLS

Be a Servant Leader - service to others warms the heart and enjoins the spirits. As Bob Dylan put it, "You're gonna have to serve somebody, yes, you are." Who do you serve? Make it your mission each day to take on the challenge of serving others, lifting them up, supporting their full engagement and sharing your gifts openly. A servant leader is someone unafraid of being vulnerable, authentic and human. When you open yourself up to serving others, you embrace godlike qualities of generosity, healing and understanding. Put aside self-aggrandizement, self-promotion and selfish adherence to exclusively serving your own needs. When you operate as a servant leader your energy and vibration fuels positive light and love.

IN CLOSING

When I set out to write this book, it was with great excitement and a bit of trepidation that I would share with you intimate and quite painful events and circumstances of my life. Yet, living true to the authenticity and vulnerability I espouse both in my writing and my speaking, nothing less than the truth was demanded of me. Opening myself up by bringing forward the pain and heartache of lost relationships, the depth of despair experienced with my addictions and the perpetual running from my deepest fears of abandonment, all intertwine to make this project a life-altering process. There were many times when reliving these events that I wept uncontrollably, experiencing anew the losses and inner suffering. Aptly, the title of the book illustrates the many times that my spirit and soul experienced death, rebirth and redemption: a contemporary Phoenix rising.

Over the past six plus decades of twists and turns, ups and downs, successes and failures, a central theme has emerged, one that quite simply boils down to loving. The love and compassion we hold for ourselves and those around us are a reflection of the divine seed we all possess. Hardship, turmoil and the many facets of fear pull us away from this truth. There have been many times in my life where darkness and depression, even the harsh reality of giving up, have infiltrated my sense of purpose and sanity. Yet, despite these treks into the dark night of the soul, I have persevered, rebounded and found enough light to put one foot in front of the other to move forward.

I know that you have faced similar and perhaps greater challenges than me. My goal in writing this book is to share with you messages of empowerment and resilience. In the context of living a full life, one that acknowledges the difficult realities of balancing personal aspirations with professional demands, my hope is that you will find in your own life strength, purpose and love. Each chapter of the book speaks to one of the seven principles brought forward in my first book as illustrated by passages of my life, from birth to the present. In telling my story in this fashion, you gain an understanding of how I arrived at the principles and most importantly, how you, too, can shift, flow and dance to the cadence of an ever-changing, complex and increasingly demanding world.

Thank you for reading my book. May you have peace, prosperity and joy.

CPSIA information can be obtained
at www.ICGtesting.com
Printed in the USA
LVHW051037041119
636244LV00002B/186/P